PSYCHOLOGY LIBRARY EDITIONS:
SOCIAL PSYCHOLOGY

Volume 2

PROPERTY

PROPERTY

A Study in Social Psychology

ERNEST BEAGLEHOLE

Psychology Press
Taylor & Francis Group
LONDON AND NEW YORK

First published in 1931

This edition first published in 2015
by Psychology Press
27 Church Road, Hove BN3 2FA

and by Psychology Press
711 Third Avenue, New York, NY 10017

Psychology Press is an imprint of the Taylor & Francis Group, an informa business

British Library Cataloguing in Publication Data
A catalogue record for this book is available from the British Library

ISBN: 978-1-138-83092-9 (Set)
ISBN: 978-1-315-69455-9 (Set) (ebk)
ISBN: 978-1-138-84444-5 (Volume 2) (hbk)
ISBN: 978-1-315-73034-9 (Volume 2) (ebk)

Publisher's Note
The publisher has gone to great lengths to ensure the quality of this reprint but points out that some imperfections in the original copies may be apparent.

Disclaimer
The publisher has made every effort to trace copyright holders and would welcome correspondence from those they have been unable to trace.

PROPERTY

A STUDY IN SOCIAL PSYCHOLOGY

by

ERNEST BEAGLEHOLE

LONDON
GEORGE ALLEN & UNWIN LTD
MUSEUM STREET

FIRST PUBLISHED IN 1931

PRINTED IN GREAT BRITAIN BY
UNWIN BROTHERS LTD., WOKING

TO

MY FATHER

AND TO THE MEMORY OF

MY MOTHER

We are by nature stubbornly pledged to defend our own from attack, whether it be our person, our family, our property or our opinion. . . . The little word *my* is the most important one in all human affairs and properly to reckon with it is the beginning of wisdom.

James Harvey Robinson

PREFACE

THIS book represents an attempt to study the psychological basis of the institution of property. There have hitherto been many psychological and social studies of marriage or of religion, for instance, but none, so far as I am aware, has yet considered the problems which arise when the institution of property is viewed from the angle of social psychology. I have set out some of these problems in the first chapter. In the remaining chapters I discuss these problems in the light of evidence drawn from the various branches of psychology and sociology. In the final chapter I indicate the importance of my conclusions for political and social theory.

I have to thank Mr. W. MacMahon Ball, Dr. W. G. K. Duncan, and Miss Pearl S. Malsin for help and criticism. Professor H. J. Laski has encouraged me by his interest. To Professor Graham Wallas I owe gratitude for much friendly and stimulating advice. Finally, Professor Morris Ginsberg has put me in his debt through the unfailing sympathy he has shown towards my studies, and through the suggestion and criticism which he has at all times freely given me. Much that is of value in these pages I owe to his teaching, and I find it difficult to set down in print my obligation to him.

ERNEST BEAGLEHOLE

LONDON 1931

CONTENTS

PROPERTY
A STUDY IN SOCIAL PSYCHOLOGY

CHAPTER I

PROBLEM AND METHOD

IN the following pages I propose to make a psychological study of the basis and nature of rights in property. Hitherto the theory of property has almost always been approached from either an historical, an economic, or a philosophical point of view, with the result that one is left in ignorance as to the real foundations of the property interest in animal or human nature. Or, if not in ignorance, one has had to be satisfied with vague speculation, prejudiced fact, or unscientific theory. There seems to be a real need, therefore, for a study which will embrace all the available material gathered from various psychological and anthropological fields and draw therefrom a body of conclusions as to the relation of property to human nature.

A quotation or two from authorities in related fields will help to stress the importance of our problem. Thus Taussig writes: "The questions between private property and socialism are . . . at bottom questions as to men's character, motives, ideals. They are questions, insofar, of psychology; in more familiar language, of human nature. They are not simple, but highly complex, because human nature is highly complex."[1] Graham Wallas suggests the same line of thought: "Almost the whole economic question," he writes, "between socialism and individualism turns on the nature and limitations of the desire for property. . . . Some economist ought therefore to give us a treatise in

[1] Taussig: *Principles of Economics.* 3rd ed. (1921–22), vol. ii, 493-494.

which this property instinct is carefully and quantitatively examined."[1] Or again, W. H. R. Rivers, remarking that the concept of acquisition is one which is very prominent in the economic and political discussions of the present day, urges the importance of knowing "how far the features of social behaviour connoted by the terms 'acquisition' and 'acquisitive' are inherent in the character of human beings as members of society; how far they are inborn or instinctive, and how far they are the outcome of social environment and social tradition. In other words, it is necessary to enquire whether Man, in addition to the many other instincts now generally ascribed to him, possesses an instinct of acquisition."[2] Finally, Drever in his *Instinct in Man* comments on the fact that no psychologist has yet made a careful study of the nature of acquisition and property interest. We have studies of the psychological basis of such social institutions as religion or marriage, but none of the equally important institution of property.[3]

The first question, then, which we shall ask ourselves in this monograph is: What is the psychological basis of the right of private property? We shall next have to consider the various answers which economists and psychologists have made to this question. How scientific is it, for instance, to speak of an instinct of property, the feeling and inclination for property, the proprietary appetite, or of an instinct of appropriation or of acquisition?[4] And if one rejects any such explanation of property in terms of specific and particu-

[1] Wallas: *Human Nature in Politics*, 36. One would like to suggest, however, that a psychologist is more likely to make a fruitful study of this problem than the economist. The economist's psychology of human motive in the past has rarely been noteworthy either for its acuteness or its truth.

[2] Rivers: "The Instinct of Acquisition." Appendix 8 to *Instinct and the Unconscious* (1924), 260. Although I disagree almost entirely with the conclusions Rivers reaches in this paper, it ranks, nevertheless, as a stimulating contribution to the subject.

[3] Drever: *Instinct in Man*, 187 *et seq.*

[4] Letourneau, for instance, vaguely and variously uses any of these

larized instinct as being too simple to fit the facts, what original elements in human nature may be combined adequately to explain what is variously known as the feeling or sense of property? Finally, even when one succeeds in analysing these elements, is one much further forward in explaining all the complexities of the institution of property as we find it, for example, in the Great Society? If not, how does impulse interact with sentiment, sentiment integrate with other sentiment, interlock with what we shall later term primary and secondary value, and the whole assume characteristic form and convention through the moulding influence of prevailing culture pattern? These and similar questions will serve to orientate us as we proceed with our enquiry.

It is of interest at this point to define more precisely what is meant by property. Property in its most general sense may be taken to mean the exclusive use, enjoyment and control of those things which are of value in so far as, directly or indirectly, they serve to satisfy the fundamental needs of the organism. It is private when these things are controlled by the individual; common when a number of individuals have several rights over things which, taken together, they hold, as a body, against other individuals. In order that this definition may cover property in the animal world as well as property in human society, it may be

expressions as a name for the element he believes to reside at the basis of the property interest: in his words, "a powerful instinct, one springing from the very bowels of humanity . . . one of the manifestations of the instinct of self-preservation, imperious and tyrannical as are all primordial impulses." *Property: Its Origin and Development* (1892), x. Much of Letourneau's work is now out-of-date and his volume is hardly to be relied upon, especially in his treatment of anthropological material. Most later writers on instinct, following James and McDougall, are content to classify among the primary elements of human nature what is usually termed an 'instinct of acquisition.' As I shall show later, it is difficult to know exactly what type of behaviour this instinct embraces. The evidence adduced in its support is usually regrettably vague, while the behaviour it is supposed to explain resolutely refuses to fit in to the Procrustes' bed of what smacks at times of an older faculty psychology.

necessary to apply it with more latitude to the former than to the latter. But in essentials, as I shall attempt to show later, this same principle of the use and control of property objects is equally a characteristic of animal, primitive and human societies and may be judged in all by the same objective standard of defence against aggression.

We have touched on the question of instinct. It may be as well at this juncture, in order to clear the way for later discussion, to explain in a few words the attitude I adopt towards this much-discussed psychological concept. During the past decade there has been a large amount of miscellaneous criticism directed against the instinct-view of human nature. This criticism has been, in general, concerned to show that the use of the concept 'instinct' in psychology involves a return to the faculty psychology, is a mere verbal explanation in reality explaining nothing, an appeal to a mysterious force, spirit or 'drive' in the mind which it is difficult adequately to characterize in scientific terms. A further criticism alleges extreme difficulty in understanding what is meant by inheritance of instinct.[1] Much of this criticism has been of considerable importance in helping to define what is meant by instinct; so that it may be suggested the time is now ripe for a more final revaluation of this concept.

Perhaps some such revaluation might be advanced in the following terms: In any consideration of the innate

[1] Much of this criticism is represented by the work of L. L. Bernard (*Instinct* (1925); *Introduction to Social Psychology* (1927)). Bernard's arguments, however, that it is impossible to understand what is meant by the statement that instinct is 'innate' or 'inherited' are biologically quite unsound. Carried to their logical extreme, they appear to deny all mental inheritance whatsoever, which is absurd. Nervous 'structure' is of course not inherited; what is inherited are unit characters which, through the process of development, appear later as nervous structure, the functioning of which results in that characteristic form of behaviour we call 'instinctive.'

equipment of Man it is important to distinguish between an inherited tendency to develop along certain predetermined lines and the actual concrete characters which are manifested as the result of the interaction between the environment and that conational unity which we call the Self. By inherited tendency is not meant any mysterious potency or animistic force but merely that part condition of development which is one aspect of the self-environment configuration. The fundamental needs or root interests of Man are comparatively few. They embrace such activities as the needs of the body as in nutrition or sleep, the need of others as in sex and maternal behaviour, and the needs of the mind as in investigation or construction. Instincts, then, will appear as tendencies to specific impulse expressed in the form of behaviour, congenitally determined and subserving the fundamental needs of the unitary organism. Typical instincts are food-seeking impulses of attraction and repulsion, sex, parental instinct, curiosity, aggression.[1] When inherited tendency is manifested in concrete acquired characters such motor mechanisms as grasping, handling, withdrawal are also integrated into the total behaviour response. As regards instinct, however, the point to be stressed is that it is a tendency to action, or, in other words, a felt drive or tension giving persistence and variability to that series of acts whereby the conational self strives to express itself. In man, innate behaviour patterns are largely lost. They exist still in such activity as sucking, clinging, grasping. It is the continuously felt tension giving this persistence to innate behaviour patterns which subserve

[1] In this view emotions are not merely the affective element accompanying impulsive activity, but are more complex tendencies arising under conditions of the conflict, delay, or thwarting of instinct. They are diffuse, contingent, variable nervous disturbances securing greater plasticity of impulse, and heightened feeling tone expressed in defined activity. Cf. Professor Ginsberg's paper on "Emotion and Instinct," *Journal of Philosophical Studies*, vol. i, No. 1, esp. 43–44.

fundamental needs that we term instinct.[1] The ultimate motives to action, therefore, may be sought in those needs, fundamental in the sense that they are primarily necessary if the dynamic continuity of the self is adequately to be realized. Instinct is a specific differentiation of the conational quality of these fundamental needs of the self.

This view of instinct will be seen to involve a particular view of the nature of the self. In other words, at the root of personality is to be found an underlying striving towards unity and continuity. The unity of the self is not the result of successive aggregation of atomistic instincts. It is the welding together of all the conscious and unconscious states of the self in a relation of conational continuity, which relation is itself based on permanent hereditary needs. These needs and their subserving instincts act selectively upon the environment and thus determine the direction of development. In so far as impulse is made clear, explicit, harmonious, through the selective handling of environmental situations, in so far as the ends of activity are co-ordinated and systematized, made comprehensive and conscious, in so far as impulse and emotion interacting with environment are ordered into the controlling organization of the sentiment—just so far is the implicit unity of the self made explicit, blind striving made conscious, and the self developed to full stature.[2]

[1] It is, of course, not correct to speak, other than in figurative terms, of instinct 'motivating,' 'moving,' driving the body. Cause implies both change and temporal continuity underlying this change. Causal connection depends upon invariable, sufficient, antecedents. Only in this sense may one speak of instinct as a cause of activity, only in so far, that is, as continuously felt tension is an invariable antecedent and part condition (bodily movement being also part condition) of the activity of the self.

[2] I must acknowledge here how much of the foregoing summary I have derived from the works of Professor Hobhouse and from the teaching of Professor Ginsberg. From the latter, especially, I have learned most that is of value in this view of the nature of instinct. Compare in this connection Appendix III to Hobhouse: *Mind in Evolution* (3rd ed., 1926) and Professor Ginsberg's survey of "The Place of Instinct in Social Theory," *Economica*, vol. xxxi (1931), 25–44.

So much for this problem of the nature and place of instinct in the development of personality. We shall bear this summary continually in mind when later we come to consider, first, the nature of the so-called instinct of acquisition, second, its relative helpfulness in explaining the interest of animal or man in property objects, and third, the manner in which integrated property values are related to personality-development and are assimilated to those sentiments which make up the 'sense' of ownership.

I have mentioned the word sentiment. It is important perhaps to add a further word in explanation of the meaning I attach to this concept. By a sentiment I understand, in McDougall's words, "an organized system of emotional tendencies centred about some object."[1] In other words, a sentiment is a complex disposition to experience various emotions in regard to the object upon which these emotions are focussed. Patriotism is an example of such a sentiment. And I shall attempt to show in later chapters of this book that the relation of the individual to his property may best be understood psychologically in terms of what I may call the sentiment of possession; in terms, that is, of the grouping of various emotional tendencies about the property object itself.

It is hardly necessary at present to say more of the problem of property. I have attempted to show there is a problem to be solved. I have indicated the leading lines of enquiry that must be pursued. I have suggested a view of instinct and of the nature of the self which will be of value in the further development of my argument. I now turn to indicate the methods I propose to pursue in order to throw light upon those problems awaiting solution.

There seem two problems of method upon which I may touch. One, of a more general nature, concerns the relevance

[1] McDougall: *Social Psychology* (11th ed., 1916), 122.

of psychological analysis to an understanding of social institutions. The other, of more particular interest, concerns the interrelations of the three principal methods I use in this monograph. I will say a few words first on the validity of the psychological approach in social investigation.

There are, perhaps, two extreme points of view on this question. One is represented by the work of a psychologist like McDougall who believes that the best way of understanding social behaviour, its forms and institutions, is to commence with what is an essentially atomistic examination and classification of the motives of activity, and then later, as a second step, to attempt a study of the interaction of these elements in characteristic forms of group life.[1] At the other end of the scale are to be found those German sociologists who urge that social science must concern itself first and foremost with the forms of social relationship, singling out the ultimate modes of social interaction and studying them, as such, in abstraction from the differing contents within which they are manifested. Among the other social sciences psychology would have to deal with the content and matter of the social life. Sociology, then, would be one social science among many, dealing with particular topics from a particular aspect; and the value to the latter of psychological analysis would necessarily be remote and only of indirect interest.[2] Nearer the German approach, though for different reasons, we would find the work of W. H. R. Rivers. Rivers, in a now classic paper on *Sociology and Psychology*,[3] was concerned to show an essential methodological distinction between the two disciplines because, for him, psychology dealt essentially with mental phenomena conscious or unconscious,

[1] See McDougall: *op. cit. passim* and his *Group Mind* (1920).

[2] Cf. Ginsberg: "The Scope of Sociology," *Economica*, No. 20, June 1927, 136–137.

[3] *Sociological Review*, vol. ix, 1916. Later reprinted in *Psychology and Ethnology* (1926)

while sociology dealt with social processes, their description and classification, their relations in time and space, irrespective of what motives prompt to these processes.[1]

Without attempting any criticism of these views, it may be suggested that the most fruitful position is that adopted in the following pages: that mental process is as much socially determined as social process, in its turn, is undoubtedly psychologically conditioned. If the former depends upon the interaction of individual minds and is the result of social life, so, likewise, does social process depend upon individual motive and become penetrated through and through with mental relations. Social data are the outcome of individual minds interacting with the physical environment and the social tradition of the group. An understanding of this point means that in the particular case we have before us it will not be enough for us to lay bare the original psychological elements of the property interest and imagine our task finished. Properly to appreciate such a social institution as property one must carry this investigation further and study the manner in which impulse is moulded by, and in its turn moulds, the economic culture patterns of the group, the fashion in which aggregated sentiment relates itself to assimilated values under the stimulus of those same culture

[1] Thus Rivers speaks of the value of a study of such a social institution as marriage written "without the use of a single psychological term referring to instincts, emotions, sentiments, ideas or beliefs, without mentioning such states as love, jealousy and constancy, which everybody knows to stand in so close a relation to the social processes in question," *op. cit.* (reprint), 4–5. Well may one doubt, with Marett, as to what virtues such treatment would possess. A similar view to Rivers' is maintained by A. M. Hocart: "Psychology and Ethnology," *Folk-Lore* (1915), vol. xxvi, 116, 126. For criticism of Rivers' sociological work, see Professor Ginsberg's paper in *Psyche*, July 1924. Perhaps a fourth approach is that of F. C. Bartlett, who believes that while sociology should confine itself to 'social facts,' psychology need not restrict its attention wholly to facts of the individual life because the social determinants of individual responses must be considered if the latter are ever adequately to be explained. *Psychology and Primitive Culture* (1923), 24 ff., 48. This distinction of Bartlett's, however, seems rather arbitrary and hardly sound in theory.

patterns to form that folk-way or institution characteristic of each culture group. It is only through this readiness to take into account psychological fact and social data that we can hope to approach the solution of our problems.

The particular methodological problem to be noticed is that which concerns the use of comparative, anthropological and individual or genetic methods of study. By enquiring into the nature of property, as judged by the objective standard of defence against aggression, among the various orders of the animal world, one may hope to gain valuable data on the primitive kinds of property objects, on their distribution, variability and specific nature. In so far, too, as we have to examine the nature of the presumed instinct of property or of acquisition, it is imperative that we should correlate all the evidence, from animal life as from human, which it is postulated to explain. Again, the use of the anthropological method will give us perspective in treating of property in our own culture; it will allow us to study the formation of sentiments of ownership about those primitive property values which, for various reasons, are not values in the Great Society; thirdly, we may hope to study the operation of economic culture patterns different from our own, and observe their moulding influence upon psychological element. Finally, it will be possible to re-examine the whole question of communism in primitive society and come to definite conclusions about this most debated form of social organization and its relation to human nature.

We may then use a third method. In the light of previous discussion we may trace the nature of property interests in the child, the dawning and slow development of property rights under the influence of home, play group, and other associations, and lastly, the close relation, throughout this period of growth, of property to personality. The great virtue in the use of these three methods is that of cross-fertilization and cross-checking of ideas, theories and hypotheses. We are studying Man, human nature, and social institutions, *sub specie aeternitatis*, so to speak. We are bringing together all relevant data. We are guarding against what would otherwise be a short-sighted tendency to concentrate exclusively upon property in our own culture. And these are no light considerations when we deal with an institution which has planted its roots so deep into original nature that proposals radically to alter the organization of property within a social group will quickly arouse bitter feeling, passionate action and violent belief; an institution before which religion has bent submissive, around which society has been organized, by which moral codes have been dictated and empires built up or destroyed. Of this great social mainspring, the only valuable study will be one which impartially and scientifically explores every known avenue and by-way, uses every fruitful method, and sets every conclusion against the most detailed of backgrounds.[1]

I would perhaps wish to emphasize this one final point. This study purports to be a psychological prolegomena. It is not concerned, save indirectly and by implication, with the history of the theories of property, nor with the philosophy of property, nor yet again with any immediate criticism of the property culture patterns of Western European civilization. These problems may be reserved for another study, and meanwhile attention is directed to the essays in *Property: Its Duties and Rights*, edited by Bishop Gore, or to Mr. Tawney's masterly analysis of property in *The Acquisitive Society*. I am concerned here only to analyse the psychological foundations and scaffolding of property in general, and to lay bare the hidden nerve of irrational

[1] Further reference to each of these three methods will be found in the introduction to each part.

animism that binds the individual to the object he appropriates as his own and defends against aggression. The aim of this study is, therefore, empirical, inductive and positive, withal psychological. In the last chapter I indicate briefly the tentative application of my conclusions to wider social and ethical issues. For the rest, however, he who runs may read. For the moment I will have perhaps done sufficient if I have indicated the possibilities and fruitfulness of this convergence of three psychological methods upon the intensive study of one social institution; if, in a word, I may in some measure make the psychological origin and development of the institution of property more clear than prejudice, passion or partiality has hitherto served to do.

PART I

In brief, in all that part of sociology which is almost one with intellectual and moral biology, or with the natural history of Man; in all that relates to the first germs of the social relations and the first institutions which were founded by the unity of the family or the tribe, there is not only great scientific advantage but real philosophic necessity for employing the rational comparison of human with other animal societies. Perhaps it might even be desirable not to confine the comparison to societies which present a character of voluntary co-operation in analogy to the human. They must always rank first in importance: but the scientific spirit, extending the process to its final logical term, might find some advantage in examining those strange associations proper to the inferior animals, in which an involuntary co-operation results from an indissoluble organic union, either by simple adhesion or real continuity. If science gained nothing by this extension, the method would.

COMTE

INTRODUCTION

In the three chapters which make up Part I of this monograph it is my aim to discuss certain aspects of the psychology and sociology of property in the animal world. As I have suggested in Chapter I, this aim can only be achieved through a consideration of two related problems. First, we must ask, what are the facts as to the existence or not of property among animals? These we may determine only through the use of an objective criterion. The most suitable criterion by which to judge relevant behaviour situations is that possession shown by defence against aggression. Accordingly, then, our first object is to determine the nature and extent of property among animals as shown by exclusive possession and active defence of such property objects against the aggression and attempted spoliation by individuals of the same related species or of entirely different species. This exclusive possession and control, which is the mark of interest in property, will have variable time limits. Among the solitary wasps and bees, for example, the nest is defended only during the activity of the reproductive cycle. While the female is actively engaged in completing and provisioning her nests, they will be defended. Later, egg laid and nest sealed, the wasp will be entirely indifferent to foes, animal or human. At the other end of the insect scale, however, one may see an ant colony flourish for many years and maintain its nest intact during this period against the attacks of marauding species. Whether ownership is shown, therefore, for three hours, three months or three years, is immaterial to our criterion. So long as a study of each case reveals exclusive possession reinforced by a disposition to defend against the interference of others, we are justified in assuming that we have before us an example of a primitive property relationship.

Our second problem, as we have already pointed out, is to study the biological evidence upon which the psychologist bases his alleged instinct of acquisition. It has long been the habit to summarize such empirical data as the storing of honey by the bee, of nuts by the squirrel, of bones by the domestic dog, of odds and ends by the jackdaw, as being all due to the 'drive' in animal nature of a postulated acquisitive instinct; and to align with this behaviour as being due to the same motive, the collecting of cigarette cards by the schoolboy, and rare books or old china by the dilettante. Yet, so far as one may judge, little systematic investigation has been carried out by the psychologist in the past to determine either the extent to which hoarding activity is characteristic of animal life in general or the nature of the stimuli prompting to such activity. This is rather surprising when we recall that unless such behaviour is fairly general among animals of all species, including, particularly, the higher apes, we have no comparative support for postulating an acquisitive impulse as one of the primary instincts in man. I hope that the following chapters will make good this omission. That, in general, my conclusions are not favourable to the acquisitive instinct theory I should perhaps state at the outset. The biological facts are too complex to be explained away in terms of an innate acquisitive tendency. One is sometimes inclined to wonder how many more of McDougall's instincts would survive an equally rigid biological examination!

To solve this second problem we have kept in mind throughout our enquiry some such leading questions as the following: What exactly is the nature of the situation leading to hoarding activity? What is the stimulus to such activity as occurs? How far is such activity generalized, and how far is it the accumulation of particular objects, e.g. food? How far is such activity to be explained on the supposition that the animal is satisfying fundamental needs?

Or how far is it an independent activity *sui generis*? Finally, even if some particularized activity suggests hoarding as an end in itself among insects and lower mammals, is it not likely that such an impulse may have atrophied during the long aeons of time our primordial ancestors spent among those tropic forests which were sole witnesses of the birth of humanity? May there not be, in fact, devolution as well as evolution of impulse? Such questions as these may serve as guide-lines to our investigation. We may not hope to present a final answer to them all. At least we may hope that a careful examination of relevant data and a rigid analysis of behaviour-situation will throw considerable light upon the animal origin of property interest.

It is hardly necessary for me to say more in justification of the use I propose to make of the comparative method, nor to enter into any consideration of detailed problems of animal behaviour. Such problems are of academic and theoretical interest. They are discussed in most text-books on Comparative Psychology. The comparative method is, after all, self-justifying. It is based on the organic view of human nature, on the underlying conviction that there is a fundamental unity of physical and psychical structure displayed in all realms of organic life. Adequately to understand the behaviour of civilized man we have to realize that the mind and body we share with all the animals are the original foundations on which are based even the most subtle and refined intellectual life. Hence the need for learning all the lessons animal psychology can teach us.

In the first chapter of this part we propose to deal with property among the insects. Though they form a terminal branch of the phylogenetic tree and have given rise to no higher orders, nevertheless it is of considerable interest to our thesis to note the reaction of the insect to those objects which may be regarded as its 'property'; and further, to examine the nature of hoarding activity among various insect orders. We will be able to use, in this chapter, a number of detailed studies which lack nothing in explicitness and careful observation. In the next chapter we may advance a stage further up the phylogenetic scale and examine bird life in relation to property. Here we have behaviour which is marked by both instinct and intelligence, and therefore all the more germane to our argument. Finally, we will consider the hoarding activities of rodents. The squirrel has long been a favourite subject for both moralist and psychologist. We will examine this hoarding activity in some detail, since it provides a crucial test for the acquisitive instinct theory. And lastly, we must consider the behaviour of the higher apes. Closely related to man himself, it will be of primary interest to find out those objects which form one term of the animal-property relation; and further, to discover the degree to which the behaviour of apes is marked by acquisitiveness. A detailed summary of the main conclusions of this study of animal life will serve as at once a comment on the whole of Part I and as a means of introducing our anthropological material.

CHAPTER II

PROPERTY AMONG INSECTS

In this chapter I propose to consider some aspects of the property relation in the insect world. For obvious reasons it is not possible to cover the whole field of insect behaviour nor to deal with many of the fascinating problems that beset the specialist when he studies the nature of instinct, the nature of stimuli to instinct action, and the nature and degree of plastic action among the various insect orders.[1] I propose, therefore, to confine this study to one or two typical insect orders: various species of wasps, bees, ants and termites. The two former species include insects living solitary, social or semi-social lives; the two latter live entirely social lives in communities ranging from a few hundred to many thousands of individuals. Thus among many of the bees and wasps what we judge by our objective criterion to be property is 'owned' individually and provisions are stored in individual nests. On the other hand, ants and termites 'own' the nest collectively, defend it collectively and provision it in the same manner. A gregarious life is lived purely in the interests of the community. The opportunity therefore presents itself of studying both the reactions of the individual insect to primitive property values and the reaction also of those communities whose economic organization may very well be classed as 'communistic,' in a later defined sense of this much-abused term.

I am aware, of course, that this selection does not mean that other forms of insect life would not provide just as equally interesting material for study. The limits of this monograph, however, exclude reference to the Coleoptera,

[1] See Wheeler: *Ants: Their Structure and Behaviour* (1913), 521, 523–524, 538–539; Peckham: *Wasps*, etc., ch. xiii; Henrick: *Neurological Foundations of Animal Behaviour* (1924) *inter alia* on these problems.

for instance, or to the Arachnids. Perhaps it is just as well; since in this measure of selection one may hope to bring into clear light the main conclusions to which we are led.

I will consider first, then, the acquisitive and hoarding activities of the solitary wasps. Following the Peckhams in their volume on *Wasps, Social and Solitary* (1905), one may summarize the life cycle of a typical species, the *Ammophila*, somewhat as follows: Each adult female *ammophila* makes a separate nest and provisions it by her own labour. In many cases, a new nest is made for each egg that is laid. The nests themselves may be made of mud and attached for shelter to leaves, rocks, eaves of buildings; or else they may take the form of burrows hollowed out of the ground, trees or the stems of plants. The adult wasp lives upon fruit or nectar, but the young grub or larva must have animal food. Here the parent wasp shows a rigid conservatism in that each species provides, without deviation, the customary food of its family. One stores the nest with flies, another with beetles, while others still seem mostly to appreciate caterpillars, grasshoppers, crickets, locusts, spiders, cockroaches or aphides.

When the egg-laying season arrives the female secures her prey and either kills it outright or paralyses it. The prey is then placed in the nest, eggs are attached to it, the nest sealed up and the female goes away to build new nests, provision them afresh and pursue the reproductive cycle as before. In some genera, however, notably among the semi-social genus *Bembex*, the female maintains a longer connection with her offspring, not bringing all the provisions before sealing the nest, but returning from day to day to open the nest and feed her larva. The female loses final interest in the nest only when the grub has spun its cocoon.[1]

[1] Wheeler distinguishes this 'progressive provisioning' of the nest by *Bembex* from the 'mass provisioning' of more solitary species. He believes it to be correlated with an evolutionary advance from solitary to social

In all species the egg develops after two or three days into a maggot-like creature which feeds on the provided store of food. It soon enters the pupa stage of development, emerging from the cocoon as the adult insect some two or three weeks later, or, in many cases, only after winter months have passed and summer has come again.[1]

This total reproductive cycle involves four subsidiary activities: nest-building, provisioning the nest with suitable food, laying the egg close to the food supply, and the final closing of the nest. Each species of wasp will have its own characteristic mode of carrying out these activities and variations are not unusual. Again, the amount of food that is stored depends upon the species concerned. *Urnaria* provides each nest with four or five caterpillars. The Peckhams found a nest of *Rhopalum subrocinctum* containing thirteen compartments each of which was stored with twenty-five to thirty gnats.[2] The number of spiders that *Trypoxylon* gathers together depends entirely on their size in comparison with the size of the nest. In any case, the quantity of food that is stored seems to be the right amount adequately to develop the growing larva. It is not improbable that spiders, caterpillars, etc., are captured and stored until they fill the nest, and the size of the nest is a matter of instinctive determination.[3]

The point to notice, however, in this summary of the life cycle of the solitary wasp is that although there is a collecting and storing of provisions, such collection forms only one

or semi-social life. It has meant not only considerably increased longevity of the adult insect but also the beginnings of social heredity among the insects. This advance from mass to progressive provisioning is characteristic also of some species of beetles and of bees of the species *Allodape*, for example. Cf. Wheeler: *Social Life Among the Insects* (1923), 40–43, 60–63, 108–111.

1 Peckham: *op. cit.*, 16–17.

2 *Ibid.*, 73–74.

3 See below Fabre's experiments on the Mason Bee and a paper by Carveth Read in *British Journal of Psychology*, vol. iv, 1911, on "Instinct, Specially in Solitary Wasps," 28–29.

aspect of the configuration of activities which form the reproductive cycle of the wasp. It is undoubtedly instinctive—the whole cycle is hereditarily determined; but it is probably far from the truth to urge that the provisioning of the nest is due to the motivation of an 'instinct of acquisition.' Further, this provisioning of the nest is not in the interests of the female wasp, it is not directed towards the aim of tiding her over winter scarcity, because first and foremost the female dies on the approach of winter. It is directed solely towards providing food for the development of the young larva, and if one could label such behaviour, one could only say it was motivated by an instinctive mechanism which was in itself one distinguishable element in an innate cycle of activities having for its end the continuation of the species.

If we turn now to a consideration of the other aspect of our subject, that which concerns the nature of property among the insects, it is possible, I think, to discover two situations in which the wasp will maintain right of exclusive possession by attack or defence. The wasp that is, will defend its prey from the attack of other insects, and it will defend its nest. An example or two of such behaviour will make my point clear.

The wasp will defend its prey from the attacks either of other wasps or of the ants. Wasps, for instance, of the genus *Nectarina* share with ants a passion for the secretions exuded by frog-hoppers. If an ant comes up to a cluster of such hoppers which are already attended by a wasp, the latter will not attempt to grapple with its rival on the leaf but will fly off, hover over the ant, and then, when its enemy is well exposed, it will dart at it and strike it to the ground. The wasp can rarely obtain possession of such hoppers from the ants, because fresh relays of ants continually arrive on the scene and the wasp soon tires of attacking its persistent enemies. But should the wasp first obtain possession it can usually keep it; for the first ants that arrive are only pioneers, and by knocking these off, the wasp prevents them from returning and scenting the track back to inform the main body.[1]

A vivid account of a wasp's attack on an ant is given in one of the Peckhams' observations. A *Pompilus scelestus* had dragged a large *Lycosid* spider to her nest; but then, finding the nest too small to hold her prey, she disappeared inside to do some more excavation. While she was employed, the Peckhams observed the spider to be attacked by a very tiny red ant, that could not by any possibility have stirred it. "When the wasp caught sight of this insignificant marauder, she fell into a fit of wild fury, and bending her abdomen under, seized the ant again and again in her mandibles, and flung it backwards against the tip of her sting. The little creature finally escaped, seeming none the worse for the rough handling to which it had been subjected, while the wasp, still trembling with excitement, grasped her spider and rushed off to a distance of several feet, carrying it upon a weed and depositing it there."[2]

Not only will the wasp fight ant, but a fight between two wasps is not uncommon. Thus in another observation, the Peckhams saw two wasps digging their nests two or three feet apart. One of them finished before the other, and being unable to find her own spider (probably it had been carried away by the ants), she seized that of her neighbour and bore that away. "The rightful owner saw, from a distance, what was happening and ran to the rescue. A violent scrimmage ensued, the two wasps clinching and rolling over and over together. The robber escaped and made off but was followed and caught again. She fought so well for her ill-gotten treasure, however, that she finally conquered the other and made off with her prize. She showed by her manner

1 Cf. Lubbock: *Ants, Bees and Wasps*, ed. Myers (1928), note 28, p. 293.

2 Peckham: *Instincts and Habits of the Solitary Wasps* (1898), 159.

that she felt the need of haste, for instead of laying the spider down and looking at the nest (as is *Pompilus*' custom), she dragged it directly in as though she feared another attack."[1]

Besides defending her prey from aggression, the wasp is equally active in defending her nest. With the species *Trypoxylon*, for example, the male discharges the duty of nest protector while the female hunts for spiders. The Peckhams frequently saw the male drive away the brilliant green *Chrysis* fly, which is always waiting about for a chance to enter an unguarded nest. On these occasions the defence is carried on with great vigour, the fly being pursued for some distance into the air. There are usually two or three unmated males flying about in the neighbourhood of the nest also, poking their heads into unused holes and trying to enter one that is occupied, but never with any success, because the male in charge seems in every instance always quite ready and able to take care of his rights.[2] On another occasion an observer, watching the final stage in the reproductive cycle of the wasp *Ammophila yarrowii Cres.*, waited until the female had gone down into her hole with a caterpillar grub and then quietly removed the door-stone that *Ammophila* had placed beside the entrance to her nest. "Returning, she looked about for her door, but, not finding it, apparently mistrusted the honesty of a neighbour, which had just descended, leaving her own door temptingly near. She purloined this pebble and was making off with it when the rightful owner appeared and gave chase, compelling her to relinquish it."[3]

From such accounts as I have just given, it seems beyond doubt that the solitary wasp will on occasion defend both her prey and her nest from the attacks of other wasps or

[1] Peckham: *op. cit.*, 133–134; cf. also *Wasps, Social and Solitary*, 128–129, 219–220, 298, etc.
[2] *Wasps, Social and Solitary*, 181–182.
[3] Reported by Dr. S. W. Williston: from Peckham, *op. cit.* 42–43.

ants. In some manner or other food and nest have some sort of meaning for the female as representing the end objects which provide satisfaction for instinctive activity. In this connection, however, it is interesting to note one or two qualifying limitations. First, the wasp will only defend her nest during the reproductive cycle. It has been noticed by many observers that when once the female has finally closed up her nest she takes no further interest in its welfare and will watch, with the completest indifference, its spoliation by the observer; and after leaving her nest, the solitary wasp never returns or takes any interest in the welfare of her progeny. Even *Bembex*, which returns from time to time with further food, does not appear to distinguish her own larva from parasitic larvae which are eating up all the food at the expense of her own grub. It would seem that the wasp, as I shall show later in regard to the solitary bee, shows a marked capacity to 'localize' her nest and return to it after foraging, but that, providing a nest is in position, it matters little whether it is her own nest or a nest provided by a curious naturalist. When once a nest is provisioned and sealed, the reproductive cycle commences again and the wasp's behaviour is concerned solely with the activities of nest-building.

The behaviour of the solitary or semi-social bee has much in common with the instinctive activity of the solitary wasps. Whereas, however, the wasps nearly always construct their nests by burrowing into the earth, the solitary bee constructs her nest and attaches it to any convenient surface, such as, for instance, a wall or rock-face or the branch of a nearby tree. The behaviour of the solitary bee *Chalicodoma* or mason bee is typical. *Chalicodoma* either occupies a disused cell built perhaps during a previous summer or else builds herself a new cell by cementing together, with secretions from special glands, tiny pebbles or sand grains.

The nest is usually fastened to a suitable rock-face. But whereas, again, the solitary wasp, being partly carnivorous, stores her nest with animal food, *Chalicodoma*—and indeed all the bees—provisions her nest with stores of honey. In both cases, however, the reproductive cycle consists of the four instinctive activities of nest-building, provisioning, egg-laying, and sealing of nest.

Fabre, in his fascinating volumes of *Souvenirs Entomologiques*, has recorded the results of some interesting experiments on the instinctive activities of the mason bee. They may be epitomized thus: Suppose a nest consisting of a cell in an early stage of construction is taken away and there is substituted for it a cell completely built and partially stored with food. Fabre found in this case that the bee did not welcome the change and go on storing food through a short circuit, so to speak, of her building activities. The bee will occupy the substituted cell and will go on building, although it is already completed, until it is made as much as a third more than the regulation height. Dr. Sharp, writing in the volume on Insects in the *Cambridge Natural History*, suggests —how seriously, I do not know—that in stopping her building after the nest is a third more than the usual size, the bee is to some extent controlled by 'circumstances,' for it does not raise the cell to twice the usual height, "but stops building when the cell is about one-third larger than usual as if, at that stage, the absurdity of the situation became manifest to it."[1] An explanation which does not attribute to bees a sense of the ludicrous and which is thus more in accordance with Lloyd Morgan's Comparative Canon is not difficult to suggest. Building instinctively, as the bee must, one imagines the size of the cell to be a matter of hereditary determination; an extra third was all that was necessary to complete the original cell. Therefore the bee, unable to distinguish between the original and the substituted cell and urged on by a

[1] *Cambridge Natural History* (1899), vol. vi, 42.

blind desire to build, follows out an instinctive 'logic' and thus adds the extra height to the substituted cell.

A similar condition of affairs results when the bee ceases to build and begins to bring provisions to the nest. A substituted cell may contain ample provisions for the young grub, but the bee goes on adding to this store although the labour is entirely superfluous. In other experiments Fabre took away a nest with a completely built cell that the bee was storing with honey and substituted for it one in which the cell was only commenced and therefore incapable of containing food. When the bee returned with its store of provisions to this incomplete cell, it seemed very perplexed, tested the imperfect cell with its antennae, left the spot and returned again. Repeating this confused behaviour several times, it finally deposited its store in the cell of a stranger. In another case the bee broke open a completed substituted cell and went on bringing to it provisions, although it was fully provisioned and the egg laid therein; finally, having completed the store, the bee laid her egg, sealed the cell and departed. In no case has Fabre found that the bee will go back from the provisioning stage to the building stage until the reproductive cycle of building, provisioning and egg-laying is completed.[1]

I am not aware as to whether or not Fabre's observations on *Chalicodoma* have been checked by any competent authority. Assuming the facts they establish to be correct, however, one cannot but be struck by the difference in the plasticity of behaviour between the wasps as observed by the Peckhams and these mason bees observed by Fabre. According to the Peckhams, 'variability' is the keynote of the behaviour of the wasps whereas Fabre's observations record the consecutive necessity of the reproductive cycle and definiteness of each sectional behaviour link. The behaviour of the bees is protopathic whereas that of the

[1] Cf. Fabre: *Souvenirs* (1914–1925), i, 365–370; ii, ch. x.

wasps is of that epicritic variety which Rivers has assured us to be the distinguishing mark of typical insect behaviour.

Fabre has some interesting pages on the manner in which the mason bee defends her nest against intruders. Thus, on one occasion he observed a *Chalicodoma murania* who, on returning home, found that another bee had, during her absence, taken possession of her partially completed cell and was unwilling to relinquish it. Thereupon "la propriétaire fond furieuse sur l'autre, . . . Elle prend pied sur le nid pour ne plus le quitter et accueille l'autre, chaque fois qu'elle ose s'approcher avec un frôlement d'ailles irritées, signe non équivoque de la juste indignation. Découragée, l'étrangère finit par abandonner la place. A l'instant la maçonne se remit au travail, aussi active que si elle ne venait pas de subir les épreuves de son long voyage."[1] From other observations of Fabre, it would appear that the two combatants do not seek to injure one another with their stings as they would fighting elsewhere, but are engaged in testing, as it were, which is the more serious in its claims to the proprietorship of the cell in dispute. It seems quite common among *Chalicodoma* for an incompleted cell to be appropriated by a stranger during the absence of the original owner, and after such a scene as described above, the owner to regain possession. Or, as Fabre expresses it: "L'intrus . . . finit toujous par être délogé tant est vif, indomptable, chez le maître le sentiment de la propriété. Au rebours de la sauvage maxime prussienne *la force prime le droit*, chez les Chalicodomes le droit prime la force; autrement ne pourrait s'expliquer la retraite constante de l'usurpateur qui pour la vigueur, ne le cède en rien au vrai propriétaire. S'il n'a pas autant d'audace c'est qu'il ne se sent pas réconforté par cette puissance souveraine, le droit qui fait autorité, entre pareils, jusque chez la brute."[2] Without professing to

[1] Fabre: *op. cit.*, i, 351–352; cf. also i, 336; iii, 104 *et seq.*; vi, 130.
[2] Fabre: *op. cit.*, i, 352; cf. also the *Cambridge Natural History*, vi, 38–39.

subscribe to Fabre's interpretation, it is material to my thesis, I think, to record the battles that take place over the disputed ownership of a nest.

Along with the nest, food is defended with equal vigour from attacks of the lazy or the marauder, but only food that has been individually collected. Each mason bee, we are told, has his nest, "domicile sacrée, où nul, dans le tumultueux essaim, sauf le propriétaire, ne s'avise de prendre une gorgée de miel. Il y a comme une entente de se respecter mutuellement entre voisines. D'ailleurs si quelque étourdie se trompe de cellule et se pose seulement sur la margelle d'un godet ne lui appartenant pas, la propriétaire survient, qui rudement l'admoniste et la rapelle à l'ordre. Mais si le magasin à miel est l'héritage de quelque défunte, de quelque égarée prolongeant son absence, alors, et seulement alors, une voisine s'en empare. Le bien était perdu. Elle en fait profit et c'est économie bien entendu."[1]

So far the conclusions seem quite clear. The mason bee defends its nest and its food stores; a further series of Fabre's experiments, however, on the substitution of nests shows that the matter is not as simple as it first appears. One of the species of *Chalicodoma* described by Fabre fixes its nests to the small boulders brought down and left by the Rhone on the waste places by its banks. This habit gave Fabre an opportunity of removing, or alternately of transposing, nests in the process of construction while the bee was absent on its foraging expeditions and of observing the effect of these alterations on the architects.

When the nests were removed from one stone to another near at hand and visible from the first position the bee failed to find its nest. It would return to the exact spot where the nest was originally located time and time again. It might actually happen that the bee would come to the stone to which the nest was attached, would visit the nest,

[1] Fabre: *op. cit.*, iii, 93.

would even enter into the cell it had left partially completed, would examine circumspectly the boulder, but would always leave it and return to the spot where the nest was originally built. On finding that the nest was not there, the bee would finally take its departure altogether from the locality. The nest, it seems, must be in the proper situation or it is not recognized as the desired object. Thus we have a condition of memory where the bee is able to return to its nest from a distance of three miles or more, but can no longer recognize it as its own when it has been removed no more than a yard from its original position.

When the experiment is so arranged that a nest is taken away while the bee is absent and the nest of another bee in about the same stage of construction is put in its place, the latter nest is at once adopted by the bee, apparently in no way incommoded by the fact that the edifice is the work of another. When nests very close together are transposed so that each bee on its return might be supposed to choose freely as to which nest to go, it was found that unhesitatingly each selected the nest which, though not its own, was in the position where its own had been.[1]

Fabre's observations on the pugnacity of *Chalicodoma* in defending nest or food would lead one to judge that the bee could recognize positively and clearly the end objects of instinctive activities. These latter experiments, however, seem to point to the opposite conclusion: the bee has a remarkably keen appreciation of locality, but little sense as to what is its own property. Pending further experiment and observation, perhaps the best explanation of this apparently contradictory behaviour of the mason bee—and indeed of the somewhat similar behaviour of many species of wasps[2]—is to be found in terms of Gestalt psychology.

[1] Fabre: *op. cit.*, i, 359–365; cf. also Lloyd Morgan: *Animal Behaviour* (1900), 129–130.

[2] Cf. Peckham (1905), 285–287, and *Cambridge Natural History*, vi, 104.

The bee seems to have a discriminating appreciation of that configuration which embraces nest in relation to locality. Should the configuration be dissolved or materially altered by removing the nest, even a distance of a few feet, the bee has not sufficient adaptive powers to react to the new configuration. On the other hand, when the nests are only transposed, the configuration is not materially altered for the bee. There is still a nest in a particular pattern-relation to a locality-background, and therefore the bee reacts, following its instinctive logic, to the new configuration, which is, for it, identical with the old. This means, of course, that the bee has a very different type of memory to our own. Within the limits of its plastic behaviour it reacts to a total situation which consists of nest in relation to background. It has not the power of reacting to nest *qua* nest irrespective of background. It cannot analyse a particular sensory pattern and react to one particular aspect of that pattern. It can only react to a total sensory situation and can only recognize as its own that which stands in a special relation to the whole locality configuration.

It is not necessary to consider other than briefly the activities of the honey-bee. The literature on the subject is so voluminous that I can only touch on one or two points that may help to throw light on my main thesis.

The active life of the honey-bee is divided between two main types of behaviour: collecting food and rearing the young. The cycle of instincts concerned in propagation and the care of the young larva need not be discussed in the present context. I may, therefore, pass directly to those activities that have for their object foraging, collecting and storing of food. The foraging bees pass from flower to flower to collect substances of three kinds. The first is honey, or, more correctly, the condensed nectar found in flowers. The second is the so-called bee-bread, which consists of the pollen of flowers, worked into a paste by the bees and stored in wax cells until it is required for the feeding of the larva. In each flight the foraging bees collect only one variety of pollen. Each load is brought to the hive and then transferred to the house bees whose duty it is in this connection to sort out the pollen for storage in different cells. There results several different kinds of bee-bread, the more stimulating and nourishing varieties being reserved for the female larvae that they may develop into queens or fertile bees or workers. The third substance collected by the foragers is propolis, a sticky resin obtained for the most part from coniferous trees and used as a mortar in building. This resin adheres so tenaciously to the legs of the bees who gather it, that it can only be detached by the help of other bees who clean with their jaws the loaded legs of their comrades and apply the propolis while still ductile to the inside of the hive. Of the substances collected by the foragers, then, two varieties are used for food, while the third is used to build or repair the hive. The wax that is used to build the cells within the hive is secreted by the bees themselves. It exudes from the segments of the abdomen, is rubbed off, and when a sufficient quantity has accumulated, the work of building the cell commences.

Bees have a mad infatuation for any sweet stuffs whatever. Lubbock, for instance, writes in a graphic fashion: "I have seen thousands strained out from the syrup in which they had perished; thousands more alighting even upon the boiling sweets, the floor covered and windows darkened with bees, some crawling, others flying, and others still so completely besmeared as to be able neither to crawl nor fly, not one in ten able to carry home its ill-gotten spoils, and yet the air filled with hosts of thoughtless new-comers." But as Lubbock goes on to moralize in true Victorian fashion: "Since their extreme eagerness for honey may be attributed rather to their anxiety for the common weal than to their desire for personal gratification, it cannot fairly be attributed to greediness."

The only agency that appears to modify the storing activities of the honey-bee is variation of climate, which also seems to modify, as I shall have occasion to show later, the instinctive activities of many other animals. Erasmus Darwin was the first to notice the effect of climate upon the bee. In his *Zoonomia* (1794–1796) he asserted that bees, when transported to the Barbados, where there is no season equal in severity to a northern winter, cease to collect and store honey. Kirby and Spence, however, contradicted Darwin's statement and asserted in opposition: "It is known to every naturalist acquainted with the fact that many different species of bees store up honey in the hottest climates and that there is no authentic instance on record of the hive bees altering in any age or climate their peculiar operations." More recent observations have shown that Erasmus Darwin was probably correct in his assertion. It is now known that European bees, transported to Australia, retain their industrious habits for the first two or three years and afterwards gradually cease to collect honey until finally they become wholly idle. The same effect has been noticed in bees transported to California. The bee-keepers have learnt, however, that they may counteract this tendency by abstracting the honey from the hive as the bees collect it.[1]

The last point seems to suggest that the honey collected in the hive serves to tide the hive bees over winter and early spring scarcity of food, but that in lands where there is a warm, equable climate all through the year the honey stored during the summer is not used during the winter months. So long as the cells are filled with honey, and not abstracted by the bee-keeper, the original accumulation of honey is likely to remain in the hive for some considerable period

[1] Romanes: *Animal Intelligence* (1882), 187–188; cf. also his *Mental Evolution in Animals* (1883), 245.

of time and thus there can be no stimulus to the foraging and storing instincts. Once, however, the hoard of honey is removed, the empty cells act as a stimulus to further exertion and so the foragers proceed once more to store the hive. This suggests that there is a tendency among the bees always to keep up the honey stores in the hive to a maximum level. During the course of evolution those hives which failed to do this would probably suffer severely during periods of bad weather conditions. In hot climates, there is no occasion to draw upon the hive stores at that period which corresponds to a northern winter, and so the storing activities languish just so long as the hive remains full of honey. Due not only to this tendency to store large quantities of honey, but also to their adaptability to the most diverse flowers, the most diverse temperatures, and to ability to maintain a high temperature within the hive during cold weather, the honey-bees have established themselves throughout the entire world.[1]

Like all the social insects, the honey-bees show a markedly exclusive spirit by the way in which they defend the hive against all those who do not belong to it. The peculiar nest odour, which is a blend of the smell of each individual with that of the nest in general, the brood, the wax and the food, is the mark of identification among bees belonging to the same hive. Sentinels stationed at the entrance to the hive examine every arrival and usually slay all strange bees who attempt to force an entrance. It is because of this that a bee-keeper, wishing to introduce a new queen to a queenless hive (without whom the hive would quickly weaken and die out), must first place her into the hive confined in a wire cage so that she may gradually acquire the nest smell. Otherwise death would quickly result.

From time to time the hive is called upon to defend its queen and its stores of honey, in fact its whole collective

[1] Cf. Wheeler: *Social Life Among the Insects* (1923), 132.

life, against those robber bees who appear to aim at lessening their own labours by pillaging the stores of other hives. If solitary burglars are successful in gaining an entrance to the nest and in obtaining plunder other bees may imitate them, and thus a whole bee community may act in concert to rob by force. In this case an army of bees precipitates itself upon the foreign hive. A vigorous defence is put up. If the invaders are successful in overcoming resistance they first of all put the queen to death, whereby they disorganize their enemies. After this they may plunder the hive with ease. The invaded hive thus fairly overcome, the owners, finding that all is lost, not only abandon further resistance but often reverse their policy and join the ranks of their conquerors. They assist in tearing down their cells and in the conveyance of the honey to the hive of their invaders. Should the defenders put up such a resistance that the battle turns in their favour, they will often pursue the flying legions of their enemies to a considerable distance from their nest. In both these cases, however, the hive is defended against the marauders. The only case in which the plundered hive offers no resistance at all seems to be that in which the robbers, having visited the same flowers as the robbed and having therefore much the same smell, are not recognized to be invaders until all resistance would be useless.[1] The queen herself is defended with as much vigour as the honey stores. She is the pivot, so to speak, of all the activities of the bee community. When the queen dies or is killed by invaders and there is none other to take her place, the hive loses both its will and ability to prosper as a flourishing community. It soon disintegrates and dies too.

One may sum up these remarks about the honey-bees by emphasizing two points. The first is that though the bees store up hoards of honey and bee-bread and collect propolis, yet because of the way such hoarding is modified by climatic

[1] Cf. Romanes: *Animal Intelligence*, 169–170.

conditions, it is probably not correct to urge, as Rivers does, that "the behaviour of the domesticated insect is ungraded in so far as the size of the hoard is concerned or more correctly that the strength of the impulse to hoard stands in no relation to the size of the hoard already accumulated."[1] On the contrary, the evidence drawn from experience in many parts of the world would lead to the conclusion that the impulse to hoard and store honey is modified to a large degree by the size of the hoard already accumulated. Further, in so far as the hive is well stored the impulse to accumulate is subject to atrophy and the bees become quite idle. One may say, therefore, that among the bees this impulse to collect honey is no protopathic impulse but shows a degree of adaptation to the peculiarities of the environmental situation. The second point to emphasize is the fact that the existence of some form of primitive collective 'ownership' among these insects may be inferred from the tendency of honey-bees to defend both their queen and their stores of honey against the aggressive attacks of either solitary or collective groups of robber insects. We may presumably interpret this 'ownership' on the same lines as we interpret it among all the other insects. Honey, hive, queen, stand in an intimate relation to specific instincts. As such they are defended when outside aggression seeks to disturb the balanced tension of the stimulus response situation.

We may now go on to consider one or two relevant aspects of the social life of ants and termites. We find among these insect orders highly organized communities living a life that in some respects is strictly comparable with our own social life.[2] I need not detail the social organization of an ant community. In many ways it is analogous to a single large

[1] Rivers: *Instinct and the Unconscious* (1924), 261–262.

[2] On the points of similarity between insect and human societies, *inter alia* Wheeler: *op. cit.*, 15–19; Bugnion: *The Origin of Instinct*, 39–40; Haldane and Huxley: *Animal Biology*, 287–297.

organism in which the soma is represented by the body of workers, the reproductive organ by the fertilized queen. The differentiation of colonial soma into castes is merely the visible result of a psychological and physiological division of labour. Further, there are two main types of instinct among the ants. The more closely instinct is concerned with growth, development and reproduction, the more fixed and mechanical it appears. On the other hand, the ancillary and more remote ethological instincts, those, for instance, concerned with foraging and nest-building, with relations to other organisms, alien ants, parasites and myrmecophiles, are more plastic and modifiable. Here again, the analogy of ant colony to a metazoon is appropriate since in the latter we also find that the activities concerned with growth and reproduction are more rigidly determined than those which adapt the organism to its multiform and changing environment.[1]

The concept of 'trophallaxis' would appear to be of considerable importance for an understanding of the social behaviour of ants and termites. Essentially, trophallaxis means an exchange of food. Social wasp larvae, for example, secrete drops of saliva which are eagerly lapped up by the workers who feed them. Ants keep aphid 'cows' and tolerate beetles in their nest on account of the secretions they obtain from them. Again, termites feed one another to such an extent that a colony may with some truth be described as bound together by a "circulating medium of glandular secretions, fatty exudates and partly or wholly digested food."[2] This concept of trophallaxis is relevant to our dis-

[1] Wheeler: *Ants, Their Structure and Behaviour*, 522–523. This distinction between the two types of instinct is relevant also for other insect orders. From a theoretical standpoint it would also throw doubt on Rivers' assumption that hoarding among bees is an ungraded, all-or-none response; and thus reinforces my contention that hoarding is essentially a plastic, modifiable activity.

[2] Wheeler: *Social Life*, etc,, 260; cf. Lubbock (Myers' ed.), 254–255, note 5.

cussion partly because of the large part it plays in the social behaviour of insects and also because it helps to explain the reason why ants use living 'honey-pots' and their extreme care for the welfare and safety of their herds of aphides.

If we review now the various activities whereby the ant community stores food in order to preserve its existence throughout long summer droughts and the cold of winter months, it is evident that some species exaggerate the insectivorous habits which they already possess and so become ravenous and highly predatory hunters. They thus manage to secure a sufficient amount of food even under the most unfavourable conditions. Many varieties keep aphides. Some ants thrive and live by cultivating fungi on underground garden beds. Other species have taken to harvesting and eating seeds. These ants still feed upon insects when these are obtainable, but seeds furnish such an inexhaustible and nutritious food supply that the impulse to collect and store them in the nest has become highly developed. Finally, a number of ants store nectar and honeydew in the crops of a special physiological caste known as 'repletes.'

I will now consider these types of storing in more detail. Honey-ants in California, Alverdes tells us, gather the sweet liquid which is exuded by the gall formed by *Cyrips tinctaria* on dwarf oaks. Any portion not immediately consumed is stored in the crops of repletes. These, in the beginning normal young workers, are fed until their crops are so full that the whole of the hinder part of the body is swollen completely out of shape. In this condition they hang for the greater part of their lives, immobile, from the ceilings of special storerooms. Should external supplies of food fail, the population of the ant nest live upon the contents of the crops of the honey carriers, allowing themselves to be fed by the latter in conformity with the principle of trophallaxis. This method of storing is found in species as widely scattered as those in Mexico, Australia and South Africa, and probably had its origin in the brief and temporary abundance of liquid food, honeydew, gall secretions, in arid regions, and the long periods during which not only these substances but also insect food are unobtainable. The honey is stored in living reservoirs for the purpose of tiding over periods of scarcity and the ants remain in their nests because they need not forage.[1]

The most primitive and carnivorous ant species, the Ponerine, the Driver and the Legionary ants, for instance, which may be taken to represent the hunting stage in the development of ant societies, live almost exclusively on insects. This means that they do not store food at all for periods of scarcity. But at the next stage of ant evolution there are species of ants which in warm, arid, xerothermal regions, where insect food is scarce, have taken to a vegetarian diet and utilize as the most accessible and nutritious food the seeds of herbaceous plants. The grain brought to the nest by the foragers is cleaned and husked by a special class of subordinate workers. The husks and chaff are deposited outside the entrance of the nest. The grain itself is prevented from germinating by the dryness of the chambers and by the ants biting off the radicles of each grain. Should the grain become damp through a sudden inundation, it is usually carried out of the nest, spread out to dry in the sun, and thereafter stored again in dry granaries. The ants probably cause the grain to germinate by moistening it before consumption.[2]

A second type of storing is carried out by the leaf-cutting

[1] Cf. Wheeler: *Ants*, etc., ch. xx; Alverdes: *Social Life in the Animal World*, 96; Lloyd Morgan: *Animal Behaviour*, 214–215; Lubbock: *Ants, Bees and Wasps*, 47–49.

[2] Full accounts of these harvesting ants are to be found among the following: Lubbock: *op, cit.*, 60–62; Lubbock (Myers' ed.): 280–284, note 24; Wheeler: *op. cit.*, ch. xvii; Forel: *Social World of the Ants*, pt. v, ch. ii; Ritter: *Animal and Human Conduct*, 128. For a summary of Moggridge's classical observations on the European Harvesters and of MacCook's on the Harvesting Ants of Texas, cf. Romanes: *Animal Intelligence*, 97–110. Harvesting Ants are not slow to utilize insect food should the occasion present itself or should vegetable food be scarce. Romanes: *op. cit.*, 108–109.

ants, who cultivate fungi on soil prepared from leaves ground down into soft lumps. The gardens themselves have to be frequently renewed and weeded to keep them free from other fungi and bacteria. The fungus that is cultivated is the sole food supply for several species of ants, and it is for this reason that a queen, setting forth to found a new nest, must take with her a piece of the plant which she carries within the infrabuccal area of her mouth.[1]

So far I have dealt with three main types of ant activity that may be brought within the generic classification of hoarding behaviour. It is important to note, however, that division of labour in the ant state forbids one to ascribe any of this behaviour to an 'instinct of acquisition.' Among the honey-ants, one caste forages and collects honey, while another caste of repletes acts the part of passive containers who return the fluid they store as it is required. Among the agricultural ants, again, one caste collects the seeds, while another division of the workers within the nest cleans them, husks them and stores them; while of the leaf-cutters, one division of workers collects the leaves while the other two prepare them within the nest and tend the growing fungi.

I will deal now with those varieties of ants who tend aphid cows and are held together in social life by the resulting trophallaxis. The ants protect and guard the aphides and, if necessary, build strong defences around them, carry their eggs into the nest in winter and in the spring deposit the young aphides again on sheltered plants. Lubbock thought this behaviour of the ants a remarkable case of prudence. "Our ants," he writes, "may not perhaps lay up food for the winter; but they do more, for they keep during six months the eggs that will enable them to procure food during the following summer, a case of prudence unexampled in the animal kingdom."[2] But as it now appears that young

[1] Cf. Alverdes: *op. cit.*, 91, 96–97; Romanes: *op. cit.*, 93–96.

[2] Lubbock: *Ants, Bees and Wasps* (1882), 73.

newly-hatched ants, without previous instruction, treat aphides' eggs in exactly the same manner as the older, experienced workers, there can be no question either of imitation or of prudence. The capacity for tending aphides on the part of the worker ants must be due to those ancillary ethological and less constant instincts which arise in the workers as the result of a psychological and physiological division of labour.[1]

This note on those ants who tend aphides has made a useful bridge across to a discussion of ant 'property' because ants defend, with considerable vigour, not only their herds of aphides and their pupae, but also their food hoards, their nest, and what one may call their territorial rights. The literature on this aspect of ant life is fairly voluminous, so I cannot do much more than summarize the main features of such defence.

Concerning the defence of aphides from marauding ants, Wheeler tells us that "the fierce watchfulness of *F. sanguinea* or *F. rufa* must be apparent to any observer who disturbs these ants while they are attending their aphides. The former at once open their mandibles and rush at the intruder and the latter throw back their heads, sit up with the tips of their gasters directed forward and discharge volleys of formic acid in the direction whence they are threatened."[2] Eidmann, again, has observed that the ant *Lasius niger* sets sentries as aphid guards over the herds, who protect them from enemies and parasites and spread the alarm if necessary to the other ants. Strange ants are seized and beaten to death. A marked sentry was observed at its post day after day for eight days, sometimes from early morning until late evening. It seemed also that, in some cases at least, each aphid had its own special bodyguard which returned to it each day. Eidmann describes combats he has witnessed between herding ants and strangers and concludes that although

[1] Cf. *supra*, 49–50. [2] Wheeler: *Ants*, etc., 353.

the protective function of the aphid guards is established beyond question, nevertheless their work has not yet been entirely settled.[1]

Many ant species, the so-called slave-owning ants, are entirely dependent upon slave ants to feed them and keep the nest in order. To obtain such slaves, the slave-owning species raid the nests of other ants and obtain from them the pupae which they rear within their own nest. The attacked ants always put up a good resistance in defence of their brood, but are usually overcome by the fierceness of the marauding species. Two typical accounts will make this clear. Describing an attack of Amazon ants on *F. cunicularia*, Lespes tells us that after a march which often lasts a full hour the column arrives at the nest of the slave species. The *F. cuniculariae*, which are the strongest, offer keen opposition, but without much result. "The Amazons soon penetrate within the nest, to come out again a moment later, while the assailed ants at the same time rush out in masses. During the whole time attention is directed solely to the larvae and pupae, which the Amazons steal while the others try to save as many as possible. They know very well that the Amazons cannot climb, so they fly with their precious burdens to the surrounding bushes and plants, whereto their enemies cannot track them. They then pursue the retreating robbers and try to take away from them as much of their booty as possible. . . . Arrived at their nest, the Amazons immediately hand over their booty to their slaves and trouble themselves no more about them. A few days afterwards the stolen pupae or nymphae emerge without memory of their childhood and immediately and without compulsion take part in all tasks."[2]

Of the attacks of *Sanguinea*, another slave-making ant, Buchner, summarizing Forel, states that the besieging army

[1] Lubbock: *op. cit.* (Myers' ed.), 262–267, note 13.

[2] Romanes: *op. cit.*, 69–70.

forms a complete ring round the hostile nest, which it guards with mandibles open and antennae drawn back. In this position the besiegers beat off all the assaults of the besieged until they feel themselves strong enough to advance for that further attack which has for its object the mastering of the entrances and outlets of the nest. A special troop guards each opening and only allows to pass such of the besieged as carry no pupae. "If a *fusca* or a *rufibarbis* fights with a *sanguinia* for the possession of a pupa it is generally very soon overcome. While the main part of the army is penetrating into the nest to steal the pupae some divisions pursue the fugitives to take away from them the few pupae which may chance to have been saved. They drive them even out of the cricket holes in which they have meanwhile taken refuge. In short, it is a *razzia* or sweeping burglary as complete as can be imagined."[1]

These vigorous battles among the slave-making ants for the possession of the immature young may be paralleled among the agricultural ants by equally vigorous battles for the possession of hoards of seeds. The importance of seeds to these ants and the consequent value which they place upon them induce the insects, when supplies are scarce, to plunder each other's nests. The observations of Moggridge upon neighbouring colonies of *A. barbara* are typical of the behaviour of practically all the agricultural ants. Moggridge records a predatory war between these two colonies which lasted for forty-six days, during which the ants of the upper nest on a grassy slope were robbing the granaries of the lower nest, while the latter tried to recover the stolen seeds, both by fighting for them and by stealing seeds in their turn from the nest of their oppressors. Hand-to-hand mortal combats between individual ants were the order of the day. One ant would seize the free end of a seed carried by another and endeavour to wrench it away. But as, frequently,

[1] From Romanes: *op. cit.*, 75–76; cf. also Lubbock: *op. cit.* (1882), 78–82.

neither would let go its grip, the stronger opponent would drag seed and opponent towards its nest. At times other ants would interfere, seize one of the combatants and endeavour to drag it away. This often resulted in terrible mutilations and especially in the loss of the abdomen, which would be torn off while the jaws of the victim retained their indomitable bull-dog grip upon the seed. Then the victor would be seen dragging along its prize while its adversary, though now little more than a head and legs, offered a vigorous though, of course, ineffectual resistance.[1]

No doubt, as Moggridge suggests, some very pressing need is the cause of these systematic raids in search of accumulations of seeds. It is probably not far from the truth to believe that the requirements of distinct colonies of ants of the same species are often different at the same season and date. Thus, writes Moggridge, "these warring colonies of ants were active on many days when the majority of nests were completely closed; and I have seen these robbers staggering along, enfeebled by the cold, and in wind and rain, when all other ants were safe below ground."

A fourth *casus belli* among the ants arises from an invasion of what I may call territorial rights. Every formicary, says Forel,which is at all considerable, has its domain, its territory, which it seems to regard as its own 'property.' This is a direct result of the fact that all formicaries, except in the case of parabiosis, are enemies to one another. Thus a large *F. pratensis* colony may 'possess' a whole meadow, several trees or a hedge; and from this domain all colonies of other *pratensis, rufa, sanguinia, truncicola,* etc. will be excluded.[2] Here, again, typical behaviour may be observed among those agricultural ants who appear to pre-empt a certain

[1] Romanes: *op. cit.*, 79, 80, 81.

[2] Forel: *op. cit.*, i, 331; also ii, pt. iv, chs. i, iii, iv. For Lubbock's account of his experiments on the attitude of ants to erratic strangers see his *Ants, Bees and Wasps* (1882), 105–106, 119–120.

range of territory around their formicary as their own and refuse to allow any intrusion within such an area. Thus MacCook, following the unpublished Lincecum manuscript, writes that one day a new ant city was observed to be located within ten or twelve yards of a long-established nest, a distance too near for peaceable possession. Only a day or two elapsed before the inhabitants of the old city made war upon the new. They surrounded it in great numbers, and were seen entering in, dragging out and killing the new citizens. Two days later the battlefield was revisited and many ants were found dead, tightly locked together by legs and mandibles, while hundreds of decapitated bodies and severed heads were strewed over the ground.

Another case of MacCook's had a similar result. Within forty-eight hours the old settlers had exterminated the new. The distance between the nests was about twenty feet. So long as the young colonists remained in concealment they were not disturbed, but as soon as they began to clear their open disc about their nest, war was declared. Another more subtle method of the agriculturals in ridding themselves of erratic ant formicaries is this: Instead of putting the issue to the force of arms, the agriculturals wait until the erratics' nests multiply beyond forbearance. Then they simply sally forth and heap up the disc with earth to the depth of an inch or so until all the erratic ant nests are covered. Though the erratics struggle vigorously against this cavalier treatment by boring through the avalanche of earth, the obstruction and blocking up of their galleries at last becomes so serious that they gather together their household stores and their pupae and quietly evacuate the domain of the inhospitable agricultural ants—a triumph of *suaviter in modo* which is as effective as it is indirect.

The territory or domain surrounding the nest may be looked upon as an extension of the nest. If so, the territory is defended for the same motive as the nest is defended;

namely, that both are instruments for the use of the ants in adapting themselves to their environment. Espinas has this idea in mind when he writes: "Les fourmis en sillonant incessamment de leurs convois un vaste terrain se l'approprient sans l'occuper d'une manière permanente. Ce terrain est le leur parce qu'elles y sont fixées et qu'elles y ont leur demeure. La propriété nous apparait donc d'abord comme un effet direct, puis comme un extension de l'industrie. Le champ où les ouvrières circulent regulièrement en longue file porte en quelque sorte l'empreinte affaiblie de l'organisation imprimée si nettement sur toutes les parties du nid. Le champ est un instrument à l'usage des fourmis comme le nid lui-même quoique à un moindre dégré. En effet les sentiers battus sont la suite des galéries, et comme les galéries, les fourmis sont prêtes à les défendre contre l'excursions étrangères. Comme les différentes parties du nid communiquent entre elles, de même un courant non interrompu d'informations unit les sentiers à la fourmilière. C'est ainsi que l'activité animale conquérit le sol et l'incorpore à son organisme."[1] Territory, food stores, aphid herds, pupae and larvae, all may be considered in one sense as means whereby the ant community adapts itself to its environment and secures its racial survival. All must be defended from aggression unless the ant society is to be annihilated by other more vigorous rivals. All in some measure are the collective property of the community, and thus minister to its continued existence.

It is not necessary to consider the activities of the termites in such detail as I have discussed the behaviour of the true ants. The social organization of the termites resembles fairly closely that of the ants, though in addition to the ant castes of winged males and females, among the termites there are wingless workers and soldiers, divided, sometimes,

[1] Espinas: *Les Sociétés Animales*, 375–376

into sub-castes, and produced at will by the workers from the sexless larva. The functions of the termite workers are nest-building, gathering food, feeding the males, females and soldiers, tending the brood and keeping the hive clean. The larger workers, as with the ants, busy themselves outside the nest, foraging and collecting food, while the smaller workers look after the inside of the nest. Among the soldiers there is a similar subdivision of labour according to size: the outer defences are manned by the larger types, whereas the medium and smaller sized soldiers police the interior of the nest, supervise the groups of workers, urging on the sluggish, if necessary, with taps of their antennae. Under this supervision of the smaller soldiers, again, the workers take charge and rear the eggs laid by the queen. Larger soldiers surround the king and queen and defend them when the sentinels posted at the entrance give the danger-alarm by their tapping and chirping. As with the social bees and the ants, individual termites belonging to the same nest know one another by a special nest odour. Strangers who do not possess this smell are usually killed should they try to force an entrance into the nest.

As I have just mentioned, foraging and collecting of food, with its consequent storage in the nest, is performed by two subdivisions of the worker caste. The larger workers spend most of their time outside the nest in an unwearying activity which involves wood-collecting, gathering lichens, stumps, rubble, etc., for the building of fungus gardens and for works of construction or eventual reconstruction. When the foragers return to the nest, the material they have accumulated is taken charge of by the smaller nest workers, who utilize it as occasion requires.[1]

Like the ants, again, the termites construct store chambers

[1] Bugnion, in his monograph on *The Origin of Instinct*, gives an excellent account of the nocturnal foraging expeditions of the termite *E. monoceros* in search of lichens and wood bark. Cf. p. 21 *et seq.*

and cultivate fungus gardens. The store chambers contain fragments of finely shredded grass, leaves or grain, seeds, lichen and bark. The cultivation of fungi is usually of prime importance to the colony, for this alone enables the higher termites to maintain queens capable of laying thousands of eggs a day, and this in turn alone assures the successful rearing, day after day, of thousands of larvae.[1]

The development of a special soldier caste, with jaws so large in proportion to the rest of their body that they cannot even feed themselves and must be constantly attended by the workers (usually by trophallaxis), is evidence of the fact that the termites are called to defend themselves on occasion against vigorous enemies. Their fiercest opponents are the ants themselves, who neglect no opportunity that arises of forcing their way into the termite nest, killing the king and queen, and carrying off the larvae and food stores to their own nest. The termite larvae in particular appear to form a welcome change of diet for the ever-hungry ants, who take heavy toll also upon the termites when, during the period of swarming, the males and females are unable to defend themselves. So impressed has Bugnion been with his observations on these ceaseless wars between ant and termite, that in his monograph already mentioned he makes an interesting, though not, I think, entirely successful, attempt to find the origin of instinctive behaviour among the termites in their continual warfare with ant communities.

Among the termites, of course, as in all the social insects, 'property' is owned and defended on a collective basis. Where the family and the tribe are merged into one, or more correctly, where there is no family at all, defence can only be successful so long as the whole insect community fights together. Petrucci has this in mind when he writes: "La propriété individuelle (chez les termites) ne s'y trouve indiquée nulle part. . . . Cet abri collectif . . . constitue un

[1] Bugnion: *op. cit.*, 33.

fait de propriété évident. Les termites mettent à le défendre un acharnement et un courage que tous les naturalistes qui les ont observés, ont noté avec soin. La possession des réserves nutritives, comme celle de l'abri, appartient à l'ensemble de la société; la disposition de cette propriété collective se distribue suivant l'organisation sociale et la différenciation du travail."[1]

Before concluding this chapter I wish to summarize as briefly and as lucidly as possible the main conclusions that it seems to me possible to draw from the preceding pages. I wish to summarize, that is, how far the so-called instinct of acquisition has any basis in the activities of insects, and secondly, what is the nature of property among the insects.

In regard to the instinct of acquisition: it is only a blurring of relevant distinctions to suggest, as Rivers does, and many other psychologists, that the foraging activities of the bee, the wasp, or the ant, may be explained as due to the motivation of an instinct of acquisition acting either in the interests of the individual or so modified by gregarious life that it acts in the interests of the community. By acquisition is usually meant the personal production or collection and accumulation of objects of some value to the individual. Only incomplete knowledge could lead psychologists to assume that the honey-bee is thus instinctively motivated as it goes from flower to flower, collecting nectar, bee-bread or propolis.

Upon analysis it seems that one can best summarize the empirical data by emphasizing once again that with the solitary insects, the solitary wasps and bees, such accumulation of food as occurs is due to the activity of one instinctive link in that chain of innate pattern behaviour which is subsumed in a total activity having for its end the reproduction of offspring. Such accumulation does not stand on

[1] Petrucci: *Les Origines Naturelles de la Propriété*, 64.

its own as a self-sufficient activity. It is modified both by the previous and by the following chain activities. It has its integral part in the whole configuration which is directed towards the perpetuation of the species. One may not reasonably cut food-collecting adrift from its total behaviour-configuration and marvel: Lo! this bee is motivated by an instinct of acquisition. Amongst the social insects the accumulating activity has not only a similar content but it is even limited to one caste, the workers in the insect community. The specialization of instinct does not finish here; because of the workers one subdivision carries out that activity which we term foraging, that is, activity directed towards the finding, collecting and bringing to the hive or nest those objects, whether lichens or grain or honey, which are in some way or other of value to the community; while another subdivision of the workers takes charge of these objects when they reach the hive and applies them to those purposes for which they are suited, whether to repair the fabric of the nest or to swell the stores in the granary. In both the solitary and social insects, such accumulating activity—in no way explained by the postulation of an acquisitive instinct—is directed towards perpetuation of the species: in the solitary insects, directly, by providing food for the growing larvae; in the social insects, both directly and indirectly, by providing food for present needs and for occasions during winter and early spring when there is dearth of insect or vegetable food-stuffs.

If such accumulating activity (in one case, to repeat, the provisioning of the individual nest, in the other case, foraging for food and other objects of value to the hive and nest) must be fitted into a limited classification of instincts of the McDougall type it is far more reasonably and scientifically subsumed by an instinct of 'nutrition' or 'food-gathering' than by an instinct of 'acquisition,' or even, perhaps, as a modification or extension of an instinct of 'hunting.' In any case, however, simple classifications of instinct into thirteen or sixteen or twenty compartments have very little value when applied to the study of insect behaviour. The innate pattern activities of the insects refuse to be thus docketed and disposed of.

The fourth and final point that I would emphasize is that taken by and large, what I will term 'primitive property values' are much the same for all insect orders. Nest, prey, larvae, food supply and food hoards, territorial domain, are all vigorously defended against aggression. One need hardly raise the problem as to how far insects 'recognize' a given object as their 'own'; or whether a wasp defending her prey 'knows' what she is defending. A discussion of this problem is not of immediate relevance to our thesis. It may be said, however, in a quite summary fashion, that although hereditary modes of response become attached to certain objects or individuals through the operation of experiential factors, nevertheless we may not infer from this a knowledge or recognition of these objects *qua* objects, or of individuals *qua* individuals. The nest is only 'known' to the solitary wasp by means of a configuration in which it is in a particular relation to a locality-background. In sum, the activity of an insect, whether securing or defending prey, is just "a form of that defining or particularizing of instinct in which is found the most elementary operations of experience."[1] Similarly among social insects as among solitary orders, nest, young, food, are collectively owned because collectively defended; but defended not as 'known,' but because these 'values' define and particularize the working of instinct patterns. Material goods are accumulated by one caste for the use of the whole community. They are defended against aggression because in their 'definition' of instinct they have acquired the status of property values.

[1] Hobhouse: *Mind in Evolution*, 138.

CHAPTER III

PROPERTY AMONG BIRDS

In the previous chapter I have discussed the facts of acquisition and property in the economy of the insect world. In this chapter I wish to approach much the same sets of facts through an examination of their relative importance in the life of the bird. I will consider first, therefore, the various accumulative activities which have at one time or another been subsumed under an instinct of acquisition. For clearness of treatment I have divided these activities into two classes: the first is concerned with the accumulation of food, and the second with the accumulation of objects of value other than food. I will deal with these two classes separately.

First, then, as to the accumulation, hoarding or storing of food among birds. For various reasons this activity plays in the economy of bird life nothing like the important part it plays in insect life, on the one hand, or in the life of the smaller mammals, on the other hand. Birds subsist on a very varied diet. Most birds are largely insectivorous, depending on insects and the smallest mammals for their food supply; only secondarily on nuts, berries or grasses. It is, of course, not possible to store animal food for any length of time. As a second reason, it may be remarked that most birds in a northern climate are migrants, with no settled home, no nest to repair to in winter and thus with no base in which to store food for seasons of scarcity. They have a temporary home only at breeding-time, which usually takes place at seasons when there is plenty of food within easy reach. With the onset of winter most birds migrate to warmer climates where there is again an abundance of food. Thus, speaking quite generally, birds have no great difficulty in obtaining the food for which they are adapted during most of the months of the year. When there is a shortage in one district, their powers of locomotion enable them easily to wing their way to districts where there is a more plentiful supply. The habit of accumulating food, therefore, in one particular spot is characteristic of the behaviour of but few birds.

The most interesting example of accumulating behaviour is found among the woodpeckers. The common Californian species of ant-eating woodpecker (*Melanerpes formicivorus*) has the disposition to dig small round holes in the bark of the pine (*Pinus ponderosa*) or the oak and to fill each of these with an acorn so tightly fitted that it is with difficulty extricated. The bark of the pine-trees, when thus filled, presents at a short distance the appearance of being studded with nails. Ornithologists are at no little variance when they try to explain this behaviour of the Californian woodpecker. Newton, for instance, asserted that the storing of acorns is not done to furnish food in winter, for the species migrates south, and after journeying a thousand miles or so only returns in spring to the forests where its supplies are laid up.[1] Pycraft, however, in his *History of Birds* (1910), believes not only that the storing is done by a considerable number of birds banded together, but also that "at irregular intervals stragglers of the original party return to inspect the store and disperse again. Finally, at a time apparently agreed upon all return to feast upon the hoard."[2] Quite possibly the true explanation is that the acorns are collected in the autumn and are eaten by the birds when they return to the northern forests in the following spring. During early spring there is often a shortage of forest food; at this time,

[1] *Dictionary of Birds*, ii, 1048.

[2] Pycraft, 140. Petrucci, *op. cit.*, 102, contradicts this theory of collective storing, however, and believes that both the woodpecker and the Mexican *colaptes* collect provisions in a purely individual fashion.

supplies of stored nuts would be invaluable in preserving life. The difficulty, however, in his theory is to explain how the birds would return in their northward migrations to the very trees where the nuts were stored the preceding autumn; though perhaps if we take into account the undoubted ability that birds show of returning year after year to the same resting-place in the same tree this difficulty may be of no real importance.

It has been urged, again, that the acorns that are stored contain imprisoned maggots; and that it is these, not the ripened nuts, which are desired as food by the woodpecker.[1] This statement has been contradicted, however, and in this connection it is interesting to note that the woodpeckers follow their instinct so blindly that in some cases they do not distinguish between an acorn and a pebble. They fill the holes they have drilled with so much labour, not only with acorns, but occasionally with stones.[2]

Equally interesting are the accounts given of the red-headed woodpecker which is abundant in Indiana only when beech-nuts are plentiful. From the time these begin to ripen, the woodpeckers are constantly at work storing nuts in every conceivable situation—the cavities of decayed trees, clefts in gateposts, and even the thatches of houses. The felling of a tree in such a neighbourhood is always sure to disclose several pints of these small nuts. In one instance when they had been dropped into a crevice, pieces of bark and wood had been driven into the aperture, presumably to conceal the hoard from poachers. These birds have also a tendency to store grasshoppers in the way the Californian woodpeckers store nuts. These insects are captured with as little injury as possible, borne to some old oak-tree or post

[1] See C. J. Jackson (*Proc. Boston Nat. Hist Soc.*, vol. x, 227). Quoted by Romanes: *Mental Evolution in Animals*, 255 and note; cf. also Pycraft, *op. cit.*, 140.

[2] Newton: *op. cit.*, ii, 1049; Jordan and Kellogg: *Evolution and Animal Life*, 433, 434.

and there wedged in between the crevices and left struggling vainly to get free. As many as a hundred grasshoppers have been found so wedged at one time. Later, the birds return to devour their victims.[1]

Another woodpecker, *Colaptes mexicanus*, a relative of *Melanerpes*, stores food in the interior of a plant which is abundant in the zone it inhabits. Insectivorous during a part of the year, says Houssay, it is forced to renounce this diet during the dry season. In the regions of Mexico where this bird is found the dry period is so absolute that it would die of hunger had it not a store of food, collected during the spring, to fall back upon. Acorns are stored therefore in aloes, yuccas and agaves, or in the sheltered cavity of a shrivelled stem of an agave, for instance.[2] The interesting points about this storing of *Colaptes* are two. First, it is the storing of food in spring for subsistence during late summer. The storing of the other woodpeckers is always done in the autumn. The second is that *Colaptes*, along with the other woodpeckers, appears to possess two distinct diets. It does not preserve for the period of famine, that is, the overplus of foods which it consumes in times of abundance. In times of plenty it lives on insects and fruits; in times of scarcity mostly on nuts.

The woodpeckers I have so far mentioned would appear to make use of their stores of food in times of scarcity. That another variety of woodpecker found in British Honduras does this is by no means clear. These birds not only store acorns in the same manner as the Californian woodpecker, but they also deposit them in great quantities in hollow trees and similar places. One observer records finding a hollow-pine tree with a cavity six to eight inches in diameter filled for a distance of nearly twenty feet with acorns dropped into a good-sized hole at that distance above the ground.

[1] Pycraft: *op. cit.*, 141–142.
[2] Houssay: *The Industries of Animals*, 89–91.

Sometimes an opening at the bottom of one of these not uncommon stores showed the earlier deposited acorns completely decayed and crumbling to dust. It is evident that they must have been in the tree for several years; probably they were not brought by the birds that completed the accumulation. In these cases, of course, it would be utterly impossible for the birds ever to make use of the acorns in any way, yet generation after generation they go on laboriously gathering them. Furthermore, in an even, tropical climate like that of Honduras, where there can be little variation in food supply from season to season, it is difficult to see how such a habit could be of any great advantage, no matter what the circumstances might be. Even granting that it is so in some cases where the accumulation is accessible, these activities show how an over-developed instinct, or more correctly, how an instinct acting out of all relation to the environmental needs, may lead to behaviour not only useless but even absurd.[1]

It has been suggested that one of the motives underlying the food accumulation of the woodpecker arises from play activities. This may certainly be so; but ultimately it would seem that the acorn-storing instinct is based on a more or less definite but blind instinct to provide food for future use. It is a modification, or better, an extension, of that fundamental impulse to obtain food which is one of the basic needs of life itself. The origin of the maladaptation in food-storing among the Honduras woodpeckers arises most probably from the fact that the Honduras subspecies is derived from a more northern form and that its storing habit is due to the survival or carry-over of an ancestral instinct useful in higher latitudes but apparently useless in a tropical climate.[2]

[1] See M. E. Peck: "On the Acorn Storing Habit of Certain Woodpeckers," *The Condor* (July 1921), vol. xxiii, 131.

[2] *Ibid.*; also Henshaw: "The Storage of Acorns by the California Woodpecker." *The Condor* (July 1921), vol. xxiii, 109–118.

I have detailed the storing habits of the various species of woodpeckers at some length because these birds show this activity in a definite and clear-cut form. However, to a greater or less degree, this behaviour is characteristic of several other species of land-birds and of at least one species of sea-birds. The North American blue jay, which feeds so much on non-perishable food such as acorns, has every encouragement to accumulate such food, and so it puts by stores of acorns and beech-nuts for food in winter. The nuts are usually inserted into all sorts of crannies in trees, fence-posts, fence-rails and deserted buildings.[1] Passerines likewise take every opportunity to store food, the Cole-Tit being particularly assiduous, when fed at a bird-table, at carrying off scraps of food and then coming back for more. A caged pair of nuthatches not only stored sunflower seeds in the chinks at the back of their large cage, but even live spiders were jammed ruthlessly on to the wires and left to kick themselves to death.[2]

This treatment of the unfortunate spiders is strongly reminiscent of the behaviour of species of shrike, which in many cases store food by impaling it alive on stakes, thorns or barbed-wire fences. It is interesting to observe that this disposition seems to be far better developed in the North American species than in the Indian species, which suggests that the original food-getting instinct is modified or extended chiefly through adaptation to climatic conditions. The same tendency towards modification of original disposition is found to hold in a similar fashion in regard to the form of the nest and the materials from which it is made.[3] As regards the shrike, however, the habit of impaling food is undoubtedly a form of accumulation since the bird is just as capable of holding its food in its foot as the hawk

1 Ritter: *Animal and Human Conduct*, 135; Finn: *Bird Behaviour*, 309.
2 Finn: *op. cit.*, 309.
3 Wallace: *Contributions to the Theory of Natural Selection*, 232–233.

is, for instance, and therefore does not require to fix it up in order to tear it to pieces.[1]

The carrion hawks of North America develop the storage habit in captivity at any rate, for both the caracara and the *Ibycter australis* (the 'Jack-Rook' of the Falkland Islands) store away food at the Zoo. Owls, again, often accumulate a quantity of prey in their nesting-places, which, unlike most birds, they use as permanent homes and not merely as temporary homes or nurseries during the breeding-season. The behaviour of these birds is thus at the opposite pole to parrots, for example, which are not only non-provident birds but wantonly wasteful of their food. It has been suggested that this suicidal tendency to squander their supplies is perhaps one of the reasons why parrots are so rare outside the tropics.

I have mentioned above that there is one sea-bird which appears to make provision for the future. This bird is the gannet. Most sea-birds live all the year round in close proximity to their food supply. They are rarely found far from the sea or from river estuaries and thus have no occasion to store food for longer or shorter periods. Gannets are peculiar, however, in that they frequently fly fifty miles to their fishing-ground. In spite of the labour involved they invariably collect far more food than they need. Ogilvie has suggested that the explanation of this accumulating activity is to be found in the fact that gannets feed on surface-swimming fish and are thus dependent for their food supply on the state of the weather, since the fish swim at a greater depth when the weather is uncertain and stormy. "If the gale continues for three or four days, during the

[1] Ritter: *op. cit.*, 137–140. Finn: *op. cit.*, 309–310. Jordan and Kellogg make the suggestion that it is the play impulse, also, that leads the shrike to impale small birds, etc., on thorns, "a ghastly kind of ornament that seems to confer satisfaction on the bird itself," *op. cit.*, 435. Ultimately, however, as with the woodpecker, it would seem that the stored food is provision for future use.

whole of that time the birds will catch nothing and it is possible that the fear of such a catastrophe occurring is at the root of the habit and that the bird's instinct teaches him always to keep a day or two's supplies in hand as long as he is able to do so."[1] Since we as yet know little about the part that foresight or fear or prudence play in bird economy it would be safer to say that the frequently recurring vicissitudes of stormy weather have served to sift out variations in the direction of this extension of the food-getting tendency. In any case, food accumulation among sea-birds is the exception and not the rule, since fish is not an ideal food to accumulate and the majority of sea-birds are not dependent upon surface-swimming fish for their sole food supply.[2]

To sum up this section: food accumulation in birds is limited to a very few species, of which the chief examples are the woodpeckers, the shrike, the jay, passerine birds, with the gannet as an example of the operation of this impulse in sea-birds. In every case there seems to be a true innate behaviour pattern at work. This is shown clearly even in the case of the British Honduras woodpecker, which stores acorns for which it has no need, since there is abundance of food in winter months. Although it has been suggested that the motive for accumulation is to be found in many cases in the play impulse, yet in an ultimate analysis it would seem that food storage is due to a modification or extension of a more primitive food-getting impulse. Least of all is it the outcome of the activity of an 'acquisitive instinct.'

I will consider now various types of behaviour which I have summed up under the heading of non-food accumu-

[1] Ogilvie: *Field Observations on British Birds*, 26.

[2] Petrucci, *op. cit.*, 139, urged that food storing in animals, including birds, shows "une prévision lointaine, et des associations d'idées, des représentations mentales qui en font un fait conscient." This view is now no longer tenable. I shall refer to it critically in the next chapter.

lation. This includes the behaviour of such birds as the raven, the rook and the jackdaw, 'collecting' habits of antarctic birds like the Adelie penguins and the skua, and finally the accumulations of the bower-bird. My object is to examine representative examples of this behaviour in an endeavour to determine how far it is due to an instinct of acquisition, as is often confidently asserted, and how far due to other motives.

One type of non-food accumulation among the water-fowl seems definitely due to a modification of the nest-building instinct. Many of these birds spend much labour during incubation in increasing the size of their nest. Pieces of grass, fragments of sedges, reeds and straw, are all collected by a sitting swan, for example, as they float past her nest and added to the nest itself. This activity may serve either or both of two purposes. It raises the nest above possible future flood-levels—a very necessary precaution in many localities—and at the same time helps to provide a warm nest for the young birds when they finally break through the shell.[1]

The accumulation of nesting material is of immediate use to bird survival. It is difficult, however, to understand the survival value of what may be termed 'museum collecting' among birds: the collection, that is, and in many cases the hiding also, of objects which cannot be mistaken by the birds for anything edible. Miss Pitt tells us that among the objects collected by her two ravens were found a coloured marble, a stump of yellow pencil, a bit of rag, the lid of a tin, pieces of broken china, a dry, whitened piece of bone, and a pretty leaf. These treasures the ravens used to secrete among the coal or else in hiding-places hollowed out of a soft sandstone wall. The concealment

[1] Somewhat similar activity is reported of Adelie penguins. Levick observed these birds gathering together large quantities of stones in order to raise their nests about the rising level of thawing ice. Levick: *Antarctic Penguins*, 66.

was necessary since the ravens loved to steal from one another when the opportunity offered. It is significant, however, that when one of these ravens disappeared "the remaining one ceased to worry so much about concealing his finds," and when once a find had been carried off and stowed away the raven appeared to lose all interest in it. It was usually quickly forgotten, though the raven might happen across it at a later date by accident.[1] This would suggest that among the more social and, by implication, the more intelligent birds and other animals, social competition and socially acquired values influence the choice of objects which are collected.[2]

The jackdaw, the magpie and the crow, three birds of high intelligence and, in consequence, of vivid curiosity, are well known for their collecting habits. Thus the crow will accumulate such objects as a glittering stone, bits of glass, a silver spoon, etc. The 'ecclesiastical' daw has collected, among other things, the following: polished pebbles, medals, coins, seals, seal rings, small porcelain cats and dogs, little silver pigs, and similar *objets d'art*.[3]

Among sea-birds, strangely enough, the same tendency is at work. Miss Turner, in her *Bird Watching on Scolt Head*, writes delightfully of the male common tern who fusses round the female all the time she is brooding and often brings her little offerings of gaily-coloured pebbles and shells or shining objects of various kinds. "These are laid round the nest and the female amuses herself by flicking them here and there as far as her bill can stretch. A very favourite gift was the flat black fish-eggs common along the seashore,

[1] Pitt: *The Animal Mind*, 200–202.

[2] Cf. on this point J. A. Thomson: *Biology of Birds*, 316, 341–342; Thomson: *The Mind of Animals*, 67–68; Pitt: *op. cit.*, ch. xx; Hobhouse: *Mind in Evolution*, ch. xiii. In the next chapter reference is made to the effect of social stimulation upon possessiveness as observed by Koehler among his apes at Teneriffe.

[3] See Hudson: *Birds and Man*, 84, and the same writer's *Birds in London*, 19–20, 37, ch. v, *passim*

known as 'mermaid's purses.'. . . I often saw them brought and laid by the sitting bird. The male sidled up with a peculiar strut and an ingratiating air. The female always examined these gifts with interest and kept turning them over during her mate's absence."[1]

This behaviour of the tern is difficult to account for, unless it is due to some modification of the mating instinct and thus has affiliations with the similar behaviour of the bower-bird. But the collecting propensities of other sea-birds like the penguin and McCormack's skua are more easy to understand. The Adelie penguins described by Levick were much attracted by bright objects. They abstracted from a heap of the black stones with which they build their nests, stones painted red and green; and from a scrap-heap such varied articles as pieces of tin and of glass, the head of a bright metal teaspoon, half a stick of chocolate, etc. All these objects were stolen from nest to nest and were thus slowly distributed in different directions throughout the rookery.[2]

To explain the collecting behaviour of birds it does not seem necessary to postulate the existence of either an instinct of property or of an instinct of acquisition. What seems to happen in these cases is that the curiosity and interest of the raven, the jackdaw, or the skua, are excited and attracted by objects which are inherently nice, bright and easily portable in the bill. This interest is focussed by the first act of seizure, or even of attention, on a particular object, and thereafter the object becomes the end object of desire. All the trains of feelings or reactions attendant on, or subsidiary to, its use are called forth in response to

[1] E. L. Turner: *Bird Watching on Scolt Head*, 33.

[2] Levick: *op. cit.*, 48–49. For an account of the manner in which McCormack's skua gull is attracted by bright portable objects, see the Report of the National Antarctic Expedition (1901–1904); *Natural History*, vol. ii, *Zoology*, Aves, by E. A. Wilson, 68–69, 74; and also Levick: *op. cit.*, 129–130.

that object rather than others. The object is thus mentally appropriated, and, should opportunity offer, mental appropriation is completed by material appropriation. As long as the object is within sight and interest is kept alive in it by social competition, it becomes a permanent basis of action, something that the bird can count upon and go back to at need.[1]

Several points of interest arise in a consideration of the behaviour of the bower-bird, since it is often stated that this behaviour can only be explained on the supposition that the bird is actuated by an acquisitive instinct. Thus Houssay, for example, tells us that "these birds feed only on grains, so that it is to a very pronounced taste for collecting that we must attribute this mania for piling up before the entrance of the bower white stones, shells and small bones."[2] A closer examination, however, of the activity of these birds as described by Gould makes it evident that least of all may one attribute such behaviour to the operation of a collecting instinct.[3] In point of fact it is not possible logically to separate the accumulation of bright colourful objects from the bower which they are used to adorn. The bower itself plays a large part in the courtship activities of the bower-bird, and therefore one may assume that the collection of bright objects is motivated by play, sexual and primitive aesthetic tendencies, rather than by any desire for a collection *per se*. The use that the male bower-bird makes of bright objects during courtship is paralleled by the activity of many other male birds in carrying a bright leaf in their beak when under the excitement of love-making. The crested grebe, for instance, present to each other dank weeds, the material from which their sodden nest is built.

[1] I follow Hobhouse here. Cf. *Property: Its Duties and Rights*, 8.

[2] Houssay: *op. cit.*, 181.

[3] For descriptions of the bower-bird, its nest, bower and courtship behaviour, see Gould: *Handbook to the Birds of Australia*, i, 444–445; Darwin: *The Descent of Man*, i, 140; ii, 75, 113, 124.

Adelie penguins, who make their nest of stones, use stones in their courtship behaviour.[1]

It is clear, I think, from a careful study of the evidence that the collecting of bright objects by the male bower-bird during the breeding-cycle is a subsidiary activity to that of building the bower and that the objects are used to decorate the bower. It is in this bower that the courtship activities of the birds take place. The bright objects that are strewn about the entrances of the bower or woven into its fabric serve in some way or other to make the bower attractive to the female, and thus help to precipitate that activity which has for its end the perpetuation of the species.[2] It is a mistake, however, to separate the collecting activities from the total activity. It is this totality of behaviour, this configuration, which gives meaning to the constituent parts. Because of this it is incorrect to state that the bower-bird is motivated by a 'very pronounced taste for collecting.' Rather does it collect because only thus can it obey the hereditary urge to mate, build a nest, and rear its young. The behaviour of the common tern described above may be due to a similar modification of the mating instincts which takes place after, and not before, mating itself. Or else, it may be due to the play impulse. Who knows but that the female tern is very grateful for bright-coloured objects to play with during that tedious lapse of hours which must pass before incubation is complete?

I come now to consider some aspects of the property relation in birds, the attachment, that is, to nest and to territory.

[1] See Julian Huxley: *Essays of a Biologist*, 105–128; Pycraft: *The Courtship of Animals*, 160.

[2] It is not my intention to trench upon controversies over the nature of sexual selection. Reference, however, may be made to the following for various aspects of the problem: J. A. Thomson: *The System of Animate Nature*, ii, 456–474; Haldane and Huxley: *Animal Biology*, 213–216; Jordan and Kellogg: *op. cit.*, 75–79; Pycraft: *op. cit.*, ch. vii, *passim*.

This is shown both by the continuous occupation of a home or a territory and by a willingness to defend both from aggression.

It is within the experience of most naturalists that the most sedentary of birds year after year occupy the same nest and territory in the breeding-season. Newton gives two remarkable instances of this persistency which seem to show that generation after generation of birds regard one particular region as their own. The nest of a falcon on the Finnish island of Avasana is mentioned by the French astronomer Maupertuis as having been observed by him in the year 1736. In 1799 the nest was rediscovered, while in 1853 the nest was again found tenanted, and from enquiries it appeared that such had been the case as far as anyone could remember. In the second instance, record shows that either in 1785 or in 1779 a pair of blue titmice built their nest in a large earthenware bottle placed in the branches of a tree in a garden at Oxbridge. With two exceptions only, this bottle, or a second which had been placed close to it, was tenanted by a pair of birds of this species from the year in which it was first occupied until 1873.[1]

No bird seems more strongly attached to its home than the spur-wing lapwing of the Argentine pampas. This bird is so jealous of the portion of ground it lives on that it furiously attacks and drives away other lapwings and even plover or other species that venture to trespass on it. Hudson tells us that winter and summer this bird occupies the same ground. "I have known a pair of these birds," he writes, "that occupied and bred on the same spot year after year, and when the ground was enclosed with a wire fence and ploughed they refused to quit, but laid their eggs in a furrow, and after the harrowing, which destroyed the first

[1] A. Newton: *op. cit.*, i, 552, note 1. See also Petrucci: *op. cit.*, 112. Hudson gives an account of a crow which nested in the same locality in Hampstead for upward of sixty years (*Birds in London*, 32).

eggs, they laid again, to lose their eggs again when the corn was hoed. And for three years they persisted in trying to breed in that one spot which was their own home. All over the country it was the same: thousands of miles of unenclosed grazing lands were all parcelled out among these birds, each pair in possession of its own well-defined territory."[1]

This attachment to home is found not only among resident birds but also among migratory species. There are many examples of migratory birds returning to the same breeding-place in successive years. A swift ringed in Ayrshire in 1914, for example, was recaptured in the same place in 1918, having, doubtless, been to Africa four times in the interval.[2] Thomson suggests that this return of migratory birds to the same breeding-place is due, not to any sense of ownership or attachment to a particular region, but to that regularity of coming and going which is so notable a feature of migration. This may well be so. Yet, on the other hand, examples are not lacking to show that the most migrant of birds sometimes appear to exercise choice in the matter. A pair of stone curlews, a very migratory species affecting almost exclusively the most open country, were in the habit of breeding for many years on the same spot though its character had undergone a complete change. It had been part of an extensive and barren rabbit-warren, and was now become the centre of a large and flourishing plantation.[3]

In many instances, indeed, this attachment to one particular locality may be ascribed to the old haunt affording the sole or the most convenient site for the nest in the neighbourhood. In so many cases, however, this is not the case that we are led to believe in the existence of a real

1 Hudson: *A Hind in Richmond Park*, 207–208.
2 J. A. Thomson: *The Biology of Birds*, 162–163.
3 Newton: *op. cit.*, i, 552.

partiality, while there are quite enough exceptions both in resident and migrant to show that choice is frequently exercised.

Along with this attachment to locality goes a vigorous defence against intruders upon the mate, the nest, the young and food supplies: the four most primitive values, and the four most primitive types of property. The cormorant, for example, resents an intruder's approach to the nest on the sea-cliff shelf, hissing violently and lunging with her formidable beak. When direct defence of the nest is out of the question because of its position or because of the nature of the bird, recourse is sometimes had to wiles. The redshank is extraordinarily successful in leading one astray, and devices for feigning lameness or a broken wing are often realistically uncanny. In rare cases the parent bird has been known to shift its eggs, the goat-sucker taking them in its capacious mouth, while the woodcock and the eagle-owl have been recorded as transporting nestlings to places of safety. Sometimes there may be combination against attack, and thus cliff swallows unite to keep at a distance the rapacious prairie falcon, and wild ducks combine to drive off eagles; wagtails, a hawk; lapwings, a buzzard, a kite or a crow. Should a wild mother fear too much for the safety of her offspring she will often remove them from danger by putting them all to death.[1]

A detailed example or two will make these points clear. Two Canadian geese elected to nest in a rather exposed spot. As soon as the nest was finished and the eggs laid therein, the goose took her place upon the eggs and the gander mounted guard. "There were so many hostiles on the warpath that he was kept on the *qui vive* during all daylight hours. At a radius of about twenty feet he

[1] Cf. Pitt: *The Animal Mind*, chs. viii. and xii, *passim*; Hornaday: *The Mind and Manners of Wild Animals*, 191–192; Hudson: *Birds and Man*, 115–116.

drew an imaginary dead line around the family nest and no bird, beast or man could pass that line without a fight. If any other goose or a swan or a duck attempted to pass, the guardian gander would rush forward with blazing eyes, open beak, wings open for action, and with distended neck hiss out his challenge. If the intruder failed to register respect and came on, the gander would seize the offender with his beak and furiously wing-beat him into flight."[1] Much the same characteristic behaviour is reported of the noddy terns by Watson. During breeding, the female guards the nest practically the whole day long, leaving only momentarily to drink. Fights between the noddies and man-o'-war birds are frequent. They are mostly brought about by the latter's attempts to roost over the nests of the noddies. Fights among the noddies themselves occur when a strange bird attempts to usurp the nest, to have intercourse with the female on the nest, to steal straws, and in general to encroach upon the neighbourhood of the nest. They will also attack any strange birds that come to their island home with the exception of hawks.[2]

Among the penguins, observations show that after arrival at the rookeries, the cocks fight first for the possession of the female and the nesting-site she has appropriated, and later both fight vigorously to gain and hold the stones and pebbles with which their nests are built. Yet thieving is very common in the rookery, and when detected the thief is always pursued and punished by the injured birds. Writing of the great rookery at Cape Adare, Wilson says: "There are many misunderstandings in these colonies over the misappropriation of property. The nests were all too close to one another and he had the biggest nest who could most successfully annex his neighbour's pebbles and prevent his own from being stolen. Needless to say, there was hardly

[1] W. T. Hornaday: *op. cit.*, 251.

[2] J. B. Watson: *Behaviour*, 116–117; cf. also Turner: *op. cit.*, 34.

a stone of his nest but had been stolen from someone else. Each bird balanced on its own little island of stones resented any interference from its neighbours, avian or human."[1]

Some birds, especially sea-birds, make a habit of obtaining their food by robbing their weaker brethren. In all cases the victim puts up as prolonged a resistance as possible to the attacks of the robber. But in most cases, might triumphs and the weak go to the wall. The robber tern, for example, gains its food entirely by plundering other terns; while the frigate pelican is a professional robber who attacks boobies, not only to make them drop the fish they have caught but also to disgorge those actually in their stomachs. This latter process is effected by the pelican stabbing its victim with its powerful beak until the boobie yields up its latest meal. One may say, however, that in bird life, as in human life, robbery is the exception rather than the rule. In the majority of cases birds are not called upon actively and continually to defend their food supplies. But should the occasion arise they are usually as willing as they are successful in the maintenance of an exclusive right to that which they have gained by their own labour.[2]

I may now pass to a fuller consideration of the part

[1] *National Antarctic Expedition Report*, ii, 34, 46; cf. also Levick: *op. cit.*, 22, 24.

[2] It has long been known that birds of prey drive away their offspring from the parental haunts as soon as the young are mature enough to fend for themselves. This behaviour is usually interpreted by animal sociologists as due to the impulse of the parent birds to preserve for themselves exclusive possession of, and control over, their nests and territory. MacCurdy, in his *Problems of Dynamic Psychology*, 332–337, suggests, however, that it is due to Nature's desire to prevent in-breeding between parent bird and offspring. This hypothesis of MacCurdy seems impossible to substantiate, though for lack of space I cannot give it the criticism it deserves. The real explanation for the behaviour of the parent birds is surely to be found in the fact that there is scarcity of food in one locality, specially when parents and offspring have occupied this locality throughout the spring, summer and autumn months. The young, therefore, are driven off to find for themselves more plentiful supplies of food. It is a very ancient saying about young ravens that "they wander for lack of meat."

territory plays in bird life. The facts, as placed on record by careful observers, are material to my thesis for two main reasons. The first is that these facts display the operation of individual ownership over territory. The second reason is that it has been confidently asserted that the process of acquiring individual rights over territory "illustrates very definitely the existence of an instinct of acquisition." I will examine, therefore, the behaviour of birds in relation to territory with a view to determining to what degree it is due to the operation of an instinct of acquisition and to what degree due to the operation of other factors. I have made use of Mr. Eliot Howard's fascinating account of the subject,[1] but have supplemented it by a further selection of relevant material from other sources.

In broad outline the animal life history of a bird is conditioned by the fundamental dichotomy of two powerful and, at first sight, opposing impulses—the one to live socially and the other to live solitary. Both these impulses have an important part to play in furthering the life of the individual and thus indirectly of the species as a whole. During the winter months many species of birds are drawn together and live a social life in flocks which come and go according to prevailing climatic conditions. This flocking is probably due to the fact that food is not plentiful and can be found only in certain places;[2] but also the birds are brought together by the functional operation of gregarious impulses. With the advent of spring, a change comes over the scene. Flocks disperse, family parties break up, summer migrants arrive, and hedgerows and plantations are suddenly awakened into life. In other words, each male bird assumes the ownership of a definite locality, defends his territory against aggression, and prepares to court the female bird.

[1] H. Eliot Howard: *Territory in Bird Life*, London, 1924.

[2] Cf. Newton: *op. cit.*, i, 554.

The behaviour of the yellow bunting provides a typical instance of the activities of a bird of a resident species. The ordinary winter routine for this warbler continues until early in February, when the male deserts the flock, seeks a position of its own and becomes isolated from its companions. The territory it selects does not embrace a large area, a few acres perhaps at the most. Within this area there is always some one point which is singled out and resorted to with marked frequency—a tree, a bush, a gatepost, a railing—and which eventually becomes the central part of the bird's environment. "Here it spends the greater part of its time, here it utters its song persistently, and here it keeps watch upon intruders."[1] The process of establishment, however, is a gradual one. For a time the bunting alternates between the composite flocks of its companions and its own territory. In any case, the process seems to depend largely on temperature. With a return to lower temperature, male birds who have acquired individual territories may return to communal life and there display none of that aggressiveness which accompanies the territorial ownership. As the temperature rises, these periodical desertions become less frequent in occurrence until the whole of the bird's life is spent on the few acres within which it has established itself.

Migratory as well as resident birds acquire a territory. It has long been known that with such migratory species as the whinchat and the nightingale, the male invariably returns before the female to the summer haunt—sometimes a few days, sometimes a fortnight before. This behaviour becomes intelligible, suggests Howard, if we explain it on the theory that the male returns early in order that it may acquire and establish itself in a territory in preparation for the breeding-season.[2]

[1] Howard: *op. cit.*, 30.
[2] It should be noticed that this explanation does not altogether cover the

It is unusual for the male bird to be left in undisputed possession of the territory it has marked out as its own, since there are always roving males, as yet unestablished, who are on the look-out for an opportunity to dispossess an unprepared or physically weak bird. Fights, therefore, are of frequent occurrence. Howard writes graphically of hostilities between willow-warblers established in adjoining territories: "A male intrudes and the intrusion evokes an immediate display of irritation on the part of the owner of the territory, who, rapidly uttering its song and jerking its wings, begins hostilities. Flying towards the intruder, it attacks viciously, and there follows much fluttering of wings and snapping or clicking of bills. At one moment the birds are in the tree-tops, at another in the air, and sometimes even on the ground, and fighting thus they gradually approach and pass beyond the limits of the territory. Whereupon a change comes over the scene; the male whose territory was intruded upon and who, all along, had displayed such animosity, betrays no further interest in the conflict—it ceases to attack, searches around for food or sings, and slowly makes its way back towards the centre of the territory."[1] Aggressiveness, that is, is shown only within the individual territory and disappears as soon as a male has been chased out of the territory into which he has intruded.

The reinterpretation of the part song plays in the life of the bird shows that it is in its origin and essential function a symbol of the possession of a nesting territory occupied by a male—to other males a notice that trespassing will not be tolerated, to females an invitation to settle, pair, and

field, since in Newton's words: "It is not difficult to imagine that in the course of a journey prolonged through some 50 or 60 degrees of latitude, the stronger should outstrip the weaker by a very perceptible distance, and it can hardly be doubted that in most species the males are stouter as they are bigger than the females." *Dictionary of Birds*, i, 556.

[1] Howard: *op. cit.*, 91–92.

nest. The old idea that the song of birds formed quite simply the serenade of the cock to his chosen hen has now been discarded. There is no longer room for doubt that the proclamation of the territorial rights of the male, the warning to respect them, and at the same time the invitation to the female, is an essential part of true song—the function of song, but not, of course, its conscious purpose.[1] In any case, the final movements of the symphony are played when the female arrives and pairs with the owner of the territory. Breeding begins, the nest is built, eggs laid and soon the two parents are busy feeding the young. The individual territory supplies them with food close at hand and thus its acquisition is an integral part in the sex cycle.

It is unnecessary to stress the value, save in general terms, of the territorial system in the bird economy. It enables the parent birds to have close at hand an area sufficient to provide food for parents and young. It obviates long and exhausting journeys in search of food. Instead of this district being overcrowded and that deserted; instead of there being too many of one sex here and too few of the other sex there; instead of a high percentage of individuals failing to procreate their kind, just because circumstances over which they have no control prevent their discovering one another at the appropriate time; instead of this, each sex has its allotted part to play, each district has its allotted number of inhabitants, and the waste of energy and the loss of time incurred in the process of mating are reduced to a minimum.[2]

Such in outline is the general nature of the territorial system in bird life. I have referred so far only to the

[1] Howard: *op. cit.*, ch. iv, *passim*; cf. also Pitt: *op. cit.*, 168–169, 176–177; Huxley: *Essays of a Biologist*, 123; and *The Observer*, March 10, 1929, and *The Times*, March 28, 1929, for further accounts of this newer functional interpretation of bird song.

[2] Howard: *op. cit.*, 174, 179–192.

Warblers.[1] But behaviour in regard to territory is characteristic of nearly every species of birds. There are, however, one or two variations on the main theme. The robin, for instance, carries the territorial question so far as to hold a territory throughout the year, while each sex has a separate territory of its own, save at mating-time, when a territory is controlled jointly by the two parent birds.[2] The sheld-duck, on the other hand, though it acquires an individual territory, is nevertheless more or less gregarious every morning and evening, resorting to the society of its fellows, until the young hatch out. Then the parent birds rarely leave their territory.[3] More or less 'standardized' behaviour, however, is typical with other water-birds, such as the crested grebe, the little grebe, the rare Slavonian grebe or the moorhen. Such birds of prey again as the eagle, falcon and hawk peregrines and buzzards all act in a characteristic fashion in regard to territory.[4]

Among various species of sea-birds such as the gulls, the guillemots, terns, or penguins it is not so much a territory which is delimited as the space which embraces the immediate neighbourhood of the nest. Sea-birds as a rule take up breeding-quarters on exposed beaches, rocky cliffs or precipitous headlands. Their nests are placed on the ground, on cliff shelfs, roughly scooped out of the sand, or equally roughly made with stones and driftwood. Since the food supply for a rookery or colony can only be found in the sea it must be shared in common. There are no means of dividing

[1] Reference should be made here to Howard's comprehensive work on *The British Warblers*, 2 vols., London (1907–1914), for further material relative to fighting in defence of territory, proclamation of possession by song, and the relation of behaviour over territory-acquisition to the total reproductive cycle of activities; cf. particularly vol. i, pt. v, 6; vol. ii, pt. xx, 12–35; vol. ii, pt. xxi, 13.

[2] Pitt: *op. cit.*, 174–176; Petrucci: *op. cit.*, 107–111.

[3] Turner: *op. cit.*, 55.

[4] Pitt: *op. cit.*, 169–174, 178–180; Pitt: *Woodland Creatures*, 213–214; Hudson: *Birds of La Plata*, i, 36; see also *The Observer*, April 21, 1929.

the sea into territorial areas as can be done with a meadow or coppice by means of trees or fences or bushes. But the delimitation of a nest area is of considerable importance, as it both provides a relatively secure area on which eggs may be laid and incubated and at the same time tends to prevent careless birds from walking about haphazardly and perhaps causing damage to eggs and helpless young. Ownership of a territory being impossible, sea-birds have compromised by being purists in regard to the exclusiveness of the area surrounding their nest. Thus Miss Pitt, in describing the behaviour of the skua gull on the Shetland Islands, writes that each pair were keenly on the look-out and ready at any moment to rise and drive off intruders. All would be calm until an intruder, probably one that did not belong to the spot, flew over. Then scores of those on the ground would rise, fill the air with clamour, and assist the first pair in driving off the intruder.[1]

Another interesting contrast to the habits of northern land-birds is provided by the Adelie penguins. Whereas with the northern birds it is the cock who arrives first and secures a territory, among the penguins it is the hen who arrives first at the rookery, chooses the site, builds the nest, defends it against competing hens until the cocks arrive and fight for the possession of the hens and the accompanying nesting-site. Round each nest is a zone which marks the limits of the property of each family and which is divided from the next zone by crossing paths. It is along these paths that the birds go to and from the open sea, often several hundred yards away from the nests. Petrucci, however, after Racovitza, talks of one zone "séparée de la zone voisine par une limite idéale"; and adds: "Cependant, les Manchots ont la conscience très nette de l'étendue de leur domaine familiale."[2] I myself find it easier to imagine that intrusion over a definite path rather than the "infraction

[1] Pitt: *Shetland Pirates*, 27.

[2] Petrucci: *op. cit.*, 124.

d'une limite idéale" is the more legitimate cause for violent quarrels among the far from intelligent penguins!

I have now considered as briefly as possible the behaviour of birds in relation to territory. Such behaviour is important, as I have suggested above, because it presents first, a clear case of the individual occupation and defence of territory among birds, and second, because it has been stated that the bird acquires such territory through the motivation of an 'instinct of acquisition.' I will examine for a moment these two points separately.

In regard to the ownership of territory among birds, Espinas has suggested that the delimitation of one territory from another, and the consequent expropriation of food and materials, can only result in the majority of cases because the birds reciprocally respect each other's rights. Petrucci has gone a step further, and adds: "En effet, il ne s'âgit plus ici des faits instinctifs mais de conceptions et d'idées qui vont jusqu'à la conscience. Et même dans les limites des domaines établis dans la façon dont ils peuvent subsister côte à côte et dont l'oiseau défend son territoire, peut-on voir apparaître la coutume sous une forme aussi précise que peuvent présenter les premiers phénomènes de la vie en société chez l'homme."[1] I take this to mean that the existence of territory occupation at a certain season of the year is not so much the outcome of the operation of instinct as of the fact that bird mind is able to use conceptions, ideas, conscience, and thus recognizes a right or custom to the exclusive ownership of such territory.

This immediately raises the problem as to what is meant by the nature of a concept, and to what degree the bird mind is regulated by concepts, as thus defined. What, then, does the formation of concepts imply? The answer surely is that generality rests on an attributive relation, on the fact that concrete wholes are qualified by attributes. The concept is

[1] Petrucci: *op. cit.*, 111; cf. also, 125–126.

the thought function which has mastered this attributive relation and, therefore, can construct what is not perceived nor ever has been perceived as a whole. To be able to form a concept the mind must analyse experience; it must make explicit the common characters on which a comparative analysis rests; and in so doing the analytic movement becomes, under another aspect, a movement of synthesis which makes possible still further synthesis. It is the power of entering into diverse combinations while still recognized as the same content that constitutes generality. Hobhouse makes this clear when he writes: "To make the general concept a reality the mind must be able to detach not only fragments of its experience but to follow that articulation of reality whereby attributes qualify substances, enter into relations, are resolvable in turn into more elementary attributes and are united by manifold and interwoven affinities. This articulation is the broad basis of the conception and the judgment, and analysis and synthesis are the processes by which the mind comes to understand and work it out."[1]

The concept implies, therefore, the fact that an element given originally in perception must come to mean something for consciousness apart from its perceptual setting; and further, that it must be applicable to a different setting. The ability to form concepts, it is evident, can only come about through the use of verbal or pictorial symbols, for the free use of symbols supposes a stock of general ideas. Description of particular facts is a means whereby those facts are brought into relation with the store of ideas. It is in the existence of such a store of ideas for use in practice, and thus the consequent ability to form concepts, that one obtains a criterion whereby human intelligence may be broadly distinguished from that of the higher animals. No symbolism, no concept, is the rule of mental evolution.

[1] Hobhouse: *Mind in Evolution*, 331.

We may grant to Petrucci's birds such capacity for dealing with the practical exigencies of their surroundings as can be attained by an intelligence limited in its scope to the concrete and the practical. Such intelligence is, perhaps, capable of forming what Hobhouse terms Practical Judgments. But at present there seems no ascertainable reason for supposing that the higher animals are capable even in a remote degree of forming conceptual judgment.[1] We are therefore justified, I think, in dismissing Petrucci's assertion that individual ownership of territory among birds rests on factors of a conceptual nature. We are justified further, it appears, in suggesting that such exclusive occupation of territory is purely the outcome of factors of an instinctive nature unmixed with any considerations of right, habit or custom.

What, then, is the instinctive basis of that occupation at breeding-time of a territory which is characteristic of the behaviour of sea-birds, water-fowl, resident birds and migrants? Rivers, it will be remembered, stated that this process of acquiring individual rights over a territory "illustrates very definitely the existence of an instinct of acquisition."[2] I would suggest, however, that in writing that passage Rivers' usual acumen temporarily deserted him, and that he was led into a false position through his over-eagerness to prove the existence of an assumed 'instinct of acquisition.' The facts, it will be recalled, are these: instinctive acquisition of territorial rights by the individual only takes place at one particular period of the year, and in connection with the sexual and parental functions. During the rest of the year most birds are gregarious and sociable; there is no aggressiveness displayed in relation

[1] Reference may be made to Herrick: *Brains of Rats and Men*, chs. xiv, xix; Smith: *An Investigation of Mind in Animals*, 177–178; Washburn: *The Animal Mind*, 270–284; Carr: "The Interpretation of the Animal Mind," *Psych. Review* (1927), 98–101.

[2] Cf. Rivers: *op. cit.*, 263–264.

to territory nor is there any tendency to exclusive occupation of a particular locality. We would summarize these data by stating that at breeding-time there comes into functional operation among birds a congenital disposition to secure and defend a territory.

The underlying basis of this disposition to secure a territory, I would suggest in opposition to Rivers, is the operation of sexual and parental impulses. If by the sexual impulse is meant the actual discharge of the sexual function which is in its turn the consummation, the final cause, the *terminus ad quem*, of the whole process of courtship and mating, then acquisition of territory and all that appertains to it is part of that process—the search for the breeding-ground, the occupation thereof, the intolerance of intrusions, are but different stages, each one of which probably has an impulse peculiar to it. Since the completion of the sexual act can only be successfully accomplished provided that success is attained at every stage, it is evident that it is only from the configuration of the whole activity that the parts attain any meaning. It is surely a gratuitous piece of theorizing to cut this total activity into parts, to take one link in the chain, the occupation of the territory, and to assert that it is the outcome of the activity of a generalized 'instinct of acquisition.' In fact, in so far as it is possible to separate the links in the chain, one may say that the occupation of territory acquires meaning only when it is subsumed under that cycle of activity which we outside observers perceive to be the reproduction of the species. It is curious that Rivers was half-aware of this truth himself, because he wrote: "This instinctive attitude towards ownership only shows itself in connection with the parental function, or as a stage in the chain of proceedings in which the parental instinct finds expression. So far as we can speak of an instinct of acquisition in this case, it is not independent, but is closely bound up with the sexual and parental instincts by means of which the race is perpetuated." Notwithstanding, this statement, however, Rivers continued to argue that the occupation of territory was *bona fide* evidence for the existence in animals of an independently acting 'instinct of acquisition.' Yet his argument as a whole is gratuitous and does violence to the facts. Acquisition of territory is not due to the operation of an instinct of acquisition. Rather is it truer to say that the disposition to secure a territory represents the initial impulse in that chain of activity whose *raison d'être* is the reproduction of the species.

Before passing to the next chapter, I will briefly recapitulate our main conclusions.

1. Food accumulation among birds is the exception rather than the rule. It does occur, however, quite definitely among several species, notably the woodpeckers, the jays, the shrike, and, among sea-birds, the gannet. It is not possible to explain this storing activity as due to an instinct of acquisition. It is due to an extension or modification of the food-getting impulse.

2. Non-food accumulation or museum-collecting is found only among the most intelligent, and therefore the most curious birds. Here the psychological basis of the behaviour seems to lie in the fact that the interest which objects excite because of their similarity to food or because of their inherent value as small, bright things, easily portable in the bill, is focussed by the first act of seizure on an object, and thereafter all the reacting train of impulse-feeling is concentrated on that object to the exclusion of any other. It is significant to remember that the raven only hid objects under the stimulus of social competition; that it frequently forgot where it had hidden things; and that out of sight was out of mind. There was probably in the first place psychological appropriation but none of that gloating over treasures which is supposed to be characteristic of the authentic miser.

3. The bird will defend from attack and violence its mate, its food, its nest, its young, and at certain seasons, its territory. These objects of defence are the end-objects which satisfy the instincts of sex, nutrition, and building, and parental impulses. They represent primitive values for the bird. It is suggested that the psychological basis of possessiveness is found in those objects which are essential to the satisfaction of these basic instincts. Possessiveness in other objects is the outcome of a process of conditioning which we shall consider later. It is not necessary to posit a special instinct to explain the acquisition of a mate or food. Acquiring food is essential to the satisfaction of the food-getting impulse; acquiring a mate is a first essential towards the satisfaction of the sexual instinct.

4. In regard to the disposition to secure and defend a territory: whereas Rivers was inclined to evaluate the facts subsumed by this disposition as evidence for the existence of an independently acting instinct of acquisition, I have suggested that these facts take on a legitimate and larger meaning only when they are considered within a configuration which comprises a total activity directed towards the satisfaction of sexual and parental impulses.

CHAPTER IV

PROPERTY AMONG RODENTS, CARNIVORES AND APES

In the two preceding chapters I have considered the facts of property and acquisition in relation to the behaviour of insects and of birds. In this present chapter I wish to carry the investigation a step further by discussing briefly these same facts in relation to the life of some of the common mammals, notably the rodents, the carnivores and the apes. I wish to determine, that is, the nature and extent of accumulation, whether of food or of other objects, among representative species of these animal orders, and at the same time discover whether these animals exercise exclusive possession or control over objects in the environment.

First, however, a word or two on the position of the common mammals in the biological scale. Physiologically speaking, mammals owe their superiority over reptiles and the lower animals in the course of evolutionary development, firstly, to the fact that they were able to regulate the temperature of their bodies in relation to environmental needs; and secondly, because they made better provision for their young, both before and after birth or hatching. Within the mammalian stock itself progress has depended chiefly upon increase of the size of the brain developing in close correspondence with more attentive pre-natal and post-natal care of the offspring.

From the psychological point of view, it has been characteristic of the mammals that although they have, as the basis of behaviour, an equipment of innate behaviour patterns—inborn powers of doing things without apprenticeship or learning—nevertheless, this common groundwork has been plastic and modifiable to a relatively remarkable degree.

The mammals have thus shown a marked ability to profit by experience, to form perceptual associations, and to be educated and trained by their parents or by man. Depending, as all higher life must, upon this groundwork of inherited instinct, the mammals have been able to subsume the groundwork by the power of intelligent adaptation to environmental difficulties which grows not less, but more important the higher the position of the animals on the ladder of evolution. The ascent of this ladder has meant the increasing replacement, or perhaps more correctly, the increasing subsumption, of automatic congenital patterns of behaviour by the power of experiential modification.

With the exception of Man himself, who stands apart and in isolation because of his ability to use language and conceptual inference, the monkeys and the higher apes are the most intelligent and adaptative of all the mammalian orders. They may be said to represent the triumph of the 'big-brain' over the 'little-brain' type of animal life in the evolutionary struggle. Gifted with a good sensory equipment, manipulative expertness, quickness of perception and plan, intense activity of body and mind, and a restless inquisitiveness, the higher apes give evidence of an intelligence of no mean order and of an emotional life which is both deep and intense. For these reasons, if for no other, it should be interesting to discover the degree of their acquisitiveness and the nature of that which they appropriate from their environment, or in other words, the nature of their 'property.'[1]

The first order of mammals I wish to consider is the Rodents, because among them we find numerous instances of food accumulation and one or two puzzling examples of

[1] For the psychological aspect of mammalian evolution cf. in general Lloyd Morgan: *Habit and Instinct*, ch. v; Thomson: *The Mind of Animals*, ch. xviii; Haldane and Huxley: *op. cit.*, 330; and Koehler: *The Mentality of Apes*, *passim*.

'museum-collecting.' As Romanes pointed out long ago, the rodents, psychologically considered, are, of all orders in the animal world, most remarkable for the differences presented by constituent species. For while the group contains many animals such as the guinea-pig, whose instincts and intelligence cannot be said to rise above the lowest level that obtains among mammalian forms, it contains also other animals with instincts as provident as those of the squirrel or viscacha, intelligence and ability as considerable as that of the beaver. The rodents are a good exemplification of the truth that only in a general fashion, and often only in a remote degree, is structural likeness related to similarity of psychological make-up. Romanes was at pains to suggest further that "similarity of organization and environment" is in a general way related to similarity of instincts, though not necessarily of intelligence. This is the case with the habit from which the order takes its name. Less obviously is it the case with the impulse to store food for winter consumption, an activity more prevalent among the rodents than in any other order of animals. A similar environment has determined modification of the same food-seeking impulse, since such a modification is not of sufficiently general occurrence among all species of rodents to allow one to infer that the species in which it does occur has derived it from a common ancestral stock.[1]

Among the various species of mice (*murinis*) we find solely food accumulation. In autumn, that is, the murines are busy laying up stores of grasses, nuts, straws, etc., in order that they may have a supply of provisions on hand to tide them over times of winter scarcity. This behaviour is characteristic of the dormouse, the harvest-mouse, the common grass-mouse, the bank-mouse and the field-mouse.[2] Miss Pitt writes of the last named: "Nearly every long-tailed

[1] Cf. Romanes: *Animal Intelligence*, 353–354.

[2] See Barrett-Hamilton: *A History of British Mammals*, pts. xv–xviii.

(field) mouse has its underground home to which it can take treasure-trove. . . . It is in the farthest corners of these that they lay up stores for the lean days of winter when it is difficult for wild creatures to find food. . . . Nuts, acorns, and grain, if it can be had, are all carried in. Sweet chestnuts are much liked too, and the minute the nuts begin to fall, long-tailed mice make for the chestnut-trees."[1] In many cases this amassing of provisions is accompanied by, and is not in the place of, hibernation as a reaction to winter weather; while again, in England, the comparatively mild climate rarely develops food accumulation to any degree.[2]

Among American varieties of Murines, however, owing to the more inclement climate, the storage impulse is highly developed, so that such grains as wheat, maize and buckwheat are often stored in considerable quantities. The gopher, for instance, stores grain, grass roots, leaves and stems in the blind alleys of its burrow.[3] Audubon noted further that several gophers kept in captivity "exhibited an extremely acquisitive disposition and constantly dragged clothing and all kinds of similar objects together, utilizing them as bedding and adapting them to such purpose by gnawing them to pieces."[4]

The various species of voles, the bank-vole or the water-vole for instance, are all reported as storing food in autumn. Miss Pitt observed of voles kept in captivity that no matter how much food was placed in the cage, superfluous food was either buried, covered with leaves and rubbish or taken into rest-holes. Out of sight was out of mind, however, and no resentment was apparently displayed when one vole raided the stores of another. Of the European voles, Brehm notes

[1] Pitt: *Wild Creatures of Garden and Hedgerow*, 124–125.

[2] Pitt: *op. cit.*., 125; Barrett-Hamilton: *op. cit.*, pt. xiv, 367–370; pt. xv, 494–495; Brehm: *The Life of Animals*, 306, 321, 322.

[3] Seton: *Life Histories of Northern Animals*, i, 484, 496, 498, 567–568, 597–598, etc.; cf. also Seton: *Lives of the Game Animals*, iv, 401–402.

[4] Quoted by Brehm: *op. cit.*, 353.

that storerooms, connected with the main burrow by tunnels, are found filled with peas, beans, onions and potatoes from neighbouring fields and gardens. So rich are these stores that the natives often made a habit of digging up treasure stores in autumn and utilizing these provisions as articles of diet.[1]

So much for the Murines. Save for the doubtful exception of the gopher, acquisitiveness is no more and no less than food accumulation. The same observation holds good for another species of rodent, the squirrel, which has been credited by most writers with an extremely well-developed provident sagacity in laying up stores of food for the proverbial rainy day; Titania's 'venturesome fairy' was to seek the squirrel's hoard and return with new nuts. Further, the distribution of these reserves, not in a single place of safety, but in several holes in different trees in the neighbourhood of its retreat, has often been regarded as circumstantial evidence of forethought. The more correct opinion seems to be, however, that the squirrel is but a careless provider at any time and no more worthy of praise in this respect than the well-fed dog that spends its spare time burying unconsumable bones. The erratic nature of the squirrel's stores was long ago commented upon by Alston after watching the storing operations of a semi-wild individual. This squirrel when fed with nuts out of doors hid them in such a capricious, casual and inconsequent fashion that 'one could hardly believe he would ever find them again, and I have no doubt that he never did find some of them.' Miss Pitt comments upon the same point. But with all due respect to these authorities personal observation leads me to judge that though the hiding of the nuts may be planless, nevertheless the squirrel seems full of 'purpose' (urged on by hunger and guided by smell) when it comes to the point of recovering its scattered hoard. I doubt whether Miss Pitt is correct when she urges that the

[1] Brehm: *op. cit.*, 346, 348; cf. also Pitt: *op. cit.*, 31–36.

squirrel recovers its nuts by luck and by nothing more than this.[1]

Although the storing of nuts is probably not of great importance for squirrels in Great Britain, in severer climates it must be a necessary action, failure to perform which may result in the death of the defaulter. This is noticeably the case with those squirrels of which Seton gives us an account in his exhaustive volumes on *The Life Histories of Northern Animals* (1910). The Manitoban red squirrel, for example (*Sciurus hudsonicus*), has three principal sources of food supply: first, stores of food and nuts that it has laid up in hollow trees or underground vaults during the previous season and over which it "exercises the surveillance of a jealous ownership"; second, mushrooms of the genus *Russula* stored in the forked branches of trees; third, the green outer bark of the aspen or poplar, which is not stored but gathered as occasion arises. The fox squirrel, on the other hand, has the same storage habits as the British grey squirrel.[2]

Since the young red squirrel remains with its parents for at least the first six months of its life, other young squirrels for from four to six months, the chipmunk (an allied rodent) for at least twelve months, and the young beaver from twelve to eighteen months, it is a not unfamiliar suggestion that with young rodents the impulse to store surplus food is not in reality a congenital response but is an acquired reaction learnt by the young under parental precept and example. Just as the song pattern of young birds is an acquired reaction, so, it is urged, the response to bury unconsumed food is similarly acquired. Accurate observation has shown,

[1] Cf. Barrett-Hamilton: *op. cit.*, pt. xxi, 711–712; Pitt: *Animal Mind*, 192–193.

[2] Seton: *Life Histories*, 323–330; cf. also Seton: *Game Animals*, i, 390–391; i, 408–409; iv, 133–134. Brehm, *op. cit.*, 309, notes that squirrels of south-eastern Siberia store mushrooms by pinning them to pine needles or larch twigs. For the activities of the common chipmunk (*Tamias striatus griseus*), a rodent related to the squirrel and storing nuts and grain on a large scale, see Seton: *Life Histories*, 356–363, and Seton: *Game Animals*, iv, 201–206.

however, that this suggestion is well wide of the truth. Lloyd Morgan, for instance, in *Habit and Instinct* (1895), quotes an observer's account of a young grey squirrel removed from the nest when young and feeble, and thereafter reared by hand. It was only when the squirrel was a month or two old that it attempted to bury surplus nuts in sheltered corners in the carpet. The squirrel "would press the nut down on the carpet and then go through all the motions of patting the earth over it, after which he went about his business as if that nut were safely buried. . . . At the time they were removed from their parents they had not only never seen the operation of burying a nut, but were totally unacquainted with the properties both of earth and nuts." Lloyd Morgan, in a picturesque phrase, terms the squirrel's behaviour "pure congenital whisky undiluted by the water of experience."[1] It is needless to add, of course, that with wild squirrels the pure whisky does not remain long undiluted. With each successive attempt at hiding nuts whisky and water become more and more irretrievably mixed.

Among the Canadian beavers food-storing is also a characteristic activity. During the autumn months suitable trees are felled. The branches are cut off and brought to the beaver lodge to be stored in either of two ways. The heavier timbers are sunk in the mud at the bottom of the pond while the smaller branches are piled in brushwood moored to any convenient support. "When utilizing these hoards the beaver takes the piece of wood into the lodge, eats the bark off and later adds the useless stick to the roof tree or to the dam."[2]

Another order of rodents are what may be termed 'haymakers and storers.' The mountain beaver collects and dries

[1] Lloyd Morgan: *Habit and Instinct*, 123–124; cf. also James' account of similar behaviour on the part of a young squirrel attempting to bury nuts in a blanket: *Principles of Psychology*, ii, 400.

[2] Seton: *Life Histories*, i, 467.

large bundles of green plant food, herbs and lilies, which are afterwards stored in subterranean burrows. The muskrat similarly treats bullrush roots, sedges, mints and young grass shoots, while the cony packs dried grasses into sheltered crevices and often makes a winter nest in the centre of its stores. This same behaviour is typical also of such rodents as the common agouti or golden hare, the crying hare or pika, and the alpine crying hare.[1] As nearly all these hay-making rodents seem to live and sleep in or on their dry collected grasses and to use this hay in times of food shortage, it would seem not improbable that with these rodents the evolution of the storage habit began first with a warm nest of hay which it was later found could be used for food when none was available. Originally, that is, these rodents fed on their nesting material. The collection of separate stores of food, apart from nesting material, is a later development and is seen more especially in the muskrat, which first tightly packs hay into narrow tunnels, afterwards plugging them up with clay.

I have been considering so far those rodents which accumulate articles of food only. Just because this accumulation is of food, because out of sight is out of mind, and because there is no evidence that rodents hoard or gloat over their stores, it seems more correct to consider this behaviour as due to a food-seeking impulse modified by climatic conditions rather than to an acquisitive or hoarding impulse. I will pass now, however, to two species of rodents, the individuals of which specialize in 'museum-collecting.'

The vizcacha, a rodent of the South American pampas, collects around its burrow a heterogeneous selection of any and every object that it may find within reach of its home; so much so that when the gauchos mysteriously lose anything they immediately go to the nearest vizcacheras to look for

[1] Brehm: *op. cit.*, 363–380; Hornaday: *op. cit.*, ch. xiv, 166–167; Seton: *Game Animals*, iv, 539, 585, 641–643.

the missing article.[1] From a superficial examination of this behaviour one might be tempted to explain it as due to acquisitiveness. W. H. Hudson, however, than whom there can be no more reliable authority upon the wild life of South America, suggests another, more searching, explanation. "On the level plains," he writes, "it is a useful habit, for the vizcachas are continually deepening and widening their burrows, the earth thrown out soon covers up these materials and so assists in raising the mound. On the Buenos-Ayrean pampas numbers of vizcachas would annually be destroyed by water in the great sudden rainfalls were the mounds less high. But this is only an advantage when the animals inhabit a perfectly level country subject to flooding rains; for where the surface is unequal they invariably prefer high to low ground to burrow on, and are thus secured from destruction by water; yet the instinct is as strong in such situations as on the level plains. The most that can be said of a habit so obscure in its origin and uses is, that it appears to be part of the instinct of clearing the ground about the village. Every tall stalk the vizcacha cuts down, every portable object he finds must be removed to make the surface clean and smooth; but while encumbered with it he does not proceed further from his burrow, but invariably retires towards them, and so deposits upon the mound."[2] In Hudson's view, then, the 'acquisitiveness' of the vizcacha is not an aspect of its possessiveness. It is merely a reaction whose aim is to get rid of obstructions about the burrow. Not a 'taking to oneself' reaction but a 'getting rid of' reaction, which, paradoxically enough, means a collecting together near to the mound. The behaviour is due to an impulse to clear the ground round the vizcachera; not to an instinct of acquisition. It would seem probable, though Hudson does not mention the fact, that this impulse of the

[1] Brehm: *op. cit.*, 372; W. H. Hudson: *The Naturalist in La Plata*, 303.
[2] Hudson: *op. cit.*, 304–305.

vizcacha to clear the ground about its nest may be a modification in its turn of the nest-building impulses. It serves the dual purpose of raising the nest above flood-level and, since the area cleared is often about half an acre in extent, of preventing enemies, human or wild, from taking it unawares as it loiters about its burrow.

How far this explanation will hold good of the wood-rat (*Neotoma cinerea*), which, living in a northern climate, not only stores food, but also collects curiosities, is difficult to decide. The food-storing is, no doubt, a modification of the food-getting impulse. The allied species *Fuscipes* domiciled in California lays up no store for winter use, since the climate arranges a constant supply of available food all the year round. The nest, on the other hand, where apparently the rat displays his collection, is a vast and growing pile of sticks, stones, leaves, pine-cones, cactus, thorns, bones, cow-dung, bark, rubbish and trash; bits of china, old cartridges, broken buckles, rags, leather scraps, feathers, skulls of small animals, and, near a camp, salt, soap, silk socks, bright neckties, perfume bottles, false teeth, boxes of matches and sticks of dynamite are, one gathers, only some of the objects which this bright little creature collects.[1] Since no one has yet studied completely the habits of *Neotoma* one can but suggest that this aspect of its behaviour is the outcome of its nest-building impulses, reinforced by that focussing of interest on bright portable objects which is so characteristic of the behaviour of many birds. It is significant that no evidence is available which would lead us to suppose that the wood-rat 'hoards' its collection, that it arranges it, spreads it out in the sun, steals from another's collection, or that the so-called collecting plays any part in the almost non-existent social life of the rat.

One other closely allied aspect of the behaviour of the wood-rat is of interest. This is its habit of exchange. When

[1] Cf. Seton: *Game Animals*, iv, 513, 520; James: *op. cit.*, ii, 424.

the rat removes some bauble from a rancher's house it commonly leaves in place a product of its own domain. For example, it will carry off silver spoons and fill the empty place with toadstools; the kitchen clock and leave in its place a rabbit's skull; empty a box of chocolates and fill it with cow-chips; leave gold nuggets for miners' cartridges and so forth.[1]

Various writers have suggested that the wood-rat is gifted with a high degree of commercial honesty and compare its behaviour very unfavourably with that of the housebreaker; or, that it is gifted with a sense of humour which delights in sharp contrasts. Both of these views, however, are not at all convincing and are tinged with more than a slight amount of anthropomorphism. Seton is more to be taken seriously when he assumes that on carrying away a spoon, for example, and depositing it near his nest, the 'mania' for carrying is affecting the rat. He seizes, therefore, the nearest object, be it stone, cone or pebble, for his return trip. Here the superior allurement of the spoons causes him to drop the pebble and take another spoon, this see-saw carrying continuing until all the spoons are removed. Without going into all the matter at all deeply since it is outside our purpose, it seems at least plausible to imagine that instead of a 'carrying mania' the rat is influenced by a 'configuration.' It sees a box of spoons as objects against a background. The box without spoons is an unfamiliar configuration since it has radically altered its appearance. The sense of familiarity is restored if *Neotoma* rebuilds another configuration of objects set off by a background of box. This he, in fact, does when he leaves in place of spoons, pebbles or cones or other objects lying to hand.

In any case it is probably more plausible to explain the rat's habit of building a nest out of a miscellaneous collection of rubbish as due to a modification of nesting impulses

[1] Seton: *op. cit.*, iv, 522.

rather than to attempt, as Seton does, to build up an elaborate analogy between *Neotoma* and the human collector. Seton urges that the rat is motivated by an aesthetic instinct; that he gets pleasure in "seeing, handling, and owning strange and attractive things"—as the human collector does from "amassing and arranging beautiful and curious objects at a special and prepared place—a place that has no relation to their ordinary functions of life."[1] It may be so. It is far simpler, however, though not so complimentary to the intelligence of the rat, to find an explanation of his behaviour in his desire to build a nest. In searching for materials his attention is focussed by bright portable objects, which *ipso facto* become building materials. Similarly, the common rat carries food and other articles to his nest. Barrett-Hamilton tells us that a single nest was found to contain three towels, two serviettes, five dust-cloths, two pairs of linen knickerbockers, six linen handkerchiefs and one silk handkerchief. Close by this nest were a pudding, sugar, carrots, turnips and potatoes. In another nest behind the wainscot of a London restaurant were found 1,728 gnawed serviettes.[2] One can only hazard the guess, of these extraordinary old clothes collectors, that the miscellaneous articles were accumulated not from pure joy in collection but as material for nest-building.

To summarize the accumulating activities of the rodents one may say that the majority store food for winter use. This may be looked upon as an extension of the food-seeking impulses brought about by climatic conditions or as the outcome of the habit of many rodents in building their nest of dry grasses which may in turn be utilized for food at times of scarcity. Few rodents neither store food nor hibernate, but subsist in winter on what is found under the snow. Two exceptions are the mole-rat or slepez and the lemming.

[1] Seton: *op. cit.*, iv, 523.
[2] Barrett-Hamilton: *op. cit.*, xix, 624.

The latter often migrates in times of dearth.[1] The vizcacha and species of rats collect miscellaneous objects. On examination, however, this behaviour turns out to be due most probably, not to acquisitive impulses, but to modifications of the nest-building impulses.

Although there are not a great number of recorded observations dealing with exclusive appropriation among the rodents, yet it is clear that there is evidence for assuming possessiveness in regard to food, for instance, or nest, or territory. The behaviour of the Canadian fox squirrel is enlightening in this respect. The following case is recorded by Judge Hargest: the Judge handed a nut to a squirrel, which ran off a short distance and buried it. Out of curiosity the Judge sought to ascertain how deep the nut was buried, and, as he stooped down to scratch away the earth, the squirrel made a sharp dash at him and knocked his hand away from the hole.[2] Seton notes further the curious fact that when given nuts and before burying them the procedure of the squirrel was always the same: "Seizing the nut in his teeth, then in his paws, he turned it over two or three times and appeared to be licking it." This suggests that the squirrel may establish ownership of a nut by licking it thus.[3]

Exclusive possession of burrow and territory seems common among rodents. The chipmunk is wonderfully tenacious of its holdings. Where one is found this year, one will find

[1] Brehm: *op. cit.*, 350, 351; Barrett-Hamilton: *op. cit.*, xiv, 390 *et seq.*

[2] *Forest and Stream*, July 4, 1908. Quoted Seton: *op. cit.*, iv, 31.

[3] Seton: *op. cit.*, iii, 487, 553; iv, 91. This recalls the fact that it is by licking that the female cow, sheep or dog establishes possession of her offspring (Fraser: "Chain Reflexes in Lambing," *British J. Psych.*, 1926, 310–313; MacCurdy: *Common Principles in Psychology and Physiology*, 37). Finally, Franklin noted how an Eskimo, receiving a gift, licked each article with his tongue as "an act of appropriation" (*Journey to the Shores of the Polar Sea* (1823), 17–18). Whereas, however, the squirrel acts by instinct in these matters, I shall urge in Part II that the behaviour of the Eskimo is to be explained in terms of magico-animistic practices and beliefs.

another next year, probably the same chipmunk. Brehm tells us there is exclusive possession of burrows even among the mild rabbits. Whereas, again, a captured brown rat will make a peaceable entry into a cage occupied by others of its species, a water-rat expects to be attacked and generally has a short bout with all its fellow-captives in turn, thus indicating that it lives in colonies or pairs apart from its neighbours and each in its own territory. Where the animals are not crowded they usually have distinct beats along the banks of a river. Entrance of a stranger to this riparian property is always resented even by immature individuals. Further, this exclusiveness usually interferes with the animal's character in captivity, since it bites furiously if its nest or its person is interfered with and cannot be handled unless thoroughly familiar with its owner.[1]

The behaviour of the vizcacha shows a similar exclusiveness. Mild and sociable as it is towards its neighbour outside the burrow, yet each one is exceedingly jealous of any intrusion into its particular nest, and indeed invariably resents such a breach of convention with the utmost fury. Several individuals may reside in the compartments of the same burrow, but beyond themselves not even their next-door neighbour is permitted to enter: their hospitality ends where it begins—at the entrance. "It is difficult," writes Hudson, "to compel a vizcacha to enter a burrow not its own; even when hotly pursued by dogs, they often refuse to do so. When driven into one, the instant their enemies retire a little space, they rush out of it as if they thought the hiding-place but little less dangerous than the open plain. I have frequently seen vizcachas, chased into the wrong burrows, summarily ejected by those inside; and sometimes they make their escape only after being well bitten for their offence."[2] It would thus appear that some degree of exclusive-

[1] Cf. Barrett-Hamilton: *op. cit.*, xvi, 494–495.
[2] W. H. Hudson: *op. cit.*, 312; cf. also Brehm: *op. cit.*, 371.

ness is well established among the rodents. Those most primitive forms of property, food, mate, nest and territory, which are the end-objects of powerful impulses, are defended with vigour against all intruders.

Turning now to the various species of Carnivora, a marked difference is at once noticeable betweeen the storing habits of this animal order and those of the rodents, due to differences of staple food supply. Whereas the typical rodent stores nuts and grasses in the autumn for consumption during winter and early spring, the carnivore, on the other hand, stores animal food at every season, but because of the nature of this food, stores it for rarely more than three or four days at a time. One may say that the impulse to accumulate food represents a more primitive modification of the food-seeking impulse among the carnivores than among the rodents.

A well-fed domestic dog will, of course, bury surplus bones, though few dogs remember with any degree of accuracy where their hidden treasure lies. The fox invariably buries the remains of his kill. The prairie red fox of North America is credited with constructing a separate apartment close to his den. In one of these storehouses were discovered two lambs, one partly eaten, a ruffled grouse, a rabbit and a muskrat. Another observer claims that during summer the fox lays up a store of wild-fowl eggs, buried in river sand bars or in beds of moss, for winter consumption. It is worthy of note also that a seven weeks old fox-cub reared by hand from the age of twenty-four hours tried to bury its first rabbit leg in the bedding of its cage. The Arctic fox likewise makes many caches of eggs, scraps of food and lemmings, marking each with its own sign, the odour of its protometric gland.

The grey wolf, the coyote, the minx, the marten, the weasel, the caugar, the jaguar, the lynx, the puma and the leopard are other examples of carnivores which store surplus food in caches underground, covered with grass or brushwood, or fastened in the branches of a tree or bush.[1] The grizzly-bear in a similar fashion will roll a dead carcass into a hole in the ground and cover it with earth, mosses and plants. Hornaday naïvely tells us of one such cache which he regards "as a very impressive exhibit of ursine thought, reasoning, and conclusion. It showed more forethought and provision and higher purpose in the conservation of food than some human beings display even at their best,"[2]—a statement which does more credit to Hornaday's ingenuous sympathy than to his critical sense.

Besides this almost universal tendency of carnivores to accumulate food there are one or two animals which indulge their tendency to make a miscellaneous collection of objects. The jackal, Brehm tells us, will not only devour everything edible, but will steal all kinds of non-eatable things from the house and yard, tent and room, stable and kitchen, taking everything that strikes its fancy. Its thievish disposition, adds Brehm, is perhaps as great as its voracity.[3] The wolverine appears to have a similar propensity to steal and hide things. Since one is not told what use the jackal and the wolverine make of their accumulations it is difficult to suggest a motive for their behaviour. Quite possibly, however, it is allied with the somewhat similar behaviour of the two rodents I have discussed above.

The carnivores are not exceptional in their defence of food, burrow or territory. Caches of food often seem to be marked with some signs of ownership. The bear, for instance, will pile fresh earth alongside a corpse or will mark a tree containing a honey nest in its branches with claw-marks along the trunk. The fox will establish ownership of a kill

[1] Pitt: *Wild Creatures*, 102, 126; Pitt: *The Animal Mind*, 206; Seton: *op. cit.*, i, 27; Alverdes: *op. cit.*, 162; Hudson: *op. cit.*, 32, 40.
[2] Hornaday: *Mind and Manners of Wild Animals*, 137.
[3] Brehm: *op. cit.*, 197.

by means of protometric musk, the wolverine with anal ointment, and the mountain lion by placing brushwood over its victim.[1] Half-wolf train dogs watch their cache all day, and in its defence often attack another animal that ordinarily they fear. Seton adds that "the big dog rarely presses his point under these circumstances but acts as though his cause were weak."[2] It is well known further that in Oriental cities every street and alley has its own pack of half-wild dogs which never leave it. Should one of these dogs enter a strange alley, the dogs domiciled there fall upon the stranger and tear it to pieces unless it has the good fortune to retrieve its mistake by speedy flight. It is possible that in the case of these packs of pariahs, exclusiveness in regard to territory is modified by the operation of impulses due to gregariousness and group solidarity.

The domestic dog defends not only his food or his kennel but also other objects to which he has been conditioned by his master. So impressed was Romanes with his observations on domestic dogs that he urged that "the idea of defending his master's property has become in this animal truly instinctive" and is not due to individual instruction. "Akin to this inborn idea of protecting the property of his master," Romanes continues, "is the idea the dog has of himself constituting a part of that property—the idea of ownership as extended to himself." That a young Newfoundland puppy should have followed Romanes through 'tolerably crowded streets' was said to be due to the dog's "instinctive idea of ownership and his consequent fear of getting lost." Elsewhere Romanes was concerned to argue that not only have all the higher animals "general ideas of good-for-eating and not-good-for-eating quite apart from any particular objects of which either of these qualities happens to be characteristic," but also that "the abstract idea of ownership is well developed

[1] Cf, Seton: *op. cit.*, ii, 31; Hornaday: *op. cit.*, 133–134.

[2] Seton: *Life Histories*, ii, 769–770.

in many, if not most, dogs."[1] Most dogs, therefore, for Romanes, are capable of forming general ideas or concepts; in regard to property, however, they have both an 'instinctive idea' and an 'abstract idea' of ownership.

I have already criticized above Petrucci's assertion that the bird mind is capable of forming abstract ideas and concepts in regard to territory. I need not, therefore, develop again this criticism. It will be sufficient to recall the facts. To 'focus the wherefore,' to form an abstract idea, means that an animal must have the power of analysing his perceptual constructions, and of forming from these, 'isolates' or abstract ideas of qualities apart from the 'constructs' of which these qualities are elements. There appears to be no ground for the assertion that the higher animals have abstract ideas quite apart from any particular objects of which either of these qualities happens to be characteristic. In the case of Romanes' dogs, even if it may be urged that a dog regards this or that man as his owner or this or that object as his master's property, yet this admission is very different from the assertion that he possesses an abstract idea of ownership. In other words, the dog may be able to form a 'predominant' against a background of, for instance, 'eatability'; but never an 'isolate' where the quality is floated off from the background, in this case, food.[2] In a word, the domestic dog defends certain objects because they are the end-objects of instinct; defends other objects—his master's property, for example—not *qua* property, but because he has been taught not to favour the intrusion of strangers within the front gate of his master's home.

I will now consider very briefly the behaviour of the monkey

[1] Romanes: *Animal Intelligence*, 233–235.

[2] In addition to the references in the previous chapter, see also Lloyd Morgan: *Animal Life and Intelligence*, 347–350; the same author's *Introduction to Comparative Psychology*, chs. xiii–xvi; and Wundt: *Lectures on Animal and Human Psychology*, 357, 359.

and the ape in relation to collecting and possessiveness. The first point to be noticed in this respect is that few or none of the apes or monkeys accumulate food for future use either in captivity or in their wild state. This is perhaps easily accounted for when it is recalled that the apes live almost exclusively in tropical climates. There is an abundance of food all the year round and therefore there is no likelihood of the food-getting impulses being modified by climatic conditions. There is thus neither accumulation nor hoarding of food for the future.

With regard to non-food accumulation, however, the case is different. The higher apes, as I have already stated, stand apart from most mammals because of their good sensory equipment, their manipulative expertness, their quickness of perception and plan, their restless acquisitiveness and their delight in experimentation. It is not to be wondered at, therefore, that their interest and attention should be continually focussed on particular objects which arouse curiosity because of their inherent attractiveness as small, portable or bright. This focussing of interest, this arousing of curiosity, leads naturally to a desire for the possession of an object which may be used as personal adornment or for purposes of play.

Brehm gives us an account of a blue-faced guenon monkey which used her roomy cheek-pouches as a storeroom for trinkets. When the monkey could be prevailed upon to disgorge her cheeks, little stones, peas, coins, came to light, as well as beans, nails, corks, thimbles and glass stoppers. This same monkey was fond of playing with dolls, balls, corks or pieces of wood. "For a long time," writes Brehm, "she always took one little stick into her basket for the night, putting others carefully away under cupboards in the draperies, etc., and regarding them as her personal property which nobody had any right to touch."[1] Another capuchin

[1] Brehm: *op. cit.*, 34, 35, 57; Alverdes: *op. cit.*, 162.

monkey which also came under Brehm's observation similarly hoarded small objects in its mouth and refused to give them up save to its master.

Of Koehler's apes somewhat the same behaviour is reported. The apes would collect and drape about themselves such articles as string, pieces of rag, rope, metal chains and twigs. Sultan would carry about a collection of empty preserve tins, while Chica specialized in carrying about heavy stones. These articles, however, do not appear to have been collected and worn because of any acquisitive impulses or habits, but solely to serve the function of adornment in the widest sense of that term. Their pleasurable effect upon the apes was "based entirely on the extraordinary heightened bodily consciousness of the animal."[1]

Other objects were collected by the chimpanzees which were not used for adornment. One ape, Nueva, "was an indefatigable collector. She scraped together stones, pieces of wire and wood, rags and banana skins into her nest, or into a tin bowl, and seemed to derive the greatest satisfaction from this procedure."[2] Should it be necessary to carry these objects about, it was the habit of the apes to wedge them between the lower abdomen and the upper thigh. Once an object was placed in this remarkable part of the body, 'its inmost spot,' so to speak, it was exceedingly difficult to get it from the ape again. In the evening it would be taken to the nest, but never given up. A valuable object, a piece of rag or the like, seemed to attain to yet more value still by being relegated to the inmost part of the body.[3] Koehler refuses to class these collecting habits of the apes as being due to 'acquisitiveness' or to delight in hoarding. More simply he explains them as forms of continuous play

[1] Koehler: *The Mentality of Apes*, 94. [2] *Ibid.*, 311.

[3] *Ibid.*, 95–96. Hornaday gives the case of an ape mother who carried about in her groin her baby chimpanzee. When the baby died the mother retained possession of the decomposing corpse against all comers for over a week. Hornaday: *op. cit.*, 90–92.

activity. The apes did not collect because they took a delight in collecting for its own sake. They accumulated objects in a greater or less degree because these objects could either be used for adornment or else as playthings. Since an ape can adorn itself or play with relatively few objects at one time, there is no stimulus to collect more than a few objects. Significantly enough Koehler writes, "None of the other apes (with the exception of Nueva, that is) had so developed a taste for collecting and putting objects together."[1]

The chimpanzee, so to speak, is an inveterate pragmatist. It will only acquire those objects which have value for it at the moment; when that need has passed, the objects are not hoarded but discarded. Rag or rope is of value for adornment; so apparently are the heavy stones that Chica would carry about the yard. A mirror or a piece of tin is of value as a plaything. Similarly a bamboo stick is a coveted treasure because by its aid the ape could reach objects three or four metres from the ground. Such a stick was given to Chica. Though separated from her toy for some time during the day, yet in the evening when Chica entered the playground where the bamboo lay "she repeatedly interrupted the (to her, immensely important) business of a meal in order to seize the coveted treasure and 'just once' snatch a hasty jump."[2]

In any consideration of the way in which objects acquire value for the apes it is important to notice, I think, the effect of what may be termed social stimulation. I have mentioned above the part this plays in the acquisitiveness of such social birds as the raven. In the life of the apes it is equally important. A case of Koehler's is illuminating in this respect. The ape Tschego was set an experiment to perform, which involved drawing within the bars of the cage food which for the purposes of the experiment was obstructed by a heavy box. For some time Tschego made no move,

[1] Koehler: *op. cit.*, 311. [2] *Ibid.*, 71.

though she was hungry enough to appreciate food. Then, however, some of the smaller apes approached from outside the cage and endeavoured to appropriate the prize. Each time they did so "Tschego repulsed them with threatening gestures, wagging of the head, stamping of the feet, and pawing of the air with her great hands; for she regarded the objective as her property though it was beyond her reach; otherwise she would not have menaced the little creatures, with whom she was generally on the best of terms. The youngsters finally gathered closely round the fruit; but the danger inspired Tschego; she gripped the box, which was like a toy in her arms, stepped up to the bars and took the fruit."[1] Another observation of Romanes on his tame capuchin monkey is equally illuminating. A thing became of value to this monkey when other people desired it. "If he gets hold of anything," wrote Romanes, "that he sees we do not care about, he soon leaves it again; but if it is an article of value (even if it be only a scrap of paper) which he sees we are anxious about, nothing will induce him to give it up. No food, however inviting, will distract his attention; scolding only makes him more angry and he keeps the article until it is quite destroyed."[2] The apes in this respect are not unlike human beings. We, too, often desire things all the more intensely when we find others desiring the same things. Social competition invariably places an increased value upon objects which at first may evoke no desire at all.

The evidence I have considered does not appear to give ground for the postulation of an instinct of acquisition among the higher apes. This is significant for our purpose when it is recalled how closely related in innate psychical make-up the apes are to man. There is firstly no food accumulation among the apes. Secondly, there appears to be non-food accumulation, but no evidence for the existence

[1] Koehler: *op. cit.*, 62–63; cf. also 31–32.
[2] Romanes: *Animal Intelligence*, 485; cf. also 487.

of a hoarding impulse. The apes collect in a greater or less degree (mostly to a less degree) miscellaneous objects. But these objects are used for the sake of adornment or for playthings. They are not collected purely for their own sake. The apes do not 'tell' them over, nor 'gloat' over them. The objects are instrumental goods which have original value as food or acquired value as adornment, toys, means to acquiring food. Furthermore, it is characteristic of the apes as of human beings that objects acquire value and are desirable when others desire them too.

A point to notice is that once interest is centred on an original value (food) or on an acquired value (a piece of paper) it does not seem far from the truth to infer that a sentiment of ownership is being built up in regard to this value. Another observation from Romanes' diary is instructive here. Of his capuchin monkey he writes: "I have long noticed that he looks upon that trunk (where nuts were kept) as in some special sense his own property. There are other things kept in the trunk as well as nuts, and if any person goes to the trunk for anything he becomes furiously angry. Indeed nothing makes him so angry as people opening the trunk, and this is not because he wants nuts out of it, for he always has more than he can eat beside him, and generally refuses to take any that are offered to him."[1]

Likewise Koehler tells us that Tschego "regarded the objective as her property though it was beyond her reach," while Alverdes states of a captive long-tailed monkey which played with rubber balls and corks that it "regarded these objects as its own property and resented any attempt to touch them or take them away as an unjustifiable infringement of its rights."[2] It is probably an overstatement to

[1] Romanes: *op. cit.*, 492; cf. also Darwin: *The Descent of Man*, i, 125.

[2] Alverdes: *op. cit.*, 162. Among various species of wild monkeys united in bands, a territory, more or less extended and favoured because of its proximity to food supply, is usually defended with sedulous care against aggression from other jungle animals. Cf. Petrucci: *op. cit.*, 149.

speak of a monkey and its rights. The point, however, is clear. The ape desires exclusive possession of objects which are of value to it. This is inferred from the fact that it shows anger at any attempt to remove such objects from its possession, or, in the case of Romanes' monkey, to handle such objects which are the centre or focus of interest.

At this stage it seems advisable to restate the conclusions we have so far reached in our enquiry into the conditions of acquisitiveness and the origins of property among the animals. The guiding thesis of this enquiry has been the assumption of the fundamental unity and solidarity of all animal life. Broadly speaking, the effect of this conception upon scientific enquiry is to render impossible the fullest understanding of any aspect of a living organism without some knowledge of its racial and of its individual history. I have been led, therefore, to consider the part that acquisition plays in the life of the animals; later I shall study the part it plays in the life history of the individual.

What, then, are the most general conclusions one may draw as to acquisitiveness in animal life? First and foremost it is established that, with a few exceptions, acquisition in the life of the insect, the bird, the rodent, or the carnivore is confined solely to the storing of food. Food-storing thus appears to be one among several of the instinctive methods of reacting to the severity, the cold, and the food scarcity which characterize the winter months in northern climates. The most hardy of animals, the reindeer for example, is a food-finding animal in winter. It manages to exist by finding moss and herbs under the snow. Most of the carnivores follow this example. Other animals hibernate during winter. During autumn they accumulate sufficient fat about their body to keep the vital organism running, albeit at a much reduced rate, during their long sleep. Other animals, again, migrate when winter arrives to places where there is likely to be a more abundant food supply. The migratory birds are the great exemplars of this method of facing a difficult season, though at least one rodent, the lemming, favours it also. The fourth mode of conquering the scarcities of winter is to store food during seasons of abundance. Most of the social insects pursue this policy, few of the birds, most of the rodents, and one or two carnivores.

Food-storing among the animals, then, is a method of circumventing the dangers of winter. To realize the limitations in the distribution of this method I will mention some of the animal orders which do not hoard: the *edentata*, sloths, ant-eaters, armadillos; the *perissodactyla*, horses, asses, zebras, tapirs; the *artiodactyla*, giraffes, camels, llamas, sheep, ibex, cows, antelopes, elks, chamois, moose, hippopotami; *marsupialia*, kangaroos, wombats, opossums; *chiroptera*, bats; *prosimii*, lemurs, lemuroids; and lastly, excluding amphibians like the whale, sea-cow and seal, the *pithici*, apes and monkeys. These orders of animals cannot and do not store food for a wide variety of reasons, chiefly, however, because their staple food is flesh and therefore not storable for long periods or because they live in tropical or sub-tropical regions where there is abundant food all the year round. The point I wish to emphasize is this: with the exception of a few cases, storing or hoarding among the animals is confined to the storing of food; it is confined to comparatively few animal orders, the majority of animals preferring to meet the winter by other methods, or else having no problem to face at all. The question which immediately suggests itself, then, is this: Is it plausible or scientific to summarize this slender basis of empirical fact by postulating the existence of an instinct of acquisition among man and the animals?

The answer seems to be in the negative. It is more plausible to explain those examples of food-storing which we find as due to modifications of the food-getting impulse brought about by particular climatic conditions—a modification which has been developed in conjunction with a tendency to settle in one locality for a longer period than is necessary merely to rear, seasonally, the young. Thus the social insects living together as one community in one particular place have developed the habit of storing honey. Birds, being exceedingly mobile animals, and settling in one locality only at breeding-time, have, with one or two exceptions, no biological stimulus to develop storing habits. The rodents, occupying settled burrows and feeding on nuts, grasses and grains, have been in a position to store food. Carnivores represent a half-way stage between non-storing and storing animals. Their difficulty has lain with their adaptation to flesh diets. The remaining orders of animals have had no biological impetus to store food. Their way of salvation has followed other paths.

What of those animals, however, which appear to have an impulse to store other objects than food: the raven and the magpie, the packrat and the vizcacha, the monkey and the ape? Is it plausible to find the evidence for the existence of an instinct of acquisition? Again the answer is in the negative. I have attempted to show in the preceding pages that in regard to all these animals there are other, more 'scientific,' explanations for their behaviour than the facile postulation of an instinct of acquisition. The magpie and the raven are social animals and therefore intelligent; their curiosity and interest are easily aroused by bright portable objects, and mental appropriation is usually the first step to material appropriation. Curiosity rather than a blind desire to collect is the motive of their behaviour. As to the two rodents mentioned above, it seems likely that impulses connected with nest-building are at the root of their collecting tendencies. These impulses, reinforced by an active curiosity, lead to accumulations being made, not acquisitiveness *per se*. Finally, the apes, owing to their comparatively close psychical affinities with man, form crucial cases to decide the point. The apes do not hoard food; but some of them do collect ropes, rags, and odds-and-ends of rubbish. But here there is no suggestion that the apes take an unalloyed aesthetic delight in collecting objects and contemplating their collections. Rather are a few objects brought together for other more 'tangible' reasons: for the sake of adornment and to experience feelings of dignity and power; or else for the sake of continuous play activity which takes delight in manipulating and experimenting with things or in using them to gain some ulterior object—a climbing-stick to reach forbidden fruit or a stone to crack tough-shelled nuts. Even with these apes, however, Koehler's experience leads one to assume that the collecting of toys in any number is the exception rather than the rule.

It will not be out of place at this juncture to take an example or two and show the facile generalizations which many psychologists consider sufficient evidence for the existence of an instinct of acquisition. James, in his *Principles of Psychology*, states categorically: "The hoarding instinct prevails widely among animals as well as among men."[1] As biological evidence he adduces the behaviour of the wood-rat. It is clear, however, from the quotation James gives from Lindsay's *Mind in the Lower Animals*, that the miscellaneous objects collected by the wood-rat are used to build its nest and not collected for the sake of collecting.[2] No other confirmatory biological evidence is brought forward to support James' assertion. McDougall is content to bring forward as evidence the behaviour of a dog burying a bone and the fact that "among those mammals which have fixed abodes and which feed on grains and nuts and other durable

[1] James: *Principles of Psychology*, ii, 424.

[2] e.g. in the centre of a mass of nails "was the nest, composed of finely divided fibres of hemp packing. Interlaced with the spikes were the following. . . ." *Ibid.*, ii, 424.

vegetable products the tendency is widespread."[1] Until one knows the exact distribution of this 'tendency' and has analysed it in detail, the bald statement that "the tendency is widespread" may mean everything or nothing. Rivers is content to discuss the behaviour of the bee storing honey and of the bird at breeding-time securing and defending a territory. As I have attempted to show above, neither line of evidence may be accepted at its face value. Finally, a psychologist quoted by R. M. Ogden in his *Psychology and Education* makes this statement, typical of many others: "*In common with the magpie, the squirrel and the bear*, children manifest a tendency to help themselves to attractive portable articles, to store them away, and later to visit the repository, contemplate, manipulate and enjoy the contents."[2] Doubtless children show a tendency to acquire portable objects and to take an aesthetic delight in contemplating and manipulating them for their own sake, but I have yet to come across the competent comparative psychologist who would ascribe such behaviour to the other animals mentioned. The magpie is attracted by, and carries off, bright portable objects; but rarely remembers where they are stored—out of sight is out of mind. The squirrel hoards food only and the bear likewise. There is no evidence available to show us either of these two animals visiting his repositories and "contemplating, manipulating and enjoying the contents."

One must conclude, therefore, that in the majority of

[1] McDougall: *Outline of Psychology*, 161. McDougall's treatment of his 'instinct of acquisition' would appear to be both illogical and confused if it leads him to the conclusion that a bird gathering "sticks, straws, hair and moss for its nest" is motivated by such an instinct. McDougall has failed to keep in mind the distinction between the 'gaining' and 'holding' aspects of acquisition: and failed to remember, too, that acquisition in the sense of 'gaining' is necessary to the satisfaction of any of the fundamental needs, though not itself an independent instinct.

[2] Mary T. Whitely: "The Child's Instincts and Impulses," in *The Child: His Nature and His Needs*. Quoted Ogden: *Psychology and Education*, 59; italics mine.

cases what strikes the theorist or the hasty observer as a direct parallel is in reality nothing of the kind. Deeper analysis and wider knowledge tend to show that there is only an apparent likeness in regard to acquisitive behaviour between man and the other animals. There are superficial resemblances, perhaps, between the squirrel hoarding nuts and man hoarding money, but no real underlying unity of behaviour. It is important to recall in this connection the fact that unquestionably instinctive behaviour in lower forms of life need not necessarily be manifest in any recognizable form in the behaviour of higher species. The general assumptions of evolution, that is, and of the solidarity of organic life on this planet, do not require that every primitive activity shall be preserved in all the higher stages of development. We must consider *devolution*, the degeneration, the transition, or the loss of an endowment, as well as development itself. While certain forms of behaviour grow and develop, certain forms weaken and decay. It is therefore theoretically and practically possible that the same empirical results which a lower species attains by definite instinctive behaviour may in a higher species be altogether a matter of acquired habit and voluntary choice. From one point of view, indeed, the whole process of evolution may be looked upon as a process of degeneration of innate equipment. The formal definiteness of innate endowment which characterizes the insects is found at one end of the scale, with the comparatively indefinite plasticity of man's innate equipment at the other end. The insects, the rodents and a few of the carnivores have been able to survive severities of winter weather because they developed as part of their instinctive endowment impulses to store food in seasons of plenty. On the other hand, the innate equipment of the apes and of man's prehuman ancestors was probably fixed and finalized, much in the same form as it is at present, in relation to a tropical climate where food was abundant year in, year out.

The absence in man's make-up of impulses to store food did not mean any rigorous weeding out by natural selection. When man came down from the trees, and later still when, driven northwards, the tentative beginnings of a primitive culture were in evidence, he was able to obtain by intelligent forethought, acquired habit or volitional choice what the lower animals could only obtain by instinctive striving.[1] On *a priori* grounds, that is, there seems no need to posit an instinct of acquisition as one of the characters in man's innate endowment.

Before concluding this chapter I will refer for a moment to the second aspect of our twofold problem. From our study of the origins of property and ownership among the animals this aspect resolves itself into the question: What conclusions may one draw as to the psychological basis of property among animals? The answer is, I think, clear: One may not find this psychological basis in the instinct of acquisition. Rather does it lie in the disposition of an animal to appropriate to itself those objects which give satisfaction to the 'possessive' instincts. To satisfy its instinctive needs a rodent, for instance, will acquire food, a mate, and a burrow. Should this acquisition be thwarted, anger is aroused and directed against the intruder. This means a defence of those objects which satisfy desire; and *ipso facto* those objects become the primitive forms of property. In other words, the psychological origin of property is based on that mental and material appropriation of those objects which are necessary for the satisfaction of those specific instincts subserving the more fundamental needs of the organism.

Food, mate, nest, territory: these are the primitive forms of property. Tentatively among the higher animals, more definitely and surely in Man, sentiments of ownership

[1] Cf. Wallas: *The Great Society*, 61; MacCurdy: *Principles*, 256; Buxton: *From Monkey to Man*, 42–44; Haldane and Huxley: *Animal Biology*, 330–331.

are built up first about these primitive property values, and later, through a process of conditioning, about new objects of value. At bottom, however, sentiments of ownership can only be based upon that appropriation which satisfies desire. We have studied this process among the animals. We may now shift the focus of our enquiry and study, among the Simpler Peoples, the fashion in which sentiment and magical belief serve to reinforce this more original, psychological appropriation of the primitive property value.

PART II

Property, marriage, the law; as the bed to the river, so rule and convention to the instinct. . . .

SAMUEL BUTLER

INTRODUCTION

In Part I of this monograph I have attempted to show that it is not possible to find a satisfactory explanation of the property relation between organism and environment in the concept of an instinct of acquisition. I have attempted to show further that the key to this relationship is to be found in a study of those situations where the organism appears to be exercising some form of exclusive control over those environmental 'values' with which it is brought into contact by its own activities. These values, these end-objects, satisfying those instincts which subserve fundamental needs of the organism, I have termed primitive property values. Broadly speaking, then, I have suggested that property is primarily the resultant of that organic striving which appropriates from the environment material for self-provision, self-development and racial perpetuation.

We are now in a position, however, to carry our study one stage further. In this second part it is our purpose to analyse relevant aspects of the life of primitive man in the hope that we may determine the manner in which primary impulses, socially determined by unconscious patterning, interact with environmental situations to build up, on the one hand, sentiments of ownership and of possession and, on the other hand, to establish the characteristic forms of property in the societies of the simpler peoples. The reasons for a study of savage society as a prolegomena to the study of this process in modern society are not far to seek. Primitive society, taken by and large, is much more simple in its social and cultural organization than a Western community of to-day. Furthermore, it has been studied in a scientific and objective fashion by skilled observers in a way that few civilized communities have been studied. The results of this intensive study are to be found in a number of the reliable monographs we have used, the best of which contain a wealth of detailed observation and a minimum amount of theorizing. Finally, the social values and economic goods of the simpler peoples are more often than not entirely different from our own. The emphasis put upon the possession of wealth and its comparative valuation, for instance, is, among many savages, the exact reverse of our own. It is not beyond hope, then, that a consideration of the property values of primitive society may help to throw considerable light upon our central problem: the manner in which impulse, interacting with the environment, is socially conditioned by, and thereby helps to build up, an institution and a hierarchy of values which, in some measure, at least, serve to satisfy the fundamental needs of Man.

Fully to understand this process, it is of considerable importance to grasp what is meant by the social patterning of behaviour. I will leave aside a full discussion of this concept until Chapter VII. One may think now of this patterning as the mould which canalizes the plastic stuff of impulse into socially accepted channels of behaviour, as the cultural organization which gives to the functional side of behaviour new forms, new increments of significance, new modes of interpretation. This patterning is unconscious just because the individual in society acts in accordance with deep-seated forms of behaviour which are emotionally felt more than intellectually known. They are not so much capable of conscious description as of automatic practice. For the individual they consist in a typical unawareness of characteristic outlines, demarcations and significances of conduct which he is all the time implicitly following. Examples of this social patterning are to be found in the field of language and gesture, in the field of morals and in the economic life of a people. Patterning plays a large part in the formation of individual and group values. By a knowledge of the culture patterns operative in any society, it is possible to explain why, for instance, the economic organization of one group is predominantly individualistic while that of another is predominantly socialistic; or why, again, romantic love is the convention of one society while a more matter-of-fact attitude characterizes its neighbour.

This much as a preliminary statement of the nature of social patterns. I shall have occasion to refer to them more than once in this part. The general nature of this section, however, is concerned with the study of the psychology of primitive forms of property. In Chapter V, I wish to consider the manner in which sentiments of possession, incorporating within themselves magico-animistic beliefs and practices, help to reinforce the original psychological appropriation of primitive property values. In Chapter VI, I continue this analysis by a study of the reactions of primitive men to such primary and acquired values as women, land, ornament. In Chapter VII, I return to a fuller discussion of the nature of culture pattern and attempt some analysis, first, of the forms of property, e.g. common, individual, private, and, second, illustrate the way in which these same forms mould the raw stuff of impulse in accordance with the conventions of each social group.

CHAPTER V

MAGIC, ANIMISM AND PROPERTY

WE come in this chapter to consider the property relation between the individual and objects which he appropriates from his environment. Before we do so, however, a caution is required as to the meaning connoted by such terms as proprietor, ownership, landed property, or rights to a tract of country. It is rarely possible to apply these words to primitive societies in the sense in which they are applied to higher societies and to our own in particular. With us, these words have a connotation presupposing the existence of highly developed systems of legal and economic conditions and sanctions which are meaningless when transferred to native society. Firth has this point in mind when he writes of primitive society that "the essential factors in the situation —the individual, the goods, and the other members of his community—remain unchanged, but the set of concepts by which these are related has been formed against a different cultural background. Hence the impression that is conveyed to a European by the simple and satisfying statement that an object is owned by a certain person may be entirely divorced from reality through his ignorance of all those rights and qualifications which to the native form an integral part of the situation."[1]

Ownership will therefore have not only a different connotation in native communities compared with civilized societies, but, further, it will have a different specific meaning in each type of native society, since in each type cultural patterning, the outcome of a variety of interacting influences, attaches a set of functions, rites and privileges to the word. The social range of those who enjoy these privileges may vary

[1] Firth: *Primitive Economics of the New Zealand Maori*, 330–331.

from pure individual ownership to collectivism with a whole graded series of intermediate blendings and combinations filling the space between the two extremes. One must remember, then, that the more correct expressions which should be employed instead of 'proprietor,' 'ownership,' etc., are such terms as 'possession,' 'claims to a country,' and so on; though for purposes of clearness and brevity it is often needful to apply the former set of words. Bearing in mind the dangers attending the description of primitive customs in the phraseology of developed law, we will have occasion to show throughout this part that primitive societies are marked neither by extreme individualism nor by extreme collectivism; for, on the one hand, the simpler peoples recognize rights over things in the same way as they recognize other rights—as claims which, if violated, give rise to approved methods of reaction by the sufferer or his group. Permanent rights in the exclusive use, enjoyment and control of certain things are recognized within variable limits which are often set by customs of hospitality, kinship or good-fellowship. On the other hand, common property and common rights in the production or distribution of goods—property or goods over which several or many individuals have rights but which, taken together, they hold collectively against the rest of the social group—this common property is no less a reality of the simpler peoples than individualism. We shall have occasion to draw attention to these differing rights over goods as we proceed in this subject.[1]

Seen in true perspective, the system of ownership in a community is essentially the mechanism which standardizes

[1] Cf. Malinowski: *Argonauts of the Western Pacific*, 117; *Crime and Custom*, 14–16, 31–32, 58–59, etc ; *The Family*, 134, note 4; *The Mailu*, 576–580, 634; Hobhouse: *Social Development*, 281–289; Max Schmidt: *Primitive Races of Mankind*, 161–164, for a more detailed consideration of this point.

and gives stability to the relation between the members of the society and the body of material culture and natural resources which they have at their command. It stands therefore at the basis of economic welfare and reacts strongly upon the efficiency of production. Our object in this chapter is to examine the psychological aspects of this mechanism as it works over generally into the private ownership of personal goods and the acquisition of hitherto non-property in land and other goods.

Appropriation, ultimately and fundamentally, is the means whereby an enduring and intimate relation between an object and an individual is initiated and perpetuated for a longer or shorter time. The appropriation is antecedent to labour, since in the first place the amulet ornament, for instance, is simply acquired because of its intrinsic interest and desirability—the shell is picked up on the seashore, the feather on the plain, the bright flower in the forest, because they awaken delight and interest in vivid colouring and ornamentation. It is only later that the application of labour to fashion an arm-shell out of refractory material or the stringing together of berries or ground pieces of shell—only later does this render the product more precious to the owner.

Property, as we have considered it, may be defined as the appropriation to persons capable of enjoying them, of goods or values satisfying fundamental needs. But what are men interested in and what do they desire? Fundamentally, as we have sought to show from the parallel of animal psychology, desire arises from such unsatisfied impulses as those concerned with food-getting, nest-building, sex, or self-assertion. Men are interested in that which will satisfy wants. Desire or interest means an imperfect adjustment to the environment and a condition of unstable equilibrium. The attainment of primitive property values stabilizes the instability and satisfies in a relative degree the sense of need.

What is desired, however, varies from man to man. This can only mean that relatively permanent sentiments or interests are formed, either through low-level unconscious conditioning of primitive impulses, or later, through the more conscious and intelligent conditioning of values which proceeds by the use of memory, imagination and forethought, the whole process being determined, so to speak, by the touchstone of feeling. Different interests, therefore, different sentiments, different life histories, different cultural patterns all go to determine the nature of the objects which are desired as property and the attainment of which confers social distinction within the group to which the individual belongs. Thus a corpse would be to most people a veritable incubus; but to the anthropophagous savage it may be an object of passionate desire, and to the medical student a not unwelcome object of interest. Similarly, to us, valuables of the *Kula* exchange, *Spondylus* shell necklaces and arm-shells, may have no more interest and value than we attribute to museum-case exhibits or tourists' curios; but to the Melanesian native within the *Kula* exchange they are objects of ultimate value, old in story and tradition, desired above all other objects, carefully treasured and tenderly handled during their short stay in their 'owner's' possession.[1]

Notwithstanding the complexity of this valuing process and the far from simple conditioning whereby primitive values are subsumed in wider and wider hierarchies, I hope to show that it is not entirely useless and unfruitful to analyse the basis of this property relation. But it must be continually remembered that the type of goods constituting property depends first upon the psychological make-up of man; second, upon the life conditions of the society to which an individual belongs; and thirdly, upon more general economic factors such as rarity or scarcity of raw materials. Thus, advances in social organization bring with them new

[1] Malinowski: *Argonauts, passim.*

desires because wider horizons of interest are opened out and therefore new types of property become of importance in a given society. Things which are property or which can become property change from time to time in both ways. New desires, e.g. for a motor-car, are acquired, but older desires for more primitive property objects, e.g. the bow and arrow, fall into abeyance. The property relation, then, is continually changing; but in spite of change, each newly-acquired object stands in a particular relation to the desiring Self. I will now consider how this relation in regard to personal goods is to be regarded in primitive societies.

Property, as I have said, is, in its broadest sense, material for 'self-satisfaction' when such material has been appropriated. It is thus not confined to items of capital which are essentially property objects of highly developed economic life. Property, being wider still, embraces a wife, a home, an amulet, an ornament, a weapon, a privilege, a magic spell, or a piece of land. How does the native consider these property objects to be related to himself so that communal authority recognizes the exterior, durable relation between him and them?

I think it is probably not far from the truth to suggest that personal property is, by the native, believed to be part of the self, somehow attached, assimilated to or set apart for the self. Thus in an extreme case the *churinga* of the Australian savage, the wooden or stone slab which belief holds to be the original home of the individual spirit before incorporation in its bodily home, is almost part of the spirit and in no case could it be alienated from the spirit. The salient feature of primitive appropriation is, then, that something of the individual's own life-spirit is integrated with that which he has taken up and handled. By contact with his personality, the thing has absorbed something of his own being. It will be remembered that the Eskimo licked all the new objects that came into his possession when he first came into contact with early explorers. It is surely not fanciful to suggest that by so doing he made these objects peculiarly his own by imparting to them something of his own spiritual essence. Not only among the simpler peoples is this so. The civilized man may dislike to wear the clothes of a dead man or he may desire possession of some personal object which has been intimately connected with a dead friend or relative. Subconsciously he may feel that part of the lost one's personality still inheres in that which was closely bound up with the latter's life.[1]

One may amplify this idea by recalling the fact that it is a commonplace of animism that the soul or ghost of the individual inheres not only to the body itself but to any severed part of the body. This is why the savage is usually careful to dispose of nail-clippings or hair in such a safe place that none may find them and thus work spells on him through the influence of the *exuviae*. Further still, all ancestors and kinsmen, since they contain the same blood as relatives and descendants, may be looked upon as detached fragments of the one life, the kin group, stretching

[1] The *locus classicus* is, of course, Tylor's *Primitive Culture*, vol. i, ch. xi, vol. ii, chs. xii–xvii. Cf. also Carveth Read: *Man and His Superstitions*, chs. ii–iii; Frazer: *The Golden Bough* (abridged edition), ch. iii; and Malinowski: "Magic, Science and Religion," essay in *Science, Religion and Reality*, for discussion of magic and the relation of magical ideas to those of animism. I have not considered it necessary to discuss in detail in the text the nature of magico-animistic ideas. They are based, I would argue, not upon the inability of the savage to think logically, as some would suggest, but primarily upon the logical fallacy of illicit generalization. And savages are not alone in their propensity to commit such a fallacy! It is surely not unnatural for a savage to imagine that if it is possible to transfer heat from one body to another, or to remove pain by the application of suitable remedies, it is also possible to transfer one's own special virtue to the objects which one possesses. Hence the danger of tampering with such objects. It is the danger of coming into contact with powerful spiritual essence, highly individualized and capable of causing all sorts of mischief. Magical animism in respect to property is thus a logical extension of an illicit generalization. It is none the less powerful for its irrationality.

back to earliest ancestor and forward to unborn babe. From this belief comes the practice of those primitive peoples like the Maori, who regard the burial of their fathers or even of their mythical ancestors on debatable ground as an incontestable claim to ownership.

This principle of the animistic attribution of a material or spiritual part of the self to those objects with which the self is brought in contact may be illustrated by one or two further examples. The African will regard the drinking-cup which touches his mouth as thereafter his own. The Maori chief would funnel his hands and have drinking-water thus poured into his mouth. Should he be given a cup from which to drink, this cup, becoming imbued with his spirit or *mana* from contact with himself, *ipso facto* becomes his own to dispose of as he wishes. Should a chief, again, knock his head on a door when entering a house and blood be seen on the door, the house automatically becomes his; should he scratch part of his body with the splinter of a strange canoe and blood flow on the wood, the canoe also becomes his.[1] Among the Dinka, articles of personal wear are regarded not so much as property but as part of the person wearing them.[2] Among the Palaungs of Further India, the child is early taught never, even in fun, to put on the clothes of anyone else lest the bad qualities of the person wearing the clothes descend upon the child. Again, among the Nagas, should a supposedly dead man recover consciousness, his own stool, wrapped in a cloth, is put in the grave instead. The spirits of the dead, cheated of the man himself, will be satisfied with something which partakes of the man's personality. Further, the stool, like the bed, is so closely associated with the virtue of the owner that it is absolutely taboo at any time to cut or burn a person's stool or bed, while to sit on

[1] Cf. Taylor: *Te Ika a Maui*, 385, 555; and F. E. Maning: *Old New Zealand*, *passim*.

[2] H. O'Sullivan: "Dinka Laws and Customs," *Journal Anthropological Institute*, vol. xl, 178.

them without their owner's permission is, to say the least, exceedingly bad form.[1] Somewhat similarly among many Alaskan Indians it is customary that those furs a visitor sits upon become his. Did the visitor not take the furs away with him, they would become valueless to any member of the tribe. Survivals of this idea of personal contact conferring ownership is to be found in legal phraseology: a person is *seized* of land; a slave is *manumitted* or *emancipated*; marriage is *cum manu* or *sine manu*, etc. Finally, for the Australian, property is so charged with the owner's personality or soul that possessions might lie in the fork of a tree for indefinite lengths of time and no one would touch them even should they rot; and when changing camp the native will leave valuable stone utensils lying about the grounds since he is absolutely sure of finding them when he returns.

As I shall show later, after death the property relation still continued with the corpse or rather with the spirit of the corpse. The deceased would want everything in the next life that he wanted here. Hence his property was buried or burned with the corpse, the savage being sure that the 'soul-stuff' of this property accompanied the ghost to the next world. What belonged to the dead was part of the ghost, and as such was variously interpreted as sacred, holy or unclean. Though later and more sophisticated practices of disposing of the property of the dead became more symbolical than real, nevertheless lip-service is paid to the law

[1] J. H. Hutton: *The Sema Nagas*, 242–243. Based upon this principle of magico-animistic attribution we find such practices as these among the Kayans of Borneo: Nothing used by or about the child—toys, garments, cradle or beads—must be lost, lent, sold, or otherwise allowed to pass out of the possession of the child or its parents; though, on the other hand, if one child has thriven, its properties, as above, are preferred to all others for the use of a younger brother or sister. Again this notion of an odour or atmosphere attaching to material objects through contact with the individual is illustrated by the fact that a "Kayan will wear for a long time, and will often refuse to wash a garment which has been worn and afterwards given to him by a European whom he respects." Hose and McDougall: *Pagan Tribes*, ii, 157–158; ii, 157, note 1.

of attribution, if not to the spirit.[1] We may perhaps sum up the relation that the savage believes to exist between the self and property objects in these words of Sumner and Keller: "That which is attached to a person's body is an observed extension of his person; his tools and weapons mechanically lengthen his reach and co-ordinate his muscles in higher combinations; his clothing is another epidermis or coat of hair; his house is a larger clothing; his beasts are an improvement upon his legs or other muscular powers; and even upon his sense of smell; his canoe is a higher potence of the power to swim."[2] Standing thus intimately in relation to his person it is easily understandable how an enduring sentiment, strengthened by animistic ideas and practices, attaches the individual self to those objects of desire with which the individual is brought into frequent and often intimate contact.[3]

In this connection it is of some interest to consider the nature of the objects ranked as personal private property

[1] Crawley has some luminous pages on the primitive attitude to the dead and to the dead man's property as determined by fear of contact with the evil atmosphere surrounding the dead. Sickness and death are, for the savage, both unnatural and abnormal, brought about by the intervention of a supernatural being or by sorcery, or by the magical influence of enemies or by evil spirits or witchcraft. If the sick or dead are afflicted by evil, it is likely, thinks the savage, that his clothes and belongings, anything with which he has come into contact, will be similarly affected. Hence the impulse to avoid contagion by the destruction of a dead man's property. Crawley: *The Mystic Rose*, i, ch. v, *passim*, especially i, 112, 114, 130–131. Cf. also Seligmann: *Melanesians*, xiii, note 2, 14.

[2] Sumner and Keller: *The Science of Society*, i, 250.

[3] The following summary is apposite here: "Along with the economic basis of the origins of property went a strong mystical factor. A man's 'virtue,' which in primitive societies meant one's *mana* or the power of one's personality, was supposed to radiate out into anything with which the individual came into continual contact. It was often believed dangerous for one man to come into contact with the mysterious virtue or *mana* of another, and hence it was risky to transfer or transmit tools and weapons freely from one person to another. Therefore usages often resembling property rights developed as a defence against the mysterious spiritual power believed to reside in the individual personality." H. E. Barnes: "The Evolution of the Great Society," essay in *An Introduction to Sociology*, ed. by Davis, 53–54.

in primitive society. Among the hunters, the Bushman owns his own bow and arrow, gourds, tortoise-shell valuables, rough earthen pots, hunting-dog, amulets, weighted root-digger, fire-stick, a rude musical instrument and a sun-umbrella to protect his children. The Australian, besides his weapons, possesses a bag of private effects containing round stones by which sorcery is worked on his enemies, the whole wrapped in bark and painted with red ochre; his wife owns the rough domestic implements. According to the Seligmanns, the inventory of a Vedda's personal estate is the following: bow and arrows, axe, flint and steel and supply of tinder, three pots, a deer-skin, a gourd for carrying water, a betel-pouch and lime-box, together with a certain amount of cloth besides that worn as clothing.[1] Among peoples of higher cultural level the examples of the Melanesians and the Maori are typical. Of the Trobriand Island household, Malinowski states that husband and wife have each their own possessions. The wife owns from twelve to twenty grass petticoats, her only clothing. The water-vessels, the implements for dressmaking and a number of articles of personal adornment are also her own property.

The man owns his tools, the axe and adze, the nets, the spears, the dancing-ornaments and the drum, and also those objects of high value called by the natives *vaygu'a*, which consist of necklaces, belts, arm-shells and large polished blades, and which play so prominent a part in the system of the *Kula* exchange. Malinowski tells us that private ownership of these objects is not without practical significance since the husband and wife can and do dispose of any article of their own property; and after the death of one of them the objects are not inherited by the partner but distributed among a special class of heirs. Further, when there

[1] Seligmann: *The Veddas*, 117, 119; cf. also 97–98. For the Punans of Borneo see Hose and McDougall, *Pagan Tribes*, ii, 190–191, and Hose: *Natural Man*, 38; cf. also Sumner and Keller: *op. cit.*, iv, 90–91.

is a domestic quarrel, a man may destroy some of his wife's property—he may wreak his vengeance on the water-bottles or on the grass petticoats—and she may smash his drum or break his dancing-shield.[1]

Somewhat the same division of personal property is found among the Maori. The man owned his tools and weapons for digging, fishing, fighting, and securing game; cordage; pieces of raw material, such as obsidian or unworked greenstone. He owned also his clothing, his ornaments for hair, neck and ear; red ochre and shark oil for decoration, together with any prized articles, such as a carved wooden box or a flute if he were musically inclined, were reserved for his exclusive use. A woman had her own garments and ornaments likewise, as well as a pounder, a pair of weaving sticks, hanks of fibre and dyes, maybe, which she used in her work. Game and fish which were secured by a man on solitary expeditions were also regarded as his own by other workers, though they were usually incorporated in the common family food supply.[2] The relation of the possessor to these articles is fairly clear. They were held and utilized for his private satisfaction, and his rights over them were respected by other members of the community. Other people were not allowed to interfere with them save by the owner's permission; unauthorized removal and concealment of them by others was regarded as theft and might be followed by severe punishment.

One type of personal private property which is characteristic of most primitive societies is the ownership of immaterial goods such as magic formulae, dance ceremony, names, crests, guardian spirits and songs. This ownership is most often shown by the customs of inheritance and the elaborate conventions which govern the sale of such immaterial

[1] Malinowski: *Sexual Life of Savages*, 20–21. For personal ownership among the Melanesian *Koita*, see Seligmann: *Melanesians*, 60–65, 88 *et seq.*
[2] R. W. Firth: *Primitive Economics*, 334; also Best: *The Maori*, i, 394.

property. Among the Mailu of New Guinea, for example, there are forms of white magic which are hereditary private property and which are forms of economic and social value distinctively personal in the eyes of the natives. This type of magic is universal in the sense that every adult man has his own monopoly and thus each knows a private spell for making coconuts thrive or bananas grow well; but at the same time it is specialistic magic, since a man will perform the magic for no one but himself. This magic is spoiled by letting anyone else know the formulae and the nature of the charm. Individual rights to private magic thus derive their importance not only from the economic value of the charm in making garden or forest produce thrive, but also from the native belief that the efficacy of the magic is likely to be altogether destroyed by its divulgation.[1] In the Trobriands, again, there are two kinds of magic: local magic, bound up with a given locality and referring principally to gardens, war, fishing or rain-making. This magic was rarely transferred outside the family. The other magic, individual magic, was not bound up with a special locality and was easily transmitted from father to son (whereas local magic descended in the female line, being matrilinear magic) or from stranger to stranger at a fair price. This individual magic was connected with such activities as native medicine, carving, canoe-making, love-making, etc. Similarly, in the sale of immaterial objects a man may, in one type of transaction, acquire goods or privileges—the title to a garden or possession of a system of matrilinear magic—which are due to him by inheritance from his maternal uncle or elder brother, but which he wishes to acquire before the elder's death. This acquisition usually involves heavy payments of native goods. In the other type of transaction a man may wish to buy a dance. Dances are owned in that the original inventor has the right to produce his dance and song in his

[1] Malinowski: *The Mailu*, 655–660.

village community. Should another village take a fancy to this song and dance ceremony it must purchase the right to perform it by a substantial payment of food and valuables.[1]

From this brief survey of the ownership of personal goods we find that primitive man owned privately both weapons, utensils and native valuables, and also systems of immaterial property, charms, spells and privileges. His right to all these personal goods was enforced by the authority of the group acting through custom and tradition. On the inner side of the relation, however, the weapons and tools with which he worked and hunted were integrated with his personality through the action of magico-animistic practices and beliefs and through the operation of other psychological mechanisms. Using a tool or weapon continuously, the savage got to know its peculiarities, whether the arrow must be aimed high or low, whether the bow shot true or the drill bit deep. He became familiar with the tool, he had a lively sense perhaps of the time and trouble required to replace a broken weapon, and thus gradually a sentiment would be built up about the object—familiarity, pride in efficient working, tradition or myth, centred upon a weapon would forge close psychological bonds which would reinforce rights conferred by the group. Further, if a weapon partakes of the *mana* of its owner, he who would acquire must brave this *mana*, supported as it is by the influence of the owner and the conditional curses of the gods and spirits. Thus another force is incorporated in our sentiment of

[1] Malinowski: *Argonauts*, 73–74, 185–186; cf. also *Baloma*, etc., 374, 388, 399 *et seq.* Seligmann: *Melanesians*, 643, note 1; Jenness and Ballantyne: *D'Entrecasteaux*, 73–74. A survey of forms of immaterial ownership is to be found in Lowie: *Primitive Society*, 225–232. For the ownership of crests and names among the Haida, see Swanton: *Ethnology of the Haida*, 107–108. Useful discussions are to be found in Goldenweiser: *Early Civilization*, 75, 190–191, 220, 245; Bartlett: *Psychology and Primitive Culture*, 90, 102, 197; Malinowski: *Crime and Custom*, 42, 47, etc.; Descamps: "La propriété chez les Sauvages," *Revue Internationale de Sociologie* (1923), vol. xxxi, 499–502.

ownership—fear of offending the gods requires that the mystical relation between person and object should be recognized and supported. As for the ownership of immaterial goods, this, too, was enforced overtly by communal authority and custom and by the respect accorded to privileges derived from ancestors or the product of dream states and trances.

I come now to consider the various psychological factors involved in the acquisition and ownership of land among primitive peoples. From the economic aspect, the land provides a home and a dwelling-place; it is the source from which the native draws the raw materials necessary for the ultimate satisfaction of his needs. The development of property from non-property is usually explained by the economist in some such terms as the following: Every appropriation involves a certain effort in the separation, keeping and defending of goods removed from the material environment. Everybody will try to avoid this trouble in so far as by so doing he does not deprive himself of the satisfaction of his wants. There is no necessity, therefore, to appropriate objects of which there is abundance and which in the event of loss can be replaced without difficulty. Common examples of such goods are those which are the free gift of nature—air, sunlight; and again for the nomad tribesman it is unnecessary to appropriate where there is pasture land, meadow and forest in abundance.

It follows, then, in economic theory, that we have reason to appropriate such objects as in the case of loss can only be replaced with a certain effort—an effort which will be avoided wherever possible; or objects which cannot be replaced at all and on which there is a manifest scarcity value. In comparison with the effort of making or finding new goods, the effort of appropriation is relatively small and economically rational. Where scarcity of goods is not evident there will be little private property. Among the Arawaks, for instance, Von Martius states that though they have the notion of private property, yet what one possesses is so simple and easy to get that each borrows and lends without much care about the returning. No one has much stimulus to win wealth by industry and trade. Supplies for a year can be acquired by three or four months' labour in the field.[1] Again, among pastoral and hunting peoples, with a growing scarcity, which may be individual or social in nature and is often the outcome of increasing population, it is necessary to incorporate labour into the soil. Ownership of land results from the operation of these twin principles of labour and scarcity; it will be private or communal ownership according as the incorporated labour unit is an individual or family or a collective group unit.[2]

So much for the statement of the economics of value. I want now to consider some of the customary modes of appropriation of land and to endeavour to state some of the psychological factors which help to reinforce such appropriation. The question of land in relation to a people, or to savages in particular, is often treated as a matter of pure economic interest. The assumption is that the sole concern of most peoples lies in the productive power which the soil manifests for them. It is on this basis that many of the theories as to the evolution of property in land are constructed. But in point of fact psychological ties and sentiments of ownership between land and people are the real heart of the rights which communal authority accords to the group. "Even among the lowest savages," says Firth, "it is probable that various kinds of sentimental associations, springing from residence, ancestral connections or religious beliefs, may provide the basis for a strong bond of union between groups or even individuals and the land, and thus

[1] K. E. P. von Martius: *Beiträge*, etc., i, 92, 692; cf. Sumner and Keller: *op. cit.*, i, 259.

[2] Cf. Lewinski: *Origin of Property*, 8–9, 10–11, 22–26, etc. Descamps: *op. cit.*, *passim.*

create property ties. Such non-material influences are often the most powerful in determining economic conduct."[1] The nature of these psychological ties will come out if we review the modes of acquiring property.

The original mode of acquisition is probably that of occupation. This is evident in the nomad's right to unoccupied land, the agriculturalist's right to the soil he cultivates and the tribe's right to the soil it occupies. Thus among the Herero, "notwithstanding the loose notions generally entertained by them as to *meum* and *tuum*, there is an understanding that he who arrives first at any given locality is the master of it as long as he chooses to remain there and no one will intrude upon him without having obtained his permission."[2] Similarly, hunting tribes, like the Veddas and the Australian aborigines, rigidly exclude other groups from the lands they occupy. This right to land based on occupation may be claimed through ancestral right, through material occupation or through conquest. Among the Maori, occupation based on *ahi ka*, or the burning fire, was deemed an important right to land, since to keep fire burning on the land meant continuous occupation, and every effort was made by the weaker tribes to keep the fires alight. In some cases this meant the abandonment of desirable sites and a withdrawal to forest-clad ranges or other places of difficult access; but in all cases, to make occupation-right valid, the fire must be kept burning.[3] Again, to take another people, among the Trobriands, a totemic sub-clan has a traditional claim to own the land surrounding the locality where its mythical ancestors had emerged from the subterranean world—the village site which often lies immediately round the 'hole of emergence,' the adjoining lands and the

[1] Firth: *Primitive Economics*, 360–361.

[2] C. J. Anderson: *Lake Ngami*. Quoted Westermarck: *Origin and Development of Moral Ideas* (1917), ii, 36.

[3] Best: *The Maori*, i, 396–397; Maning, F. E.: *Old New Zealand*, ch. v.

economic pursuits and privileges associated with the locality.[1]

Ancestral right is one element in ownership based upon occupation. Another important element lies in the fact that keeping possession of an object may make it the property of the possessor even though the occupation of that object gave him no such right. As the time of possession lengthens, the object becomes more and more a part of the self, feelings of familiarity and affection grow up between the self and the object, so that the latter is psychologically appropriated, if not legally. Thus Hume wrote: "Such is the effect of custom that it not only reconciles us to anything we long enjoyed, but even gives us an affection for it, and makes us prefer it to other objects which may be more valuable but are less known to us. What has long lain under our eye, and has often been employed to our advantage; *that* we are always the most unwilling to part with; but can easily live without possessions which we never have enjoyed, and are not accustomed to."[2] This feeling of familiarity and consequent affection is, of course, the psychological basis of the legal principle of prescription.

We see, then, that feelings of familiarity based upon habit and custom and ancestral traditions are elements in the building up of a sentiment of ownership which unites an individual or a group to the land which has been occupied. It is this undercurrent of deep feeling which provides a strong emotional basis for the right as objectively recognized.

The second major principle that has been formulated to justify acquisition of property has been that of the incorporation of labour. In Russia it was the custom to say that the land was property "as far as the axe, the scythe, and the

[1] Malinowski: *Sexual Life*, etc., 418 *et seq*.

[2] Hume: "Treatise on Human Nature." *Philosophical Works* (1874–1875), ii, 274. Cf. Sir John Salmond: "Such is the tendency of mankind to acquiesce in established usage that we have here a further and important source of *de facto* security and possession." *Jurisprudence*, 303.

plough go," and, to take another example from another continent, the Institutes of Manu, classified in India about 500 B.C., gave it that "the sages declare a field to belong to him who first cleared away the timber as the deer to him who first wounded it." In this connection it is interesting to note that in some communities (Java, Russian Buriats, etc.) the land is subject to different rules according to the degree of labour necessary to cultivate it. Thus of the Buriats, Krol writes: "It is impossible not to notice that they differentiate carefully between those fields the tillage of which required much labour (clearing of stones, forests, etc.) and those fields the occupation of which has not necessitated a great amount of it. With regard to the first, the right of property is recognized without discussion; the second class of fields only belong to the occupier so long as the enclosures stand round them, or a little longer; only in exceptional cases are they considered property."[1] In general it may be said that among primitive peoples in regard to the ownership of implements, weapons and land, what is acquired or made by a man or woman by personal exertion is regarded as his or her private property. Similarly what is acquired or made through combined labour of a group is usually the common property of the individuals forming the group.[2]

The psychological elements involved in a sentiment of ownership supporting property, the acquisition of which has involved the mixing of labour, are not far to seek. In the making of a tool or weapon or a house there is the satisfaction of the impulse to construction; in the decoration or carving of the implement there is aesthetic pleasure and joy in good craftsmanship. Memory of the energy, time and labour

[1] Krol, quoted Lewinski: *op. cit.*, 18; cf. also 13–14, 60–61.

[2] It is hardly necessary to consider in this connection which principle is primary in the appropriation of property—occupation or labour; cf., however, Hume: *Philosophical Works* (1874–1875), ii, 276, note 1, and Westermarck: *op. cit.*, ii, 36.

spent in fashioning the tool from raw materials strengthens the feelings of satisfaction at having produced something that is useful or beautiful and perhaps both. Since an object of this nature may be envied or praised by other members of the group, the sentiments grouped round the self are proportionately strengthened and reinforce in their turn those feelings centred about the newly created object.

The case is likewise when we consider the incorporation of labour in land. Through such mixing of labour, the individuality of the worker and the land he acquires becomes mingled in feeling, if not in fact. The roots of this feeling have been nowhere more vividly described than by H. N. Brailsford when, of the Russian peasants after the Revolution of 1917, he writes: "The peasants have what all landworkers desire; they count their acres their own. That desire was for them a primitive passion, which ranks among their physical instincts, so deep is it, so closely linked with the sensations of hand and feet as they spread out the roots of their seedlings in the soil or tramp through the furrows behind the plough. The true countryman feels for the soil a love comparable to the ties that bind him to wife and child, a passion that can heal when it is satisfied and corrode when it goes hungry. . . . The instinct bred in the placid solitudes of these great plains is one of conservatism which will tend to hold and to keep what has been won."[1] It is this passion for the land, the outcome of labour, trials, disappointment and success, which is the basic reality of that ownership which, annexing labour to the common state of nature, excludes the common right of other men.[2]

[1] H. N. Brailsford: *How the Soviets Work*, New York (1928), 153. It is the powerfulness of this psychological tendency 'to hold and keep what has been won' which makes the efforts of the Russian Soviets to collectivize the farm lands of the peasant such an interesting psychological experiment for the outside observer.

[2] Cf. Locke: *Treatise on Civil Government*, ch. v, *passim*. Two further but secondary modes of acquiring property, i.e. by gift, sale, exchange or contract, and by accession, need not be considered in the present context. Cf., however, Hume: *Works*, etc., ii, 279, and Salmond: *Jurisprudence*, 304.

That claims to land based upon various varieties of occupation involve a connection between the personality of the claimant and the property claimed may be illustrated from some of the customs and practices of a nature folk like the Maori. Though the main claims to land were based on conquest, occupation and ancestral right—these not mutually exclusive grounds of ownership but often concurrent or supplementary—yet other claims depending upon magico-animistic beliefs were frequently advanced to prove a title to disputed property. Thus a person might have a certain right in the lands of another tribe if he happened to have been born thereon, if his blood had been shed there, if an ancestor of his were buried there, or if his umbilical cord together with a small stone had been buried there. Similarly, a chief from whose head-dress a feather had fallen while travelling stopped and built a little fence round it with twigs, thereby establishing a claim to the land. Another chief, pleased with the catch of eels on the river of a strange tribe, threw the albatross-down tuft from his ear into the water, thus securing an interest in the land and in the periodical eel-fishing. There is recorded, too, the act of a chief who by leaving the combings of his hair in a small bundle on a pole thereby made the locality *tapu* to himself and henceforward occupied it.[1] The essential underlying idea in all these examples seems to have been that the act in question connected the personality of the man with the land and he was therefore entitled to a share in it.

The same explanation is at the basis of the Maori practice of claiming land through its bespeaking. This custom, called by the natives *taunaha whenuia* (the bespeaking of land), was followed when land was obtained by conquest and men of standing claimed certain areas thereof for themselves or their tribe. A favoured method of doing so was to name the

[1] Cf. Firth: *op. cit.*, 380. For the umbilical cord *motif* among Melanesians, cf W E Armstrong: *Rossell Island*, 101.

desired area after some part of the claimant's body. It is recorded in the story of the coming of the first canoes to New Zealand that when land was at daybreak sighted one chief claimed a rocky headland as "the bridge of his nose"; another claimed more land as "the belly of my son Waitaha"; another used the words, "this land is my throat." Thus all the land in sight might be annexed by no more than several men.[1] A tree wherewith to fashion a canoe might be preserved as bespoken by the same method as was employed for land. A stone might be placed at the base of the tree, or some other sign employed, and the embargo verbally notified to the people. Thereafter the tree was reserved (*rahuitia*) for its owner's use.

The practice of bespeaking was very like another method which the Maori used to acquire property, the practice of *tapatapa*. The essence of this practice was that by definitely associating a desired article with himself a chief thereby isolated it for his own use. This could be done by connecting clothing with the object, by calling the object by one's own name or by referring to it as part of one's body; then, if the property was that of any person of one's own or a friendly tribe, it would be at once handed over to the claimant. A canoe might be thus bespoken or pigs or kumara crops, and in all cases, since they thus became part of the claimant's personality, they would be given up. Pigs called by a chief's name could never be eaten by any other persons, since this would be equivalent to eating him. Hence it was the chief's duty to remove them for his own use. This logic is not hard to understand. When once the object by direct contact or by association with the name or body of the chief has become infected with his *tapu*, the safety of the erstwhile owners and the preservation of his own dignity both require that it be handed over to him. In the matter of initiative, only a chief with some rank, consequence and *mana* could

[1] Best: *The Maori*, i, 400; Firth: *op. cit.*, 377.

employ the *tapatapa*; and obligations of reciprocity constrained him to give an adequate return to goods so bespoken. In two ways, therefore, a very definite limit was imposed upon powers of acquisition under schemes of *tapatapa* or *taunaha*.[1]

I have been trying to show so far that other factors besides those purely economic are involved in the relation between an individual and a property object. Scarcity and utility may be the major elements in economic value; but from the subjective point of view, value is more complex than the economists would allow. It is my thesis that objects become values when they are desired; they are desired primarily because they satisfy major impulses; and secondly, objects are desired because they have become assimilated to, or integrated with, primary values and thus new values have become integrated with the personality. Valuing, however, is a two-sided process. Objectively, new objects may be assimilated to primary values, and new values are formed either when these objects stand on their own or when they become fused with the primary values. Subjectively, many feelings, impulses or desires may become centred about a primary value. In this way a sentiment is formed which helps to give stability and comprehensiveness to the operation of the value in the integration of personality.

Of this second process in the formation of values, a consideration of the sentiments and feelings that grow up about the land of a people will prove illuminating as showing the factors which form such a sentiment. I have already noticed the way in which incorporation of labour in land helps to build up sentiments of ownership for that land. But among a native people other more mystical ideas strengthen feelings of familiarity and affection. With the savage, as with the peasant of to-day, land has economic value in that upon its

[1] Cf. Best: *op. cit.*, i, 349 *et seq.*, 391; Taylor: *Te Ika a Maui*, 164–165; Shortland: *Traditions of the New Zealanders*, etc., ch. v; Firth: *op. cit.*, 337–338.

productivity both must depend in a greater or less degree for subsistence and support. Whereas, however, mystical or magical ideas or feelings are probably absent from the European peasant's attitude towards his land, yet among such culturally low savages as the Australian aboriginal we are probably justified in believing that the savage hunter's sentimental[1] attachment to tribal land was based not only upon its value in providing food but also upon the fact that it was once the hunting and ceremonial grounds of his *Alcheringa* ancestors. Individually the Australian savage was attached to a portion of the local district through a right which was mystically intangible in character and which drew strength and vitality from the whole series of customs, beliefs, traditions and creeds grouped about the cycle of totemic ideas concerning reincarnation and supernatural conception. Likewise with the group. "We are justified," says Malinowski, summarizing all the evidence, "in supposing that everywhere the rights of the local group . . . were the sum or resultant of such individual rights of magical or religious character, or that the group as a whole was attached by such ties to its area."[2]

If we take the Maori again and study from his proverbs, laments, traditions, beliefs and legends the sentiments which grew up between him and his land, we may find other elements to group alongside those of mystical and religious feeling, physical contact, or familiarity which we have already distinguished as part of the warp and woof of the sentiment of ownership. The Maori had a great respect for land in itself (a primary value) and an exceedingly strong affection for his ancestral soil. But this sentimental valuing can be by no means correlated solely with its fertility and immediate value to him as a source of food. Such economic

[1] I use the word *sentimental* as the adjective of the psychological term *sentiment*, i.e. with a definite scientific connotation.

[2] Malinowski: *The Family among the Australian Aborigines* (1913), 153; cf. also 143–144, 149, 209 *et seq.*, 290–291, etc.

values would fuse with the psychological values, but the latter were something more important to the Maori than the former. The lands whereon his fathers lived, fought and were buried were ever to him an object of the deepest feeling. His feeling is summed up in the cry: *Noku te whenua o oku tupuna* (Mine is the land, the land of my ancestors).

This deep-rooted affection of the native for his land is found, for instance, in many of his proverbs. 'Man perishes but the land remains' is one such proverb contrasting the fleeting nature of man's life with the eternal stability of man's heritage, the land. Another proverb stresses the importance of land, together with women, as the cause of tribulation and distress: *He wahine, he whenua a ngaro ai te tangata* (By women and land are men lost). Another old saying, illustrating the affection of the Maori for his land, is, 'I greet my only surviving parent in the world, the land.' This same feeling for the land is evident also in tribal records and traditions. Cases have been known where a Maori, taken prisoner and enslaved by enemies, has sent a message to his tribesmen: *'Tukuna mai he kapunga oneoneki au hai tangi* (Send me a handful of soil that I may weep over it). Even so would his request be granted. Or a captive would ask to be allowed to drink of the waters of a stream flowing through his tribal lands; and in many instances he was so allowed to drink before being killed. Such a prisoner, says Best, has also been known to say to his captors: 'Conduct me to the bounds of my land to sing a song of farewell ere I am killed.' Again, when the chief Rakuraku was too old to travel, his young people, on returning from his tribal lands, would bring him a branch of the *Kotara* tree for him to greet over.[1]

Finally, in times of great stress the courage of the people

[1] Best: *The Maori*, i, 397; Firth: *op. cit.*, 361; Firth: *Folklore*, xxxvii, 152–153; cf. also for the part proverbs play in Maori life, Colenso: *Transactions, New Zealand Institute*, vol. xii, 108–147; Smith: *op. cit.*, vol. xxii, 111–118.

was sometimes stirred by an appeal to their affections for their land. Instances are recorded in Maori history of how a chief, seeing his people about to break ranks and flee in disorder, would strike his spear into the ground and stand firm with the words, 'Let me die on my land.' Rarely has a tribe failed to respond to such an appeal. To take one more instance: the transfer of territory to the white man in the early settlement days was often accompanied by affecting scenes of farewell between an assembled people and their tribal lands, songs, laments and speeches being token of their grief. The associations between a land and its people are shown by such a quotation as the following made by a surveyor investigating a dispute between two Waikato tribes: "Every spot of ground is associated with some particular deed connected with their many engagements and triumphs. One is sacred because a man of rank fell there; another because it is the place where he is buried; and another is named to commemorate the place where they ate their enemies. This history of these places is handed down from father to son, the retaining of them in their possession has become more dear than life."[1] And so when discussing the demarcation of the boundaries the Maori proposal was to run a crooked boundary-line between the graves of the chiefs fallen in the preceding struggles. In this way they would keep as many of the disputed places as possible.

The few examples I have given will be sufficient to indicate the outlines of the type of sentiment that grew up between a primitive people like the Maori and his tribal lands. To a certain extent, of course, as I have suggested already, the existence of this sentiment must be correlated with a recognition of the primary value of land as a source of food for self-support and for the exercise of that hospitality which is so marked a feature of savage life. Nevertheless, over and

[1] C. W. Ligar, Surveyor-General, from *New Zealand Spectator*, February 20, 1847. Quoted in Firth: *Primitive Economics*, 364.

above means of subsistence and the fulfilment of social obligations one must recognize the large part that other psychological factors play in the formation of values in land. Aesthetic appreciation, memories of former years, tribal battles, sacred practices, memories of home and family—in fact all those interests which are the resultant of the interplay of social sympathy with traditional teaching and aesthetic emotion combine to create a sentiment of ownership for the land.

So much for the part that magico-animistic practices and beliefs play in the generation of property rights. So much also for the complex fashion in which impulse and emotion are fused into a sentiment of possession centred about the land. In the next chapter I wish to carry further this study of the nature of the sentiment of property by analysing the reaction of primitive man to the ownership of woman, ornament and more specific objects of native wealth.

CHAPTER VI

SENTIMENTS OF OWNERSHIP IN SAVAGE SOCIETY

In the last analysis both primitive and civilized man will only take the trouble to acquire objects because they have value for him. The process of valuation in its widest sense may be considered as a subjective appreciation, and at higher levels of mental development a conscious judgment, based upon the functional interrelation between a person and an object of desire. A previously neutral object or good must acquire interest and become a desirable object or good.[1] In being desired, such object has become an object of value. The agent strives to acquire and preserve such objects because, being valued and desired, they can bring satisfaction when finally obtained. They may give satisfaction either as primary values when they are desired for their own sake; or as secondary or instrumental values when their attainment makes possible the gaining of values at a further remove from the agent.

From the point of view of this thesis, certain constant and fundamental root-interests work out in practice as motives of acquisition; and the end-objects of these root-interests I look upon as the primary organic values. Typical interests are those connected with hunger, sex, vanity, social recognition and fear; or more broadly still, those of self-maintenance, self-perpetuation and self-gratification. In the actual living individual few actions are the outcome of any one of these root-interests *in vacuo*, so to speak. Neither life nor the organism is as simply made as all this. In prac-

[1] "In practice, value is a personal attitude of welcome or the reverse towards an object of interest." Schiller: art. "Value," *Hastings' Dictionary*, vol. xii.

tice motives present a tangled web in which various interests cross and interweave in a fashion that is the reverse of simple. But for the purposes of analysis one may classify the primary motives of man, and, by implication, the primary values which interest him, as I have done above.[1]

It is my purpose in this chapter, having given an account of what I believe to be the psychological basis of the appropriation of property values in personal objects and land, to continue my analysis by taking further examples of property values to show, first, the way objects have become values, second, the assimilation of values often through a process of unconscious patterning of behaviour, and third, the manner in which motives and interests have been integrated in a generally complex fashion about the primary or secondary property objects. I am conscious, of course, of the difficulty and complexity of this task. But the fundamental problems in any consideration of the psychology of property are to be found, I believe, in the origin and integration of values. It is only by an attempt to reveal the nature of this process that one can hope to give a definite meaning to that otherwise 'tabloid' phrase which finds the basis of the right to property in some such words as 'necessary for the development of personality.' Without particularizing why and how property is necessary for the development of

[1] In this and in the preceding chapter I am using the term 'value' as roughly equivalent to the phrase, 'object that is desired.' I am aware, of course, that this equivalence can only be justified in terms of the psychology of the valuing process. From the point of view of the epistemology and ontology of Value, the nature of value is probably quite other than mere equation with 'the desirable.' A discussion of the wider implications of the Theory of Value, however, would lead far afield into the realms of logic and philosophy and would not be to our present purpose. Here I am concerned solely with the psychology of the process of valuation; but with the premise understood that values which are psychically data and psychologically immediate may always be logically mediated and made objects of valuation processes and explicit value judgments. They then function as facts to be evaluated. For the wider Theory of Value reference may be made to the standard works of Urban and Perry. A useful summary is to be found in Clarke: *The Logic of Value* (1929).

personality, such a phrase is meaningless. I think, however, and it is my aim to show, that it is possible to see in terms of psychology why the acquisition of property values is necessary to secure a harmonious development of the self. The amount and kind of property values is another problem altogether, and one which does not interest us at the present moment.

I will first consider the basis of one of the most fundamental property values of both savage and civilized society. I refer to woman as a property object. Leaving on one side a consideration of the status of woman in this respect as it is conceived in civilized society,[1] one may briefly mention some of the facts which relate to the conception of woman as property in savage communities. In Fiji, for instance, Wilkes tells us that "the women are kept in subjection. . . . Like other property, wives may be sold at pleasure, and the usual price is a musket."[2] Among the Shoshones, "the man is the sole proprietor of his wives and daughters and can barter them away or dispose of them in any way he may think proper."[3] Again, among the East African Wanika, a woman "is a toy, a tool, a slave, in the very worse sense; indeed she is treated as though she were a mere brute."[4] Among the Kirgiz, the woman is quite definitely conceived as her husband's property and loses contact with her own family; while again with the Ho, an Ewe tribe of Togo, West Africa, there is a series of payments and services which establishes a proprietary title to the wife. In a very definite sense the woman is a form of property, since she may serve as a pawn in a creditor's custody and is inherited by her husband's brothers while herself barred from inherit-

[1] John Galsworthy, in the *Forsyte Saga*, has analysed with a wealth of subtle illustration what is probably a typical attitude—the sentiment of ownership which, for the Man of Property, was centred about the woman he married and desired exclusively to possess.

[2] Wilkes: *Narrative of the U.S. Exploring Expedition*, iii, 332.

[3] Lewis and Clarke: *Travels to the Source of the Missouri*, 307.

[4] New: *Life, Wanderings and Labourings*, 119.

ing any of his possessions.[1] Of a pastoral people like the Kalmouks, Renard tells us: "Une femme valait quinze chevaux, quinze vaches, trois chameaux, vingt brébis, si bien que posséder des filles qu'on vendait à l'age nubile était un moyen d'accroître ses troupeaux."[2] Finally, discussing marriage on Rossell Island, Armstrong states that the completeness of the husband's ownership is shown by the fact that it is common for a man to be punished by the killing of the woman, i.e. his wife, who cooks his food, and this without necessitating revenge by the girl's clansmen or her father's clansmen, nor even a demand for compensation. A variation of Rossell Island marriage is the institution which enables a number of men to combine and buy between them a woman (*ptyilibi*) for their collective use. Though the system of purchase is the same as for the individual wife, nevertheless the *ptyilibi* may be hired out to others, and the money received shared by the owners.[3]

I do not wish to discuss the institution of marriage by purchase at length, nor to enquire into the facts as to how far it is misnamed, how far *coemptio* has evolved from *raptus*; or how far it is a development from the practice of bride gifts or *vice versa*.[4] But in essentials, it seems uncontroversial to state that marriage by purchase is the

[1] Cf. Lowie: *Primitive Society*, 18–19, 32–33, 186, and Westermarck: *Origin and Development*, etc., i, 629–630.

[2] Renard: *Le Travail dans la Préhistoire*, 258.

[3] The groom pays the bride's relatives a valuable native coin (No. 18 *ndap*) and further money at two marriage feasts, while they, on their part, make no reciprocal payment to the relatives of the husband. This practice should be compared with that of the neighbouring Massim, where it is difficult to find the bride price in operation. In place of it are mutual obligations between a man's and his wife's relatives extending over an indefinite number of years. Cf. W. E. Armstrong: *Rossell Island*, 93–99; Malinowski: *Argonauts*, etc., 54; *The Mailu*, 566–567.

[4] For these and cognate topics reference may be made to Sumner and Keller: *Science of Society*, iii, 1643–1646; Westermarck: *Human Marriage*, ii, 393–396 *et seq.*; Crawley: *The Mystic Rose*, ii, 138–139, 140–142, 237–239; Hobhouse, Wheeler and Ginsberg: *The Simpler Peoples*, 154–156; Müller Lyer: *History of Social Development*, 267–270.

prevalent form of primitive marriage, constituting a mean between the capture and the dowry systems. It is based upon the general alignment of woman with other property values. The unmarried girl is the property of the family or of the family's representative. She is an asset whose value depends partly on her attractiveness, partly on her capacity for work, partly on the scarcity of the article, but chiefly on the fact that she is an object of sexual desire. This article can be sold for so much, and the purchaser naturally expects to become wholly possessed of what he buys. Where the consequences of such a sale are pushed to their furthest extent her family lose the power of protecting her, and the wife is at the mercy of the husband. He may dispose of her at pleasure; he may sell her, give her away or lend her, and she has no right of redress against him. At best she may escape from him if her family is willing or able to return her price and buy her back.

Not every case where property passes is an example of marriage by purchase. Gifts to the bride's parents are made to win favour and consent, to atone for capture or elopement, to repay parents for the expenses of the girl's rearing, to reimburse the loss of her services or to buy the right to beget children by her and include them in one's own tribe. Under endogamy and mother-right especially, if the man goes to the woman's group, gifts to her parents, kinsmen or herself have meaning only as winning favour and acceptance. It is in exogamy and father-right, when a man takes his wife from her tribe to his own, that payments are most genuinely purchase money. In this case a woman is lost to her own people, as a thing bought leaves the hands of its former owner.

From another point of view it seems a not improbable assumption that bride purchase among primitive peoples is broadly correlated with the institution of pre-marital chastity. If this is so (and the assumption can only ultimately be validated by an extensive comparative survey), then it follows that both the common insistence upon fidelity in a wife and pre-marital chastity in a bride may be regarded as property taboos, explicable on the ground that unfaithfulness and laxity before marriage may result in property complications incident to notions of illegitimacy.[1] It is sufficiently established that a man, where *patria potestas* is marked, by owning his wife owns also her offspring. In such a case the man is generally resentful of any infringement of his rights over his daughters or of any assumption by them of rights over themselves. He may allow what he wishes, he may assign them in hospitality to a guest, but he is jealous of his authority. He sells his daughters with specifications, explicit or implicit, as to their quality, and he is responsible in a definite material way if they do not measure up to specifications. He must replace a daughter who proves on accepted tests not to be satisfactory, or restore the price paid for her. "Where daughters are property even though they may resist by elopement, and where the conception of property has been sharpened into a pretty definite shape, the taboo against trespass reaches beyond a prohibition of mere abduction, which was early resented as an invasion of rights, to include sex relations, unless they are expressly permitted by the father or other owner."[2] Thus to take two examples: Wellhausen tells

[1] This is, in general, correct. The explanation will not hold, however, for native peoples like the Trobriand Islanders or Australian aborigines, where competent observers have suggested that the native is entirely ignorant of the facts of physiological parentage, and where, in consequence, notions of illegitimacy are hardly relevant. In any case, among the Trobriands pre-marital chastity appears to be quite unknown, though unfaithfulness after marriage is severely punished. Cf. Malinowski: *Sexual Life of Savages*, *passim*.

[2] Sumner and Keller: *op. cit.*, iii, 1680. Thus Bancroft writes of the Chinook Indian woman that after marriage, too, "female virtue acquires a marketable value, the possessorship being lodged in the man and not in the woman. Rarely are wives unfaithful to their husbands; but the chastity of the wife is the recognized property of the husband, who sells it whenever he pleases." *Native Races of the Pacific*, i, 242.

us that "suspicious jealousy, not of the love of their wives, but of their own property rights, is a prominent character of the Arabs, of which they are proud." The blood kin guard their property rights in the maiden as jealously as the man guards his rights in the wife.[1] In the Torres Straits, again, irregular intercourse is known as 'stealing a girl'; fornication or adultery as '*puru* theft.' Unchastity is regarded as a breach of the property rights of the father or guardian and is often punishable, especially if it results in pregnancy.[2]

The institution of bride purchase and the payment of wealth for the woman has a psychological reaction upon the woman herself. Where marriage by purchase is the prevailing form a girl is justly proud of the price she brings. She would be despised if she cost nothing. So the Kaffir despises a wife taken for love, that is, without payment, comparing her with a cat, which is the only animal got for nothing. Zulu women are said to be proud of the price they bring; while again, among the Yakut reindeer-tending nomads, the bride price is shared by the parents, older brothers, uncles and guardians of the bride, and, in case of orphan working girls, by the master. Each gets something, be it ever so little, as a recognition of surrender by him of a claim to the woman. "Not a single well-bred Yakut girl would consent to go to her husband without a bride price. She would be degraded in her own eyes and according to the views of her people.

[1] Sumner: *Folkways*, 358.

[2] Haddon: *Cambridge Expedition*, vol. v, 275. Westermarck (*Human Marriage*, i, 317) hazards the suggestion that pre-marital chastity, fidelity during marriage, and faithfulness of wife after the death of husband, have their origin in feelings of retrospective and prospective jealousy. This demand partly "owes its origin to the same powerful feeling as keeps watch over the purity of the marriage bed." The wife sacrifices herself on the funeral pyre of her husband or never remarries because of the idea that she belongs exclusively to her dead mate. There may be an element of truth in this suggestion. The correlation of chastity with the institution of bride purchase seems less far-fetched, however.

It would mean that she was not worth any price, was friendless or an outcast."[1]

From the above considerations it will be readily seen to what degree among primitive peoples woman is regarded as a form of property value. Speaking generally, woman is used, enjoyed and controlled by her husband, parent or guardian, before and after marriage; but though the rights of the latter are generally limited by customary authority and may be in few cases entirely absolute, nevertheless, to all intents and purposes, the woman in savage society may be looked upon as a value of some considerable importance.[2]

We may ask, next, what is the origin of the value of woman and to what degree are sentiments of ownership built up about her. First and foremost, of course, woman acquires an intrinsic and primary value as the biological complement of the sexual impulse in man. She is valued ultimately because of her capacity naturally to satisfy the insistent cravings of sex. But only in terms of ultimates; because being human as well as a biological species, emotions of affection, interest, joy, sorrow, anger and fear quickly grow up about crude sexual desire and become centred about the member of the opposite sex. The desire for possession, which is one aspect of sex, is integrated with

[1] Sumner: "The Yakuts," *Journal Anthropological Institute*, vol. xxxi, 85; cf. also Bancroft: *op. cit.*, i, 277.

[2] Of the Australian aboriginal Malinowski writes: "The idea of individual sexual overright and control over his wife is strongly present in the aboriginal mind. This right is undoubtedly realized as a privilege, and the natural tendency to keep his privileges for himself, or to dispose of them according to his will or interest, must create a strong opposition to any encroachment. In other words, the sexual act has its intrinsic value, and it is considered as an unquestionable advantage. And the right to this advantage constitutes a kind of private property. The feeling of jealousy exists here in its economic sense: the proprietor of a certain object begrudges the use of it to anyone whom he does not invite to it and who is not otherwise entitled to the privilege . . . The facts . . . show that the husband vigilantly watches over and keeps his overrights." *The Family Among the Australian Aborigines*, 127.

other emotions into a sentiment of ownership, which, intimately connected in the individual with sentiments of self-valuation, serves to forge a bond of union between man and woman. At this stage, though woman may still be regarded as a primary value, yet the existence of powerful sentiments of ownership is revealed in the operations of emotions of jealousy whenever possession of the valued good seems likely to be disrupted.

After Shand's acute and definitive analysis of the nature of jealousy,[1] it will be sufficient for our purpose to point to the elements which are grouped together in this sentiment. First, fear: we desire exclusive possession of a woman and feel fear or anxiety because we are in danger either of losing her or of not attaining her. Fear leads to aggressive anger in an endeavour to retain control of the threatened object of desire. Since, again, sexual love cannot be separated from self-love in that the self is intimately bound up with the satisfaction of desire, it is due to the desire of self-love to possess certain goods exclusively for the self, women, power, reputation, that jealousy principally arises. The loss of possession to which jealousy refers, as well as the failure to obtain possession, is of such nature as carries with it a lowering of a man's self-valuation. This is accompanied by humiliation and consequent shame at the failure of the self. Thus jealousy (and jealousy is important for us because of the light its analysis throws upon the sentiments grouped about one of our primary property values) is derived from the influence of self-love and its system of self-valuation, evoking the emotions of shame and humiliation, fear and anger, and the sorrow consequent upon the loss—the loss of trust in, or the anticipated loss—of the desired object. Though difficult to define by subjective criteria, since jealousy

[1] A. F. Shand: *The Foundations of Character* (1920), 257–260; cf. also Westermarck: *Human Marriage* (1921), i, 301 *et seq.*; and an interesting study of "Jealousy" by Gesell in *Amer. J. of Psychology*, vol. xvii; Sumner and Keller, *op. cit.*, iii, 1764–1776, should also be consulted.

is sometimes more fear, sorrow and shame, and at other times more anger, suspicion and humiliation, yet, defined in terms of function, jealousy is "that egoistic side of the system of love which has as its especial end the exclusive possession of the loved object, whether this object be a woman, or other person, or power, reputation or property."[1]

I have given this brief analysis of jealousy to suggest the complex manner in which motives and emotions gradually integrate themselves about a primary value. Instead of a blind impulsive biological desire for the possession of a good, we have a desire for possession which has assimilated about the good a number of other emotions and feelings. A sentiment of possession or of ownership has been formed which only requires social recognition to become a right to ownership. A further point of interest, however, is this: that although this sentiment of ownership is usually very strong where sexual prerogatives are involved, nevertheless, in many savage societies, it has been socially and unconsciously patterned along lines which are the reverse of our own. I refer, of course, to such a practice as wife-lending. This is not uncommon among primitive peoples.[2] The husband who would kill or mutilate the wife whom he discovered in clandestine intercourse with a lover will also lend her as an act of courtesy to a guest. In the one case she infringes his right of property, in the other case it is as his property that she is acting.

In terms of psychology the natural tendency towards exclusive sexual control over the woman is moulded by social opinion and modified into a set tribal pattern by

[1] Shand: *op. cit.*, 260; cf. also Santayana: "Love is indeed much less exacting than it thinks itself. Nine-tenths of its cause are in the lover for one-tenth that may be in the object." *Life of Reason*, ii, 22.

[2] The records, for instance, of the early missionaries to New Zealand contain many examples of the embarrassing and delicate situations in which these sturdy Christians were placed by their refusal to take full advantage of the open-handed hospitality of the Maori chief in these matters. Cf. also Bancroft: *Native Races of Pacific*, i, 169, note 1.

the collective ideas, customs and conventions of the group. In many cases public opinion compels a man to waive his rights in an act of hospitality and good will. Sometimes this is so because it is thought that a stranger may bring great blessings to the group; or, if not pleased, great evil on his host.[1] Again, it may be a case of ceremonial duty to lend the wife; impulse may be modified by primitive ideas on the magical character of the sexual act; and with many peoples the waiving of rights is made easier by the absence of knowledge regarding the facts of physical paternity. Whatever the reason, however, primitive feelings of sexual exclusiveness and sentiments of ownership based thereon are overruled by social patterns having for their purpose hospitality, advantage, utility, ceremonialism or magic. The Eskimo will be jealous of infidelities occurring without the husband's cognizance or permission, for both the sentiments of self-valuation and of ownership have been violated. Jealousy is in abeyance with unfaithfulness by permission or by order, since neither *amour propre* nor property rights are in question. Indeed, in the latter case, the one is being qualified and the other exercised to the full.[2]

So far we have been considering woman in terms of what I have called primary property values. It will provide an easy transition to my next section, the discussion of wealth as a property value, if I pause for a moment and briefly consider woman in primitive society in her rôle as an instrumental value, as an interest or value, that is, to the husband, because of the part she may play in the acquisition of wealth. We are not yet concerned with wealth as a value in savage society; but provided wealth is a value desired and sought after, it is evident that the daughter, through

[1] Thus of the Masai it is reported: "A Masai cannot refuse hospitality to a stranger (of his own age), for he is afraid that the other members of his age group will curse him and he will die." Hollis: *The Masai*, 288.

[2] Cf. Westermarck: *op. cit.*, i, 225–229, 230–234, 303 *et seq.* Also Malinowski: *op. cit.*, 125–131, 300; Lowie: *Primitive Society*, 46.

the institution of the bride price, may often bring to her father appreciable wealth and influence, while to her husband she is of a value because of the children she bears and the labour she performs.

In savage society, as in civilized, wealth enables its possessor to acquire all kinds of power and advantages which the poor must do without. In itself, therefore, it constitutes a source of new distinctions. From the point of view of the husband, we find that in those Melanesian societies which are based on elaborate conventions of reciprocity and mutuality of service, "marriage puts the wife's family under a permanent tributary obligation to the husband, to whom they have to pay yearly contributions for as long as the household exists. From the moment when they signify by the first gift that they accept the marriage, they have to produce, year after year by their own labour, a quantity of yams for their kinswoman's family. The size of the offering varies with the status of both partners, but covers about half the annual consumption in an average household."[1] Though monogamy is the general rule in Melanesia, nevertheless polygamy is allowed by custom to people of higher rank or to those of great importance. In order to wield his power and to fulfil his obligations a chief must possess wealth, and this can only come to him through his plurality of wives. Power in the Trobriand Islands, for instance, Malinowski tells us to be essentially plutocratic. Since there are no emoluments or tributes attached to the office of chieftainship as such, the chief must rely upon the annual marriage contributions of his several wives for the wherewithal to carry out his executive functions, to give great feasts, to finance all the major tribal enterprises, to pay craftsmen for making precious ornaments, to hire dangerous sorcerers and assassins—in short, to do all that is expected of a person in power. Though personal prestige,

[1] Malinowski: *Sexual Life*, etc., 103.

respect for his holy character, and abilities as magician contribute to the power of the chief, yet in every case this power rests at bottom upon the practice of polygamy, the rich dowry due to a woman who marries a chief and the subsequent contributions levied upon the wives' kinspeople.[1] The woman who marries a Trobriand chief has, in fact, become an instrumental property value.

The same conceptions are at work among the Indian hunter folk, where a plurality of wives means so many more labourers. An Indian with one wife "cannot amass property as the wife is constantly occupied in household labours and has no time for preparing skins for trading."[2] Therefore a plurality of wives is required by a good hunter, since the more wives a man has the more and larger fields he can cultivate and the more robes and furs they can tan for him. Again, in Indian society, the dowry of the wives directly contributes to the wealth of the family. When the children grow up they add to the riches of their father through their labour, and thus give him prominence and respectability in society. Daughters bring their fathers wealth and influence through the purchase price given for them and through the number of new relations which their marriage usually adds to the family.[3] These two examples show what I have sought to stress, namely, that in some primitive societies woman must be regarded not only as a primary value in her capacity to provide satisfaction for functional activity, but also as an instrumental value in the production of wealth for the use of her husband and family.

I now wish to carry our discussion of primitive economic values a stage further by considering the origin and nature of value as embodied in primitive objects of wealth. Examples

[1] Malinowski: *op. cit.*, 110 *et seq.*

[2] Dorsey. *Sioux Sociology.* Smithsonian Reports, xv, 225. For the correlation between the wife or wives and the amount of property of the husband among a pastoral people, cf. Sumner: "The Yakuts," *op. cit.*, 94.

[3] Cf. Buxton: *Primitive Labour*, 32.

of such objects in savage economy are food, houses, clothing, canoes, tools, ornaments and articles of a religious or magical interest. Though it is rarely possible to find among primitive communities a valuation of such objects in terms of exchange, nevertheless the savage does rank many of these objects in the order of their relative worth. My aim is to show that, apart from ideas of practical usefulness and apart from their interest as primary values, factors of an aesthetic, social and traditional nature enter as practical determinants of property value, making the appreciation of the worth of the objects as much the resultant of association in terms of sentiment, and complex set of emotional attitudes, as of any consideration of rational advantage.

Too often the savage is credited with being the convenient prototype of the modern business man, guided solely by ideas of a purely rational and calculating nature. The adoption of this assumption as a subconscious major premise has vitiated much of the work of Bücher and his school on primitive economics. Food is thought to be of interest to the savage only as it satisfied his hunger, clothing so far as it covered his nakedness and protected him from the elements, tools to the extent they assisted him to manufacture or procure other articles of need. Yet when one comes to the study of native life blinded by no prejudicial major premise one discovers the degree to which rational considerations are reinforced, sometimes overwhelmed, by non-rational motives in the determination of value. Food is accumulated for the purposes of display as well as for consumption. The possession of it is correlated with rank and power. Certain types of clothing and ornaments, whose value is based upon traditional factors, act as social insignia quite apart from their use in protecting or enhancing the beauty of the body. Decoration lavished on tools and implements, sometimes so much so that it hampers their efficiency, bears witness to the non-practical interest with which they are invested. Finally, the nature and extent to which wealth is accumulated and preserved in savage society is determined by a complex set of culture patterns whose effect is more often than not to stress the social importance and value of the distribution of acquired goods rather than their hoarding.

An instance or two will make these points clear. Jenness and Ballantyne tell us that the natives of the D'Entrecasteaux ornament canoe-heads, pottery, mats, armlets, grass skirts, combs, lime-gourds, lime spatulae and water-bottles, "not to sell, for there is no one to buy them, but merely to satisfy their artistic cravings."[1] "One might almost say of these people that whatever they touch they adorn, although their method of adorning naturally follows the line of their own ideas, not of ours."[2] The Kiwai Papuans will take infinite care in the manufacture and decoration of a fine harpoon. A good harpoon has a magical value in fishing; it has a social value also in that the entire community participates in a successful catch; and its importance is finally sealed by naming it, a process only accorded to the most highly valued native implements.[3]

Again, the Trobriand Islander "works prompted by motives of a highly complex, social and traditional nature, and towards aims which are certainly not directed towards the satisfaction of present wants or to the direct achievement of utilitarian purposes."[4] This same appreciation of decoration and aesthetic elements is seen in activities as widely separated as those of gardening, on the one hand, and the manufacture of ornaments and implements, on the other.[5] In regard to the Maori, Firth and others have shown the aesthetic, social and religious factors that help, along

[1] Jenness and Ballantyne: *The Northern D'Entrecasteaux*, 169.
[2] Jenness and Ballantyne: *op. cit.*, 197.
[3] Landtman: *The Kiwai Papuans*, 124; cf. the whole section 120–124 and 203.
[4] Malinowski: *Argonauts*, 60
[5] Malinowski: *op. cit.*, 58–59 and *passim*; Seligmann: *Melanesians*, 36.

with those of utility, to determine the value of ornament, clothing and tools.[1]

So much by way of general introduction to our study of the psychology of property values in wealth. I will now discuss one or two of these primitive wealth-values in order to show the fashion in which the drive of vital needs to their attainment is blended with a complexity of other motives and incentives, some largely impulsive in their origin, others the product of education, tradition and the general social milieu. The work of the new functional school of anthropology has been to some extent centred about the ceremonial treatment of primary values, for example, economic or vital, and here, it will serve best my purpose if I state the main conclusions to which the investigations of this school have led.

I take first the motives and values grouped about the accumulation and preservation of food. There is an important sense, of course, in which food as a primary value is acquired through economic activity, because it is necessary to satisfy hunger drives. Starvation and extinction are the reverse side of this process. To maintain life, however, a relatively small amount of work in the cultivation of food plants is required by those savages living under favourable climatic conditions. Yet one often finds that these savages accumulate food out of all proportion to minimum vital requirements and will expend a large amount of time and energy in the care of their gardens and the cultivation of their principal sources of plant food. The question then arises, on the one hand, as to the importance, in the eyes of the natives, of the values centred about food; and on the other hand, as to the assimilation of motives, impulses and feelings, to the primary activity which is directed towards the satisfaction of hunger.

[1] Cf. Firth: *Primitive Economics*, 387–390; Maning: *Old New Zealand*, 2, 94, 95; Colenso: *op. cit.*, 144.

With a native people like the Trobriand Islanders, undoubtedly the greatest factor which reinforces mere economic activity is that culture pattern which emphasizes the social recognition and importance that must accrue to him who can display abundant food. Food-stuffs, that is, are accumulated not only for use as nourishment, but also for purposes of display. Malinowski talks of a "deep, socially standardized sentiment" centering about the display of garden produce: a sentiment which is evident in the ceremonial handling and double display of food, first in the gardens and later in the storehouses, in extensive mortuary distributions, in food contests between two villages at harvest-time, and in the social psychology of eating, where the centre of gravity of a feast is not so much the eating as the ceremonial display and preparation of the food itself. Since pride in possessing abundant food is one of the leading characteristics of these natives, one of the greatest insults that can be offered is to call someone 'Man with no food.' Such an insult would be bitterly resented and probably a quarrel would ensue. To be able to boast of having food is one of their chief glories and ambitions, and their whole conduct, as regards eating in public, is directed towards ensuring that no suspicion of food scarcity can possibly be attached to the eater.[1]

As for the display of food in yam houses, these are so built that the quantity of food can be gauged and its quality ascertained through the wide interstices between the wooden beam walls. The yams are so arranged that the best specimens come to the outside and are well visible. Special varieties of yams, writes Malinowski, "are framed in wood and decorated with paint and hung on the outside of the yam houses. That the right to display food is highly valued

[1] Cf. Malinowski: "Primitive Economics," *Economic Journal* (1921), 8–9; *The Mailu*, 667–668; "Baloma," *Journal Anthropological Institute* (1916), 365, 372, 377.

can be seen from the fact that in villages where a chief of high rank resides, the commoners' storehouses have to be closed up with coconut leaves so as not to compete with his."[1] That this accumulation of food is prompted not only by economic foresight but also by the desire for display and consequent enhancement of social prestige through possession of wealth is further illustrated by the institution of harvest magic (*vilamalya*). This magic is performed at harvest-time in order that the inhabitants of a village may lose their appetites. In this way food may be accumulated in the yam houses until finally it rots, and then replaced by a new display.[2]

In effect, among these Melanesian natives, food is valued for its own sake as the preserver of life; but it is also regarded as an instrumental value in that its possession in sufficiently large quantities gives to a chief definite status, is a sign of high rank, and satisfies ambition. It has value as property because of its enhancement of power in the same manner as the possession of property has value with us. In other words, the sentiment which has grown up about the display of food is rooted in the conscious satisfaction that comes from the pleasure of eating. But this value, again, makes accumulated food a symbol and a vehicle of power. Hence the need for storing and displaying it, and hence the result that value is not so much the outcome of either utility or rarity or of any intellectual blending or compound of these two, but is the outcome of a sentiment grown up about objects. The sentiment has formed because these things of interest not only satisfy human needs but are also capable of evoking feelings and emotions.

That this sentimental attitude to food values is not found solely among one native people is shown by the work of A. R. Brown in his correlation of the ceremonial observances of the Andaman Islanders relative to the turtle and other

[1] Malinowski: *Argonauts*, 168–169.

[2] Malinowski: *op. cit.*, 169.

foods, with the social life of the native.[1] Firth, too, in his systematic examination of the material bearing upon the economics of the Maori stresses the same point. In his chapter on the "Psychology of Work" he shows that in regard to such widely separated activities as bird-snaring, fishing and carving, both social and aesthetic motives are interwoven with utilitarian in successful operations. My point as to the assimilation of motives and interests about a property value may be stressed by this quotation. Discussing the magical and religious beliefs and secular customs grouped round 'food values,' Firth writes: "Not only are they an expression of the social value of food, they also react directly upon its acquisition. They give an emotional tone to the otherwise drab round of economic life; on their social side they offer enticing prospects of parade and excitement, the lure of public appreciation; in their religious and formal aspect they steady and stiffen the activity and supply a backbone of regulation and order. In short, by the introduction of a totally new set of motives into economic pursuits, they facilitate work and thus promote the satisfaction of the vital needs."[2]

Just in the same fashion as sentiments expressing the functional relation of individual to object are grouped about food values, so, to take another instance, are sentiments centred about the native canoe and the native ornament. The native canoe is an instrumental value. It is built as a means and not as an end; but withal, through its use, it quickly takes upon itself, in the native mind, an atmosphere of romance built up of tradition and personal experience, it becomes an object of cult and admiration, a living thing, possessing its own individuality. Thus the Maori still remember the names of the various canoes that brought the great

[1] A. R. Brown: *Andaman Islanders*, 98 *et seq.*, 270–272, 279 *et seq.*
[2] Firth: *Primitive Economics*, 159.

fourteenth-century migrations to the shores of *Aotearoa* and have woven them into many a legend and tribal myth. Likewise with the ordinary everyday canoe, the native spins a tradition about it and adorns it with his best carvings.[1] The elements that go to make up a sentiment of attachment to a canoe are well illustrated by this vivid passage from Malinowski: The canoe is, to the native, "a powerful contrivance for the mastery of Nature, which allows him to cross perilous seas to distant places. It is associated with journeys by sail full of threatening dangers, of living hopes and desires to which he gives expression in song and story. In short, in the tradition of the natives, in their customs, in their behaviour and in their direct statements there can be found the deep love, the admiration, the specific attachment as to something alive and personal, so characteristic of the sailor's attitude towards his craft."[2] In other words, it is an over-simplified psychology which would express the value of a canoe to the native purely in terms of economic usefulness. For such a psychology neglects to take into account the most important factors in the relation of the native to his canoe. It neglects, that is to say, all those factors of personal feeling, experience, tradition, magic and ceremonial which, fused together and centred about the canoe, form the real emotional core of the property relation. The right of property, so to say, is the objective expression and recognition of this more fundamental sentiment of ownership.

I have treated the psychological factors involved in the relation of the native to his canoe in somewhat summary fashion since a more important, and in many ways more interesting, illustration of my thesis is to be found in a consideration of the psychology of personal ornament. Why, for instance, does the primitive Malay collect beads,

[1] Cf. James Cowan: *Maoris of New Zealand*, chs. v. and xiii.

[2] Malinowski: *Argonauts*, 106.

the North American Indian scalps, or the hunter trophies of the chase? Why, again, does the Bornean woman collect beads, the Trobriand Islander *Spondylus* necklaces and arm-shells, the Andaman Islander ornaments made of netting, or the Megalithic peoples articles made of gold, cowrie-shells and precious stones? The answers to these questions are no doubt various. By studying this question of property values in personal ornament, however, it is at least possible to show that it would be a *reductio ad absurdum* to believe that these questions might be answered by appeal to the drive of some alleged acquisitive or collecting instinct. And if it is possible that other elements than the acquisitive instinct are the basis of accumulation among primitive peoples, it is, to say the least, not unlikely that the reduction of all collecting activities among civilized peoples—from the accumulation of money to the collecting of stamps or old silver—to the drive of one impulse is equally absurd. In effect, as I will seek to show, the psychology of the collection of articles of personal ornament in primitive as in civilized societies must be considered in terms of a complex of sentiments of ownership interacting with varied behaviour patterns. It is a false simplicity which seeks to reduce the acquisition of property values to the operation of one particular instinct.

Coming now to a consideration of the kind and nature of native ornaments, it is of interest to hear Malinowski tell us that in his discussions with his native informants over questions of inheritance or of marriage gifts he repeatedly found the natives had a totally different scheme of values compared with his own. While the Western ethnologist was inclined to attach the greatest value to land, for example, and to enquire what were the rules of inheritance concerning the distribution of land, he found the native interested in land only to a remote degree. To the Mailu natives, that is, garden land had little value since there was no limit to the land that might be acquired by each individual from the common forest land, and, further, since no rights in land were ever acquired or exchanged. What the native was primarily interested in was, first, the ownership of native ornaments, and to a lesser degree, the ownership of the more immaterial privileges and rights—the right, for instance, to sing certain songs, perform certain dances, or to give the order for the burning of grass over certain areas. Over native ornament there was most concern and discussion when dividing a dead man's property among his heirs. Among the Mailu, arm-shells, shell discs, boars' tusks, dogs' teeth, bird of paradise feathers—these are the most desirable property, while property in pigs, dogs, coconut palms and similar food values follow closely in relative interest.[1] The Mailu as a native people are not alone in this emphasis upon value in ornament. The Trobriand Islander, as I shall show later, is immensely interested in the valuables of the *Kula* exchange; the Dyaks and other Bornean tribes find the most important class of property objects in heads and beads; the Maori, again, places high value upon objects made of greenstone. Among all primitive peoples there is not, of course, the same relative 'disvalue' placed upon land as is found among the Mailu. I have already indicated the important position that land may occupy among the property values of savages. But the stress that nearly all natives place upon personal ornaments shows that their ownership must occupy a place of importance in the relative cultural and economic values of primitive society. In treating this aspect of the subject I will divide ornaments into three classes: hunting trophies and badges, articles of personal ornament, and articles of protective value or amulets. I will endeavour to show what factors are at work in the acquisition and ownership of articles of each class. This will conduce to clearness of treatment. But it must be

[1] Cf. Malinowski: *The Mailu*, 636–637, 643–645, etc.

remembered that the native probably never makes a clear-cut distinction between objects of these three classes; and in many cases some articles are objects of personal adornment as well as serving as amulets, while others stress ability as a hunter as well as adorning the person and indicating social status. I hope, therefore, in concluding this section to draw the threads together and give, so to say, a total view of the relation of the native to property values in ornament.

First, then, as to hunting trophies and badges. The possession of such trophies in primitive life is a powerful factor in contributing to the attainment of personal distinction. Of the honour which a man gains for himself through his exploits in the chase or in war, the trophies of which he has become possessed serve as tokens. Memorials of bravery and personal prowess tend outwardly to manifest the superiority of one tribesman over his fellow-tribesmen who cannot make a display of similar decorations. Hirn expresses this point succinctly when he writes that the chief aim of decoration "is, of course, not to make the man more beautiful and charming, but only to show off his skill and courage, and thus to inspire respect and fear. It is needless to point out that in times of war such decorations must be of eminent advantage by inspiring their wearer with pride, at the same time that they strike his enemies with terror."[1] If we understand the term 'decoration' to cover hunting trophies and war trophies, scalps, and some forms of decoration by painting or tattooing, then the statement expresses an undoubted truth, though it by no means applies to all types of personal decoration and ornament.

Likewise from the same motives, badges or similar traditional tokens often take the place of trophies as indicators of personal valour. Among some tribes gold earrings or

[1] Hirn: *The Origins of Art*, 222.

bracelets are worn to denote the taking of heads; other tribes specialize in badges made of cowrie-shell, feathers, incision marks or tattooing to serve as marks of heroism. In nearly all cases such badges constitute a direct reward for the performance of brave and honourable deeds. The possession of them leads to influence in the tribe. The man who wears numerous badges is "one whose voice is loud in council." It is because the culture patterns of the tribe allow social prestige and influence to him who wins many trophies, that these trophies and badges become objects of desire.[1]

In particular, trophies denoting the vanquishing of human enemies are of great value in establishing the social recognition of courage and resource, without which virtues the tribe could not hope to survive or maintain itself in the struggle for existence. This is one reason why head-hunting seems to be popular among certain native peoples. The Dyaks, for example, are said to practise head-hunting in order to show their bravery and manliness. The Ibans, again, "seek above all things to take heads, to which they attach an extravagant value, unlike the Kayans and Kenyahs, who seek heads primarily for the service of their funeral rites; and they not infrequently attack a house and kill a large number of its inmates in a perfectly wanton manner and for no motive other than the desire to obtain heads." So strong is this 'morbid desire' that Iban war parties will often "rob the tombs of the villages of other tribes, and after smoking the stolen heads of the corpses will bring them home in triumph with glowing accounts of the stout resistance offered by the victims."[2] It is extremely likely, however, that motives for head-hunting are exceedingly

[1] Cf. Spencer: *Principles of Sociology*, ii, ch. ii, ix, x; Sumner and Keller: *op. cit.*, iv, 1188–1191; Landtman: *Primary Causes of Social Inequality*, 39–40, 48, 59.

[2] Hose and McDougall: *op. cit.*, i, 185.

complex. Besides emphasis upon social recognition of bravery and courage, it is not impossible in the first place that the practice of taking heads of former enemies arose by the extension of the custom of taking the hair for the ornamentation of the shield or sword-hilt. Among the tribes of Borneo, hair was commonly applied to shields in order to complete the representation of a terrible human face believed to be a valuable aid in confusing and terrifying the foe. In other cases the habit arose from the custom of slaying slaves to accompany a dead chief on his journey to the other world. Considerations of economy might lead the mourners to prefer slaying hostiles to slaying their own highly valued and affectionately regarded slaves. In such a case it would be less troublesome to slay the enemy on the field of battle and return with the head alone than to bring him home alive and then slay him.[1]

These possible explanations are not mutually exclusive. They may have co-operated in bringing about the custom of collecting human heads. It is significant, however, that Iban women urge on the men to the taking of heads, so that a girl will taunt her suitor with not being brave enough to take a head should he be one who prefers discretion to valour. Other lines of explanation still open out when we recall that whereas among the Nagas of the Indian Hills the skull is kept as a memorial of vengeance, in parts of Melanesia the idea of human sacrifice is prominent and we are nearer to cannibalism.[2] Whatever explanation or aspect

[1] Hose and McDougall: *op. cit.*, i, 187–190, ii, 20–24, 38; Crawley: *The Tree of Life*, 106. If we may believe Bancroft, however, among the Ahts, the warrior who has taken the most heads is most praised and feared; while among the Nittenahts, heads of enemies slain in battle are regarded as *spoila optima*. *Native Races*, i, 189, note 65.

[2] Cf. Hobhouse: *Morals in Evolution*, 242. But we have the authority of Rivers for the suggestion that in the Solomon Islands heads are sought after in order "to propitiate the ancestral ghosts on such occasions as building a new house for a chief or making a new canoe, while they were also offered in sacrifice at the funeral of a chief." Apparently, too, the institution of head-hunting has had wide ramifications amongst the social

is more prominent among various peoples, my point is clear: that the motives involved in the collection of human heads, on the one hand, and of general war and hunting trophies, on the other, are exceedingly complex in character. Social recognition is intertwined with ideas of vengeance, ideas of magic with ideas of the other world, and it is out of this matrix of confused motives that a culture pattern emphasizing the value of property objects in heads or trophies is formed and operates in a particular group.

Continuing this analysis of native ornament, I will deal now with the factors at work in the acquisition and ownership of objects of personal adornment. Examples of such objects from a people like the Southern Massim are armshells made from *conus millepunctatus*, necklaces, nose ornaments, lime spatulae, spiral pigs' tusks (*dona*) and ceremonial axe-blades.[1] Ornaments of Lower Hunters like the Andaman Islanders are more simple, comprising, for instance, belts of rope and necklets of string, ceremonial belts, bracelets, necklaces and garters of netting with strings of human or animal bones to serve magical or protective purposes.[2] As I have stated above, it is often difficult to distinguish objects of this class from objects which may be more correctly described as amulets or charms. The Vedda youth wears a number of bone beads made from the ground-down teeth of a dead bear partly out of personal vanity, but also, no doubt, because the bones are regarded as possessing magical power and are a protection against an attack by wild bears. His father, again, the shaman of the tribe, wears on his wrist a silver cylinder not only as an object of vain show, but also because he believes this same cylinder once cured

life of the Islands and was a stimulus to canoe-building, horticulture, pig-breeding, religious rites, feasts and social ceremony. Rivers: "The Psychological Factor," in *Essays on the Depopulation of Melanesia* (ed. Rivers), 101–102. Cf. also Rivers: *History of Melanesian Society*, ii, 259–260.

[1] Seligmann: *Melanesians*, 512–513.

[2] A. R. Brown: *Andamans*, 125–127.

him of an illness.[1] Objects such as these cannot be classified into any hard and fast division. For practical purposes, however, it is of some importance to attempt some such division on the lines I have indicated above, since it is only by this method that one may hope to disentangle the complexity of motive underlying primitive ownership of these objects.

The value to the native of objects of personal adornment is determined by two sets of factors, one set governed by conditions of utility which interacts with the other set determined more exactly by psychological conditions. I am not concerned here to deal in any detail with conditions of utility value. In sum, it is reasonable to believe that the value to a Massim native of a *conus* arm-shell is in part determined by such factors as the refractory nature, the durability, and the rarity of certain raw materials. Thus, the most valued Massim articles are made of stone or shell, the hardest materials of which the natives have knowledge. The rarity of certain raw materials, e.g. spiral pig-tusks, as well as the skill to work them, is of importance in determining value. Finally, the refractory nature of the material, e.g. shell or bone, from which ornaments are made, must be considered since the more refractory the material relative to primitive tools, the more prolonged is the labour required to produce the finished article.[2]

Here, however, factors of utility shade over into factors of psychology. It is important to take into account, that is, in any assessment of value, the manner in which, as an outcome of energy expended, sentiments of attachment to the created object are likely to be built up in the mind of the native. Having a keen appreciation of good material and of craft-perfection, a native worker will lavish talent, fancy, skill and patience upon the creation of objects of

[1] Seligmann: *The Veddas*, 193, 205–207.
[2] Cf. Seligmann: *Melanesians*, 514–521.

worth. This loving attitude towards material and work must produce sentiments of attachment to rare materials and well-worked objects. Thus of *vaygu'a* objects, specially valued in Trobriand economy, Malinowski writes: "It is not rarity within utility which creates value, but a rarity sought out by human skill within the workable materials. In other words, not those things are valued which, being useful or even indispensable, are hard to get since all the necessities of life are within easy reach of the Trobriand Islander. But such an article is valued where the workman, having found specially fine or sportive material, has been induced to spend a disproportionate amount of labour on it. By doing so he creates an object which is a kind of economic monstrosity, too good, too big, too frail, or too overcharged with ornament to be used, yet because of that, highly valued."[1] It is this 'loving attitude,' this 'sentiment of attachment,' the outcome of the exercise of skill and patience, of the focussing of self-feeling upon the accomplishment of a difficult task—it is this that is one of the chief components in that sentiment of ownership directed towards the possession of objects of worth.

But factors of utility, rarity, durability and incorporation of skill are by no means the sole and only determinants of value and desire for possession. Other, and perhaps more potent, factors are the outcome of motives grouped round the drive of vanity, the desire for social recognition, and the fact that value is often the outcome of what, for want of a better term, I may call 'historic sentimentalism.' First as to the drive of vanity. There can be no doubt that the desire to possess ornament in many cases derives from the opportunity it offers for the gratification of personal vanity and for the consequent heightening of self-feeling. The dancer painted and hung over with ornaments becomes pleasantly conscious of himself, of his own skill and agility,

[1] Malinowski: *Argonauts*, 173.

and of his striking, or at least satisfactory, appearance. He becomes conscious of his relation to others, of their actual or possible admiration, and of the social approval and good will that go with admiration. In brief, the ornamented individual is pleasantly conscious of his own personal value, and his vanity is satisfied by the wearing of those ornaments which serve to mark him off from his fellows as one sufficiently fortunate and superior not to be of the common herd. The function of personal adornment is, therefore, to heighten self-feeling and thus to mark or express the personal value of the decorated individual. In so far, however, as the occasions on which much personal ornament may be worn are strictly defined by custom, i.e. on such occasions as tribal dancing, the completion of marriage, initiation and funeral ceremonies, the decoration and adorning of the body may become at once the expression of increased social value as well as of increased personal value.[1]

From this same point of view it seems to be extremely likely that the 'clothes' of primitive man were assumed not so much because of the need for protection but because of this same motive of vanity and self-adornment.[2] Hence it follows that, among lower cultures, ornament is of far more importance and value than clothing. It is because of the vanity of the savage that he places such exceptional value on bodily ornament, that he will often undergo the greatest discomfort and pain to attain it. From every source within reach he desires to possess and wear what to us seems at times to savour not a little of the barbaric and bizarre.[3]

Westermarck is inclined to believe that most ornamentation other than that worn as trophies of war, signs of social

[1] Cf. A. R. Brown: *op. cit.*, 254–256.

[2] It is interesting in this connection to recall the behaviour of Koehler's apes in adorning their bodies with brightly coloured rags and streamers. Cf. above, part i, 130.

[3] Cf. Grosse: *Beginnings of Art*, 84; Sumner and Keller: *op. cit.*, iv, 1185–1187.

status, or as protective charms and talismans is definitely worn to increase sexual attraction. He quotes with approval Burton's *Anatomy of Melancholy* to the effect that "stronger provocations proceed from outward ornaments, than such as nature hath provided," and goes on himself to state later: "We can easily imagine that among a tribe of naked savages when someone, whether man or woman, put on a bright coloured fringe, a few gaudy feathers, a string of beads, a bundle of leaves, a dazzling shell, or a piece of cloth, this could not fail to attract attention and served as an invitation."[1] There can be no doubt that much ornament worn by both primitives and civilized serves to accentuate sexual attractiveness. But on the other hand it is important not to overstress this form of explanation to the exclusion of those other motives I mention in this discussion. Primarily, I think, ornament is desired because it gratifies personal vanity and self-feeling, though later it may become a secondary or instrumental value as a means to sexual conquest. It must be remembered, finally, that the explanation of personal ornament as a function of sexual feeling has an extremely narrow validity since it fails to account for those occasions on which the wearing of ornament is obligatory and its nature and kind determined by culture pattern.[2]

It fails, too, to account, save in a far-fetched and indirect manner, for value ascribed to ornaments which in native life play the part that is played in civilized economy by crown jewels, heirlooms, or trophies and sporting-cups. I am thinking now of the *Kula* valuables as described by Malinowski or the valuable old beads and gongs that are so sought after by the pagan tribes of Borneo. A word or

[1] Westermarck: *Human Marriage*, i, 554–555; cf. also i, 500 *et seq.*

[2] Brown makes this point also in his discussion of marriage and initiation ceremonies. He concludes: "There is therefore I believe no special connection between the dancing and personal ornament of the Andamanese and sexual feeling." *The Andamans*, 256.

two, therefore, on each of these two types of native valuable. The *Kula* objects or *vaygu'a* consist principally of such objects as ceremonial axe-heads, necklaces, or red *Spondylus* shell discs and arm-shells of the *conus* shell.[1] The material of which these objects are made is rare, difficult to obtain, and much time and labour must be expended in working it. Once made, however, the objects are very durable, almost indestructible. Their main economic function is to be owned as signs of wealth and of power and from time to time to change hands as ceremonial gifts. As such, they are the foundation of certain kinds of native trade and constitute an indispensable element in the native social organization. The value of these *Kula* objects, however, does not depend solely on their rarity or durability. The social forces of tradition and custom, rather, give the imprint of value to these objects and surround them with a halo of romance. Just as the white man strives to possess gold nuggets and pearls—to the native, objects filthy, insignificant and treated with contempt—so the native will strive to acquire *Kula* objects and the consequent conventionalized power and renown attaching to their possession. In other words, these objects are cherished by the native because of the 'historic sentimentalism' which surrounds them. Though an object may be to all intents and purposes ugly and useless, yet if it has figured in historical scenes and passed through the hands of famous chiefs it becomes in the native mind an object with an individual name, an unfailing vehicle of sentimental association, an insignia of rank, wealth and prestige. At bottom the same psychological and sociological forces are at work in giving value to the heirloom of the sophisticated white man as to the *vaygu'a* of the New

[1] I am taking for granted a general knowledge of the objects, methods, motives and ceremonial of the *Kula* exchange. Further description of this important native institution would hardly be in place here, and could not do justice to the skill, vividness and detail of Malinowski's now classic treatment of the subject See his *Argonauts of the Western Pacific, passim.*

Guinea primitives—and it is the same mental attitude which makes both heirloom and *vaygu'a* worthy of possession.[1]

The *Kula*, however, implies a new type of culture pattern in regard to possession. The ownership of these valuables is not permanent but temporary, intermittent and cumulative. Because of the half-commercial, half-ceremonial, nature of the *Kula* exchange, each man has an enormous number of articles passing through his hands during his lifetime, and these he only temporarily owns, with the obligation very soon to hand them on again to his partners in the exchange. Though incomplete in point of permanency, the ownership is, in turn, enhanced by the cumulative ownership of successive possessions. In any case, temporary ownership of this nature allows the native to derive a great deal of renown, to exhibit his valuable, to tell how he obtained it, to plan to whom he is going to give it. "And all this forms one of the favourite subjects of tribal conversation and gossip, in which the feats and glory in Kula of chief or commoners are constantly discussed and re-discussed."[2] Furthermore, there is another element of pride in ownership, since success in Kula, i.e. good fortune in securing a highly valued article, is ascribed to special personal power obtained through the use of magic. This is the increased personal value. Increased social value comes about when the native community glories in an especially fine *Kula* trophy obtained by one of its members. In this respect the *Kula* valuables may be compared with the sporting-cups and trophies of our own culture which are kept by the winning group or individual for a limited period, bring pleasure through the fact of temporary ownership and

[1] Malinowski: *Argonauts*, 214, 351–352, 510, etc. *Economic Journal* (1921), 9–13; *Baloma*, 376–377. Cf. also Seligmann: *Melanesians*, ch. xl. Turner writes of Samoan mats: "They are preserved with great care; some of them pass through several generations, and as their age and historic interest increase, they are all the more valued." *Samoa*, 120.

[2] Malinowski: *Argonauts*, 94; cf. also article in *Man* (1920), 51, 100.

reflect glory on the community whose representatives have been thus successful in open competition.

Less need be said about the social value of the beads of the Bornean tribes. It appears from Hose and McDougall's account that old beads, formerly one of the principal forms of currency, are much valued and sought after. Certain rare kinds are especially valued, of which those known as *lukut sekula* are the most precious of all. The ownership of each such bead is accurately known throughout a large district as the ownership of the masterpiece of ancient art in our country, and any change of possession is keenly discussed among the inhabitants of the 'long houses' throughout the country. The wife of a rich chief will wear as many valuable beads as she possesses on any occasion of display; they are made into tassels, girdles, necklaces, earrings, applied to head-bands, sword-sheaths, cigarette-bones, and worn on the waist. In all cases their ownership and display are a source of renown and prestige to the native, arising from their rarity, their value as ornament, and the history, romance and tradition which have grown up around the oldest and best.[1]

I have throughout this discussion recognized that many objects of personal ornament may be, at the same time, of value as amulets and preservers of life. A brief consideration of this magical side of what are mainly objects of ornament will serve as a bridge to our discussion of the factors which make up the value of the amulet proper. Take, for instance, such a simple object as the native comb. This has a purely utilitarian value as a means to keep the hair in order; when decorated, it may serve purposes of personal adornment; finally, it may be a vehicle of protective power against sickness and demons. Thus the marks on a Semang woman's comb are both ornaments and magical signs indicating the diseases she wishes to be spared. In Malacca, again, combs

[1] Hose and McDougall: *op. cit.*, i, 227–228.

are carefully preserved from one generation to another, since the decorations carved on them make them, as it were, sacred.[1] To return again to *Kula* articles: it appears that *vaygu'a* valuables may at times be treated in a ritual manner, with veneration, respect and affection. They are placed before a malignant spirit, when, assuming the shape of snake or land crab, it is discovered near the village. During the *milamala* festivals, when the *baloma* spirits visit the land of the living, *vaygu'a* are exhibited sacrificially on platforms, "to make their minds good." In these two examples there is clear expression that valuables are not only regarded as potential wealth, ornaments or instruments of power or status, but as supremely good in themselves. For the natives "to possess *vaygu'a* is exhilarating, comforting, soothing in itself. They will look at *vaygu'a* and handle it for hours; even a touch of it, under circumstances, imparts its virtue."[2]

Furthermore, the soothing value of these valuables is shown by the native custom of surrounding and covering a dying man with them. Here the underlying emotional attitude, rationalized as gifts to *Topileta*, keeper of the nether world, is to be found in the native notion of the pleasant, comforting, fortifying action of them. They inspire with life; at the same time they prepare for death. They hold fast the dying man to this world; they equip him for the next. Above all, they are the supreme comfort. To surround a man with them even in his most evil moment is to make that moment less evil. *Vaygu'a* are desired as ornaments and objects of wealth; they are also desired because they are 'objects of cult,' handled in reverence and awe.[3]

1 "It was said that each disease had its appropriate pattern (of comb) and hence in some cases several combs were worn simultaneously, apparently to protect the wearer against several diseases at once." (This refers to the combs of the Kedah Semang women.) Skeat and Blagden: *Pagan Tribes of the Malay Peninsula*, i, 149; cf. also vol. i, 419–448, 606–624.

2 Malinowski: *Argonauts*, 512.

3 Malinowski: *Argonauts*, 513; cf. also Malinowski: "Spirit Hunting in the South Seas," *Realist* (1929), vol. ii, 406.

An interesting parallel to the Melanesian native's attitude towards these valuables is also afforded by the attitude of the Australia aborigine towards the bull-roarer. Besides being of value as the vehicle of magic power, the bull-roarer possesses mystical efficiency as a soother and comforter in time of trouble. Mere contact with it, as, for instance, rubbing it against the stomach, will make a man 'good.' 'This act softens the stomach' is the native expression for the resulting emotional state.[1] In this, again, the efficacy of the bull-roarer resembles the magical virtues which people of megalithic cultures and of the cultures of dynastic Egypt are said by Perry and Elliot Smith to have ascribed to ornaments made of gold, pearls, cowrie-shells and amber. All these substances, of value first as ornament, came later to be valued more as means of prolonging life, of gaining good health and good fortune in this world, and of securing immortality in the next. Not that this second function of these ancient valuables ever entirely displaced the first; but at certain periods in culture-development, gold and cowrie were more important as promoting life than in increasing self-feeling.[2]

This reference to megalithic 'life-givers' brings us directly to a brief consideration of our third division of personal ornaments, that is, the charm or amulet. With the same motive as before, I now wish to examine the nature of the psychological elements which make such amulets of value to the native mind and which, by entering into a sentiment of possession focussed upon such objects, help to strengthen that principle of attribution which I have urged lies at the basis of the property relation.

There are probably four types of qualities that lead to

[1] Cf. Marett: *Threshold of Religion*, 165; Spencer and Gillen: *Native Tribes of Central Australia*, 170–179.

[2] Reference may be made in this connection to W. J. Perry: *Origin of Civilization*, chs. vii, xxiv; Perry: "The Search for Amber in Antiquity," *Journal Manchester Egyptian and Oriental Society* (1918–1919), 71–80; G. Elliot Smith: *The Evolution of the Dragon*; and his more recent *Human History*, *passim*.

a natural object being recognized as a suitable amulet and therefore as capable of exercising a beneficial effect upon a particular class of objects, persons or powers. These qualities are, first, similarity in shape or contour to the object to be influenced. Under this head would come yam or banana charm-stones, and also charms made of animal bones. Second, the quality of rarity, e.g. irregular fragments of stone, coral, quartz, bone or wood. Third, unusual shape in not very uncommon objects, e.g. stones with natural holes in them. Fourth, a varied class of objects selected on more devious principles still: amulets selected through guidance of dreams, trance states or extraordinary experience; or again, amulets selected from materials used in hunting, fishing or food-gathering because of animistic power assumed to reside in such material. In general, however, it is usually the unusual object which so attracts the savage that he attaches it to his person. Since any such object may be the abode of a spirit whose influence in winning luck or avoiding harm is appropriated through this attachment, the object is preserved as a primitive form of insurance against the large element of chance in life. It becomes an amulet, which, when worn, marks one out among his fellows and thus heightens self-consciousness. The power residing in it commands respect, excites emulation. At the same time, the knowledge that mysterious power is on one's side in all conflicts with one's fellows and with the hard reality of nature promotes self-confidence, self-respect and courage.

The amulet-ornament in its quality of amulet is regarded among all native peoples as inalienably one with the personality of its owner. Some writers, for instance, Lippert, are inclined to regard 'ghost fear' and consequent belief in the efficacy of amulets as the oldest and most primitive source of property. The things needed by the dead man were left to him without dispute as sacred and holy. Since nobody dared to use them they were his more exclusively than in life. Thus land was set aside for the individual; his grave became his own personal property in a very real sense. Without, however, examining this thesis in its extreme form, it is not unreasonable to imagine that this 'ghost fear,' this fear of the unknown and the desire to possess exclusively for the self those objects believed to have special power over the unknown, is one of the strongest elements in the sentiment of possession growing up about the ownership of personal objects. In other words, it is because the amulet represents some sort of favourable relation with spirits or with the extra-ordinary world that it acquires value in its would-be owner's eyes. In many cases, it is selected or made at birth by the shaman or sorcerer and becomes a lifelong talisman. Or again, objects originally appropriated from motives of utility come to take on the fetichistic quality which attaches them indissolubly to the person. In all cases, the amulet is that type of primitive property which is most reluctantly parted with.[1] The owner's being is all concentrated in the possession of it and his existence may, in his own conviction, be staked in the defence of it. Hence the most intense passion is often evoked

[1] Two examples, typical of many, will make this clear. Of a Vedda charm designed to protect against the attack of bears, Seligmann writes: "A youth, Kaira of Bingoda, wore a number of bone beads on his waist string. He refused to sell these or exchange them for other beads or cloth, and though obviously not desirous of discussing them, stated that he had made them by grinding down the bones of a bear which he had found in the jungle." *The Veddas*, 193. Again, Skeat and Blagden summarize De la Croix as follows: "A young girl who had disposed of her seed necklace to him came back in a hurry to ask for it to be returned. He thought she was not satisfied with her bargain and was about to give her some knick-knack or other in addition when she informed him that all she wanted back was the set of small spirals of copper wire attached to the necklace. In spite of the most extravagant offers of tobacco, which certainly ought to have persuaded her, she would not allow him to retain the spirals, and evidently attributed a far greater value to them than could be accounted for by the mere worth of the copper. De la Croix subsequently asked the Chief of the tribe (Bah Itam) about it and the latter told him, with evident conviction, that the girl would certainly fall ill if she ceased to wear these metal rings." *Pagan Races*, i, 141.

by any encroachment or desire 'unlawfully' to expropriate. Sumner and Keller sum up this aspect of the case in these words: "The amulet has a high utility to its wearer in the midst of the chances of life; the ornament or trophy is interwoven with the pride and prestige of its owner. Hence this article of property is exclusive and individual; it pertains to its possessor only and distinguishes him as fortunate, powerful, secure, noble, heroic."[1]

In the eyes of the native, then, the most important element in the sentiments built up about the possession of amulets and charms is probably the desire for security and protection. Any unusual object or object marked out by dreams or trances which becomes associated by means irrational, 'pre-logical,' or the like with the sense of protection serves to satisfy this desire and therefore takes on all the physical and emotional qualities of the amulet. The same desire to obtain good fortune is not, of course, confined to savages. It is evident in the pathetic way the modern world clings to mascots, emblems, charms and lucky stones. It is because this desire for security among the changes and chances of the world is almost universal that this element of the demand for protection is primary and fundamental in the ownership of these amulets. From this point of view the interpretation of amulets by members of the functional school of anthropology seems both highly intellectualized and not a little unreal. A. R. Brown, for instance, interprets the customs connected with this belief in the protective power of amulets as a means whereby a 'sentiment of dependence' is maintained. It is important, he argues, that in primitive society cohesion and conformity to custom and tradition should be enforced. Where, as in the Andamans, "society is not sufficiently concrete and particular to act as the object of such a sentiment (of dependence)" the individual is made to feel his dependence

[1] Sumner and Keller: *op. cit.*, i, 267.

upon society through dependence towards "every important possession of the society, towards every object which for the society has constant and important uses."[1]

Thus, Brown urges, sentiments of dependence grow up about amulets made of the materials used in food-getting, wood used in arrow-making, fibres used in hunting turtle and pig-fish, or fibres used in the making of ropes, threads, bow-strings and the like. Or amulets are made of animal bones which are said to have protective powers in that "they are visible proof of the ability of society to protect itself and its members from the dangers that are believed to threaten the human being in the most important activity of his life, the obtaining and eating of food."[2] Finally, amulets are made from human bones for the same reason. They are at once visible signs of past dangers overcome through the protective power of society and the manner in which surviving relations express their sense of value in those who have passed away.[3]

As I have already suggested, this functional interpretation of the ornament-amulet seems more arbitrary than conclusive. To me it suggests the reading of complex theory into what, after all, are essentially simple facts. It does not seem entirely reasonable to imagine that whenever the Andaman Islander makes an amulet necklace of the bones of his grandfather, he is explicitly thinking of 'past dangers overcome through the protective action of the society' and of the ability of society to guarantee similar protection in the future. Nor is it likely that this thought is implicit in his mind and has been rendered explicit by the intuition of the gifted anthropologist. Rather is it that the grandson thus shows his respect for the grandfather and so keeps alive his memory; just in the same fashion as a civilized person likes to have in his possession relics of a dead parent

[1] Brown: *op. cit.*, 257–258. [2] *Ibid.*, 274.
[3] *Ibid.*, 292–293; cf. also 322–323.

or friend and, if he is superstitious, will attribute to those relics magic or protective powers.

I am concerned to maintain, that is, in opposition to the functionalist explanation of Radcliffe Brown, that the amulet serves to crystallize a special relation between the individual and that 'other world' system of powers and magic forces on the benevolent attitude of which the safety, success and good fortune of the individual is believed to depend. Born of the 'dusty answer' that the soul gets "when hot for certainty in this our life," the individual attaches to himself some object which has irrational associations with good fortune and safe success. Thereafter, on the one hand, this object is magically associated with the personality of the owner. It becomes one of the objects upon which the sentiment of self is focussed. On the other, the good luck that it is supposed to afford is the means whereby the emotional bonds between it and the individual are at once broadened, deepened and made more intense. Every increment of success strengthens this emotional bond; no ill-fortune weakens it since ill-fortune is explained by the fact that the protecting spirit has been angered through the breaking of taboos or the omission of necessary action.[1] In every instance the protecting spirit is really protecting even when this protection is not explicitly evident.

Throughout this section I have been dealing with the nature of property values in personal ornament, and I have endeavoured to indicate the manner in which it is possible to envisage the formation of sentiments of possession centred about such values. It is a commonplace of psychological theory, first, that the development of the sense of self is closely connected with the deepening perception of

[1] "Though a fetich might fail its wearer in time of need, it was never admitted to be useless, but the failure was explained by saying that some greater power, perhaps the fetich of a greater god, had been at work on the occasion." J. Roscoe: *The Bakitara*, 46.

the nature, limitations and individuality of one's own body; and that, second, the development of the moral and social sentiments in man is dependent upon this prior, or perhaps concurrent, development of self-consciousness and self-feeling. From this standpoint, personal ornament and its regulation by the social patterns of a particular group are the means whereby society acts upon, and thus modifies, regulates, develops the sense of self in the individual. In all three types of ornament distinguished above this heightening of self-feeling takes place. Hunting-trophies and badges, however, emphasize more particularly the aspect of social status and the social recognition that society accords to courage, bravery and resource. Articles of personal adornment have utility value as evidences of wealth and as instruments for the award of that social recognition accorded in most societies to 'men of substance.' They have further value in more particularly developing self-consciousness and satisfying personal vanity. Finally, other ornaments are more important as amulets and charms. These are worn for their protective powers either against particular dangers, i.e. childbirth, or as more generalized givers of good fortune and success in all the manifold vicissitudes of life.

It is clear, therefore, that it would be far from correct to attribute the native desire for property in personal ornament as due to the drive of an alleged instinct of property. There is rather the drive of social impulses in this desire: the need for social recognition, to give and receive response; or there is the overwhelming need for personal security and the belief that this may be obtained through the attachment to the self of spirit-powers resident in amulets. In consequence, various and varying sentiments of ownership, with one or other of these social feelings as their nucleus, are formed to give a deeper value to the original attachment to the self of these objects which the culture patterns of a group class as articles of ornament. The individual is born into a social group where certain classes and types of objects have traditional value as ornament. The desires and feelings which find satisfaction in the possession of such objects are the same in the latest member of the community as in the earliest ancestor. Thus when an object possessed is looked upon as an extension of the personality, animistic ideas and feelings strengthen the operation of social impulses. Identification of an object with the self is deepened and strengthened by the formation and interconnection of sentiments with the co-ordinating sentiment of the self. From the point of view of social philosophy, rights in property may be looked upon as social 'canalization,' as the assimilation of these sentiments and ways of behaviour into culture patterns which at once subserve the development of the human personality and adapt the social structure to the demands of the material environment.

CHAPTER VII

THE SOCIAL PATTERNING OF PROPERTY VALUES

IN the two preceding chapters of this second part of my monograph I have dealt at some length with the sentiments, feelings, impulses and motives which examination has shown to underlie acquisitive activity among primitive peoples. I have examined, that is, the psychological factors involved in the ascription of value to property objects, and the sentiments of ownership that grow up between the individual and the property objects in which he is interested. In other words, I have been considering man's relation to property objects from a functional point of view.

Undoubtedly this functional aspect is of primary importance when we consider any facet of human behaviour. Yet just as undoubtedly, it is not of sole importance since complete behaviour must be defined in terms both of function and of form. Functions of behaviour, i.e. emotions, sentiment, impulse, may often be entirely transformed or at least take on new increments of significance through that formal patterning which society imposes upon each of its members. Thus a consideration of some of the more characteristic forms by, and through, which the acquisitive activities of man, and especially of the savage, are patterned into a standardized system seems to be necessary if we are to give a final completeness to our work. It is the aim of this chapter, therefore, to show to what degree acquisition in the interests of the individual, no matter how it is determined functionally, is modified and moulded in response to social needs by the forms or culture patterns of group life. In other words, it is proposed to give a very brief survey of the social patterning of property values among primitive peoples.

Perhaps first, however, a further word may be required in definition of these culture patterns. As I have already suggested, it is just because original functions of behaviour are so readily modified or assimilated by new forms, that social behaviour must be studied from a functional as well as from a formal point of view. Looked at in this light, culture patterns may be defined in Goldenweiser's words as "attitudes, concepts and procedures grounded in the psyche of man, but given definite form by social determinants and specific for different times and places."[1] The use of this concept stresses the fact that in most behaviour the individual is reacting to the control of deep-seated cultural patterns not so much consciously recognized as felt, not so much capable of self-conscious description as of naïve practice. The unconscious nature of this patterning is not, of course, any mysterious activity of a racial, social or group mind. If I may repeat an earlier description, it is merely a typical unawareness on the part of the individual of outlines, forms, demarcations and significances of conduct which he all the time implicitly follows. Examples of such patterning abound in every field of social activity—in the fields of language, of religion, of morals, of personal relationships (the Western pattern of romantic love, for instance) and of economics. More specifically in relation to our own thesis, patterning of activity in pursuit of property values occupies considerable importance among the various forms of economic organization. There is evident among societies, both primitive and civilized, an unconscious patterning of economic motive in terms of a characteristic economic endeavour.

The preceding chapters have endeavoured to emphasize the complexity of motive underlying the acquirement of property objects. Here I wish to stress the point that the tempo in accumulation of property and in the deference

[1] Goldenweiser, essay on "Psychology and Anthropology," in *The Social Sciences and Their Interrelations*, 71.

of immediate enjoyment of wealth is set not so much by the individual but by the society to which he belongs. It is the culture patterns which regulate these activities and inhibitions, not private caprice. This is immediately evident when we recall that many primitive societies are quite innocent of an understanding of the accumulation of wealth in our Western sense of the phrase. Even where there is a definite feeling that wealth should be accumulated, the motives which are responsible for the practice and which give definite forms to the methods of acquiring wealth are often signally different from those of our own immediate experience. An example to which we shall recur later is, of course, the patterning of economic behaviour among such a primitive people as the West Coast Indians of the American Pacific States. The dream of the modern individualist—that of amassing wealth as an individual pure and simple with the expectation of disposing of it in the fullness of time—this dream would be entirely meaningless to the majority of savages.[1]

A preliminary consideration of the patterning of economic behaviour immediately reopens the controversial problem of the relations in primitive society of common to private property, or in other words, the degree to which such society is communistic or individualistic in its organization. As I shall seek to show in this chapter, generalizations in regard to such a problem are not at all easy to formulate—this notwithstanding the practices of some earlier investigators. Yet first carefully defining what is to be understood by the ownership of property in common and by individuals, I hope to reach fairly definite conclusions as to the degree in which common and private property respectively is standardized by the culture patterns of savage societies at each culture

[1] Cf. Sapir: Essay on "The Unconscious Patterning of Behaviour" in *The Unconscious: A Symposium,* 1927; Goldenweiser: *Early Civilization,* 17–18.

level. I may add here in anticipation of later pages that it is not difficult to refute those economic individualists concerned to defend our present acquisitive society. They, primed with the least possible amount of psychology, or more often with none at all, are given to the assertion that a social life based upon common ownership of property is contrary to human nature, therefore 'unnatural' and foredoomed to shipwreck upon the rocks of the acquisitive instinct. Even had we not the evidence before us of some of the not unsuccessful communitarian religious and socialistic societies which flourished during the last century throughout the Americas,[1] at least we should find that the culture patterns of many primitive societies recognize the existence of a greater or less amount of property common to the various members of the group. The truth of the matter is, of course, that man is both an individualist and a communist in regard to property. He becomes relatively one more than the other according as the culture patterns of his group stress the one or the other of these limiting types of property ownership.

Before proceeding to define what is meant by the terms 'common property' and 'communism,' I ought perhaps to say a word or two about the materials and methods by which the tables in the appendix to this chapter have been compiled. Taking the now classic monograph of Hobhouse, Wheeler and Ginsberg on the *Simpler Peoples* as an example in method, I have endeavoured to draw up tables from which one may infer the culture patterns of any group in regard to the various items of property of that group. Again, from the incidence of thieving, the taboos on property, the nature of inheritance, alienation, etc., valuable information may be obtained as to the manner in which savages regard property, personal or real. Land I have not reconsidered, since exhaustive tables in regard to this are to be found in the *Simpler*

[1] Cf. Gide: *Communist and Co-operative Societies* (1930), chs. v–vii, *passim*.

Peoples.[1] The primitive groups I have chosen to report upon are necessarily few, yet they are taken from each culture stage and represent a fair sample. The conclusions one infers from a study of such tables would not, I think, be very materially altered by a wider casting of the net. I need not add anything here in the way of a detailed explanation or defence of the methodology employed. A full and impartial discussion is to be found elsewhere.[2]

As regards the materials themselves, I have confined myself in compiling the tables as far as possible to the more authoritative anthropological studies. But even here it must be remembered that no investigator had my scheme of enquiry in mind when reporting upon his social group. The result is that though some monographs give adequate information, others are silent on just those points where one would desire the fullest evidence. Over and above this difficulty there are sources of error, obscurity and confusion which arise from the intermixture of cultures, the rise and decay of patterns under outside stimulus, whether native or civilized. There is always the probability, further, that the peoples with whom observers come into contact are just those members of the group who lie nearest to the white man and are most influenced thereby. The tables I have drawn up, therefore,

[1] *The Material Culture and Social Institutions of the Simpler Peoples,* 251 *et seq.*

[2] *The Simpler Peoples,* ch. i, *passim.* I am aware, of course, that one could draw final conclusions only from a comprehensive tabulation which would cover all and every primitive people about which we have anthropological record. And that in a controversial subject like this, embracing the relative incidence of communism and individualism in savage society, it might not be unexpected if an opponent were to insinuate that by choosing one's examples with care, one can prove anything one desires. The social sciences, for lack of quantitative methods, suffer from this desire to prove a case more than sciences which employ exact quantitative methods. However, I may state that the peoples listed in the tables were chosen at random from the Bibliography of the *Simpler Peoples.* They represent a fair, logical sample of the material and may with safety, I think, be relied upon to give a sufficiently accurate conclusion. I hope later to make a more extensive study of the forms of property in primitive society by a comprehensive use of this quantitative method.

probably suffer not so much from quantitative considerations as from the necessary and inherent imperfections of the anthropological materials. Within these limits, however, I venture to think that they are sufficiently accurate to enable one to draw major inferences as to the kind, degree and importance of the property culture patterns of primitive groups at each culture stage.

I may now proceed to explain what is to be understood by the terms 'communism' and 'common property.' I believe that the term communism as a sociological concept is best restricted to that use where it implies the common ownership of property objects within the three concentric economic realms of production, distribution and consumption. As such, communism may be usefully distinguished from various forms of co-operative ownership. Co-operative production or distribution is not communism, since under the former system each individual—for example, in an agricultural community—is the owner of his plot of land, cultivates it himself and keeps the produce; only, he is bound to other cultivators by various forms of association for the distribution of their collective goods. Even if the plots of land are owned by the community, yet if each tills his plot, keeps the produce and lives in his own household, there is still co-operation and not communism. It is only where the ownership of the soil is vested in the community, where the produce of individual labour goes to the community, and, further, where there is community of consumption and habitation—it is only under these circumstances that we find a complete, logically developed communist system of life.[1] Among very

[1] The *New Oxford Dictionary* defines *Communism* as follows: "A theory which advocates a state of society in which there should be no private ownership, all property being vested in the community and labour organized for the common benefit of all members; the professed principle being that each should work according to his capacity and receive according to his wants." This is a much better definition than those which take the criterion of communism to be equality of distribution, since equality in this respect is compatible with various forms of co-operative ownership;

few societies, either savage or civilized, do we have this complete communism. The Russian Soviet system is more an example of co-operative enterprise than of communist, if we define communism in some such terms as the above. Perhaps religious communities and orders are the nearest approach to complete communism that we may find in the modern world.

From another point of view—that which starts from the distinction made by Hobhouse between property for use and property for power[1]—the principle of communism may be best regarded as one which would confine all rights in property to those of the first type, rights to property for use. The community, under a regime of communism, would take over all rights in things that are not being used and give to the individual members of the group only those rights which are coincident with prescribed uses. "A successful state of communism," says Lindsay, "would imply that all care of property when it is not being used, all provision of property in anticipation of its use, and the reconciliation of all conflicting claims to the use of the same property would be the business of the community. The individuals would only have to think what they wanted to do, to manifest their needs, and if the communal organization was adequate, these

and communism stresses distribution according to need. But needs, however, may not be equal. Mill (*Principles of Political Economy* (1871), i, 254), Sidgwick (*Principles of Political Economy* (1919), ch. vii, par. 3), and the writers of articles on *Communism* in *Hastings' Dictionary* and in *Palgrave's Dictionary* have sinned in this regard. I have followed Gide: *op. cit.*, 14, 54, 114 *et seq.*, in stressing common ownership within the realms of production, distribution and consumption. A popular definition of 'communism' will not unusually extend the connotation of the term to cover the common ownership and possession of women within the group. And in so far as women are looked upon, practically and theoretically, as no more than property objects, this extension is logically not incorrect. But it would seem that there never has been an organization of society in which there has been promiscuous intercourse between the sexes. And at present I am concerned to get a working and not merely a theoretical definition of the term 'communism.'

[1] Hobhouse: Essay on "Evolution of Property," in *Property: Its Duties and Rights*, 9–11.

would be supplied."[1] In other words, control over wealth in a system of communism, when it is not being used, is assigned to the community. The right to use wealth is assigned to individuals who participate according to need. A definition of communism from this point of view, therefore, will cover much the same ground in common with the view adopted above.

In the context of this chapter, however, I wish to deal with the problem of communism and common property more particularly as set over against the background of savage society. It is necessary, therefore, to ask first: What is the nature of rights in a primitive community? Briefly stated, the answer is this: That rights are essentially claims to this or to that thing, to be allowed to do this or the other thing. If such claims are violated there is usually some socially approved mechanism for restoring the *status quo*. This mechanism may be put into operation either by the sufferer or his group or by representatives of society as a whole. As regards rights or claims to the ownership of property, it is usual to find among the simpler peoples permanently existing rights to the more or less exclusive use, enjoyment and control of what I have termed property values. These rights, as I shall show later, vary from case to case. Although some of the incidents of control known to us, e.g. alienation or inheritance, are practically unknown, nevertheless the body of such rights may be called property culture patterns, established and maintained by customary regulation. So long as the owner is identifie dand his rights to property objects respected, many examples of alleged communism prove on examination to be rather extreme limitations on property prescribed by rules of hospitality, kinship, good-fellowship, or magical beliefs, than evidence of strict communism as I have defined the term. When, however, custom

[1] A. D. Lindsay: Essay on "The Principle of Private Property," in *Property*, *op. cit.*, 77.

requires the returned hunter to share his game with an entire group according to specified rules, themselves probably the outcome of original relative need, it is not unreasonable to classify this custom as evidence of communism. This all the more so when the game is hunted in common and, after distribution, not unusually consumed in common.[1]

If we return now to the explicit statement made above that property in a communist system is held in common, we may ask a second question: What does this notion of common property imply? It implies at least two points. First, common property is that over which several individuals have rights to use and control. Second, these rights are held collectively over against the rest of the group or against other communities. Both points are of equal importance. The latter point distinguishes common property from no man's property which is held neither by individual nor group. Land amongst many nomadic tribes seems to be of this nature. The individual rights are similarly to be stressed. They may be equivalent, at one end of the scale, to the indiscriminate right of each to use property objects at will. Or, since in regard to limited supplies of food, for example, indiscriminate right may lead to shortage and inconvenience, we have, at the other end of the scale, various rights of sharing designed to satisfy no need at the expense of others' needs. It is interesting to note in this respect that "shares, if not at once consumed like food, become for the time private property, and if the time is extended, common property may in this way be gradually transformed into private."[2] So long, however, as the community retains to itself the control of wealth when not in use, and so long, further, as the apportionment is temporary and regulated by customs of universal sharing, property is held in common and is in

[1] Cf. Hobhouse: *Social Development*, 282.

[2] Hobhouse: *op. cit.*, 283.

no way private. It is not to be imagined, however, that communism and common property require for their realization the existence of an extended social group. There may very well be common property and common participation in production, distribution and consumption of wealth among two individuals. The family or joint household is probably the nearest approach to communism among savages or civilized. In theory, if not in practice, the area of participation may be extended to include clan, tribe or community of tribes. Each case of alleged communism must in fact be examined on its merits. In all cases our criteria are to be those of common property and those of common participation in the three so-called realms of economic behaviour.

Where, among primitive peoples, there is an approach towards common property rights, as among hunting tribes, for instance, in the ownership of land or in the distribution of food, it is not altogether impossible to infer the circumstances under which this approach would be made. There is, first, the reality of primitive group solidarity with corresponding, but implicit, ideas as to group or family responsibility. In native society the individual is essentially a unit within the larger family or clan group. Both these latter absorb the individual in that he strengthens, while his property serves to augment the wealth of, the family or clan. The wealth of each member makes up the wealth of the larger group, which may make demands on the individual just as he may avail himself of its wealth and protection. Miss Kingsley writes of West African tribes thus: "Every person is a member of some family and all the other members of the family are responsible for him and to him, and he to them; and every family is a member of some house and all the other members of the house are responsible for and to the families of which it is composed. The natural tendency of this is for property to become joint property, family property, or to be absorbed into family property."[1] Numerous examples might be quoted to illustrate this reaction of group solidarity upon property culture patterns. But the principle is clear: and it is within the closed family group that we find among primitive, as among civilized, the closest approach to communitarian social organization.

A second factor in this communization of culture pattern is to be found in motives either of prudence alone or of prudence based upon religious or magical ideas. Seligmann speculates upon the manner in which the custom of exchanging food between neighbouring Melanesian villages may have arisen through far-sighted prudence. Of ceremonial exchange he writes: "It seems likely that it arose as a convenient way of disposing of surplus food, it being assumed that the recipients would return the compliment when they, in their turn, had more food than they could consume."[2] It seems unfair for Sumner and Keller to dismiss this theory as 'thin speculation' or rationalization *post hoc*, since it does not seem an unnatural way in which such distribution might arise. The sharing of food among individuals, due in the first place to notions of group solidarity, would be reinforced by magical motives. This quotation of Jenness and Ballantyne, of the D'Entrecasteaux natives, is typical of many savage peoples: "A hungry man would naturally ask anyone whom he saw eating to give him a little food. The person asked would hardly venture to refuse, lest the other in his anger should secretly strike his shadow with a spear and cause his death."[3] Whatever might be the motives, therefore, of such sharing of food, the practical result would be that of common participation in the distribution and consumption of food.

[1] Miss Kingsley: *West African Studies* (1899), 429; cf. also Vinogradoff: *Outlines of Historical Jurisprudence* (1920), vol. i, 261–273.

[2] Seligmann: *Melanesians*, 141–142. Cf., however, Sumner and Keller: *op. cit.*, i, 274. Spencer and Gillen seem to uphold some such theory as Seligmann's in regard to Arunta 'communism.' Cf. *The Arunta*, i, 37.

[3] Jenness and Ballantyne: *Northern D'Entrecasteaux*, 205.

A third factor which is of importance among hunting tribes and nomads is the fact that it is impossible to store much of their staple food. It must be consumed almost immediately, otherwise it will perish and be useless as food.[1] Therefore, in a manner, the distribution of game or of flesh is forced upon these natives, and it is to be expected that customary rules would be developed to regulate this distribution. Once such behaviour is given the sanction of custom, however, it becomes part of the established order of society. And a Yakut pastoral nomad will express the utmost surprise when he hears that poverty and want exist among Western peoples,[2] or, again, a Melanesian will treat as a joke Rivers' statement that European customs do not demand that he should share his sovereign with all his kith and kin.

There is therefore good reason to expect that, however the customs have originated, we should find, when we examine savage society, a number of culture patterns indicating a greater or less amount of common property, and likewise a certain common participation in the production and distri-

[1] For example: we are told that the pastoral Yakuts live on kumiss and horse-meat. But kumiss is spoiled in winter by frost, in summer by heat; it does not bear transportation. Further, the Yakuts have never known how to preserve meat by drying or smoking. "Hence," writes Sumner, "it was in the highest degree convenient for them to live in groups of such a size that the kumiss and meat obtained could be used as soon as possible. They even have a tradition that horse-thieves in ancient times tried to organize themselves into bands large enough to divide and eat up in a night the animal they had stolen. We must believe that in ancient times the fundamental grouping of the people consisted of bodies constituted upon the basis of a convenient common consumption of the product of a proportionate number of animals." Sumner: "The Yakuts," *Journal Anthropological Institute*, vol. xxxi, 70. Cf. also Malinowski: *The Family*, 283–286, 289.

[2] "The Yakuts would not believe the author when he told them that in his country there were rich and populous cities in which people sometimes died of starvation. They asked why anyone should die when he could go to eat with his neighbours." Sumner: *op. cit.*, 69. This question of the Yakuts reveals more of their economic culture patterns than pages of laborious description.

bution of native wealth. Just so much, however, and no more. I think one will rarely find among savages that complete approach to communism, defined as I have done it, which has often been alleged but not as often substantiated. In the first place, valid generalization about the communitarian organization of primitive groups is not at all easy. Apart from our inveterate tendency to assume a single line of evolution, when, in fact, development follows different lines; and again, apart from the fact that many commit the error of attempting to describe the customs of the simpler peoples in the phraseology of a highly developed system of law and ethics—apart from these two potent sources of error, it must be evident from a consideration of the accompanying tables, that the facts are too variously complex for simple generalization. Before I discuss in detail one or two cases of alleged communism, I will consider the facts contained in the tables appended to this chapter.

For the sake of completeness, however, it may be well first to summarize the tables and graphs regarding property in land as set forth in the *Simpler Peoples.* These tables would seem to indicate that among hunting tribes the land is usually held in common tribal ownership by a section of the tribe, by the clan, sib or local group. Such common ownership means that every individual and every section of the group is free to hunt the entire area of this land; but that no outsider would be allowed in this area without special permission and would be liable to death at sight unless he satisfied the tribesmen that he came as suppliant, envoy or trader. This common ownership may be correlated with a culture pattern enforcing customary distribution of the products thereof and thus tending to equalize the chances of obtaining food, the sharing of superfluity and obviating some of the risks of starvation.[1] But along with common ownership we may find the existence of private ownership

[1] Cf. below; and Table III, appendix to this chapter.

of hunting lands, as among the Veddas and some Australian tribes.

Among pastoral peoples wealth is usually measured by flocks and herds; the ownership of land is of less importance. It is usually common property. With agriculturals, however, the tables show that though the right of hunting remains with the whole group, yet possessory right, though not permanent private ownership, is the rule in regard to forest clearings for agricultural purposes. With developing tillage, cultivated lands acquire value and tend to pass into permanent possession. The old communal right may be asserted by periodical redistributions as amongst the old Russian *mir* or else communal rights lapse and the lots become family property. *De facto* occupation is merged in private ownership. Finally, with the rise to power of a class of nobles, the latter own the land, while peasants, serfs or semi-free cultivate it. Thus it is among natives of the Pacific Coast and Polynesian peoples. In effect, common ownership of land declines as we rise through the cultural scale to the most advanced Agriculturals (A3). Individual ownership is fairly constant throughout the agricultural grades, partly in association with the communal principle, partly qualified by the rise of chiefs and nobles with an early approach to feudal or semi-feudal land tenure.[1]

TABLE I.—Referring now to the tables in the appendix and the evidence they bring forward as to the nature of ownership among primitive peoples, it will be evident from Table I that the protection of private or personal property by personal marks, taboos, magico-animistic signs, and, again, by the social disapproval of theft, is extremely widespread among all grades of savages.[2] Likewise is the

[1] I have summarized these tables from the *Simpler Peoples*, 251–253. Cf. also Hobhouse: *Social Development*, 323 *et seq*.

[2] Regarding the taboo, Crawley writes: "The whole series of phenomena helps to disprove the common idea that early society possessed a socialistic or communistic character. The rights of the individual in property,

condemnation of theft. This extends to the condemnation of unlawful appropriation of food and garden products as much as to personal property.[1] As is to be expected, this disapproval has not a definite extension to extra-group activities. Its extension has reference to activities within the group. This is no more than the expected result of the idea of primitive group solidarity. The writ of tribal morality does not run beyond the bounds of the close-knit homogeneous group unit. With some peoples, stealing outside the group is definitely approved. This is the exception rather than the rule. Westermarck is probably not incorrect in suggesting that it is only when stealing is associated with cunning and bravery that it is approved; and then this approbation refers more to the display of cunning and skill than to the light-handed attitude to other's property. With other peoples, however, e.g. in British Guiana or the Kayans of Borneo, we are told that the same code of honesty applies to strangers as to fellow-tribesmen. I should add that where there is no information available, e.g. among the Todas, relative to the use of property taboos, this does not necessarily indicate the absence of such taboos; merely that it has proved difficult to obtain conclusive evidence either way.

TABLE II.—I have drawn up Part I of this table, that relating to the ownership of the dwelling, in order that, read in conjunction with Table III, inferences may be made as to the existence or not among savages of community of

marriage and everything else were never more clearly defined than by primitive man." *The Mystic Rose* (1927), i, 181.

[1] "Not the mere fact that individuals are in actual possession of certain objects but the public disapproval of acts by which they are deprived of such possession, shows that they have proprietary rights over those objects. Hence the universal condemnation of what we call theft or robbery proves that the right of property exists among all races of men known to us." Westermarck: *Origin and Development of Moral Ideas*, ii, ch. xxviii, 1. Cf. also Thurnwald, "The Idea of theft presupposes the valuation of economic goods and private ownership of them." Art. "Diebstahl" in Ebert's *Reallexion der Vorgeschichte*. Ref. may also be made to Landtman: *Primary Causes of Social Inequality* (1909), 38–39.

consumption—the common habitation and the common consumption of the food supply being one of the criteria of communism. The table indicates that among Hunters and Gatherers, with the exception of the Central Australians, there is usually a common dwelling for the clan group together with family and, therefore, private occupation of houseroom therein. Among the Andamans, the Central Eskimo and the Veddas, family ownership of separate huts or caves exists along with this common dwelling. Among Agricultural peoples, however, there is evident a marked preference for the separate family dwelling, often with common ownership of the tribal meeting-house. With the Kenyahs, Kayans and the pastoral Yakuts only, among the higher cultural grades, do we find the clan or sib living together in the common house. With the Kayans and Kenyahs, however, this communism may be more apparent than real, since each family has its own set of rooms with family hearth; while the common meeting-place outside the rooms partakes of the nature of a raised, covered-in village street. It is interesting to note also of these tribes of Borneo, that rice plots are cultivated by each family and the rice stored in private rice barns. Food is usually prepared and consumed by each separate family group.

As to the ownership of canoes, it is noticeable that most savage peoples show a decided preference for family or individual as opposed to common ownership. Where canoes are owned in common by the clan, these are usually war canoes or canoes built to carry representatives of the clan on trading or 'diplomatic' visits to other groups. In the nature of the case these canoes are so large that they could be neither made nor owned by single members of the clan. This evidence, apart from Malinowski's later and more detailed analysis of the concept of canoe ownership among the Trobriand Island natives, seems definitely against Rivers' insistence upon common and widespread communism in regard to the ownership of canoes in Melanesia. Unless Rivers meant by common ownership, ownership common to a larger or smaller family group, and this is hardly consistent with Rivers' customary use of the term communism, one is compelled to suspect that Rivers was led astray in this, as in other matters, by theoretical preconceptions which could not fail to give a bias to all his investigations in the Pacific Islands.[1]

TABLE III.—Community of production and distribution of economic goods is one of our criteria of communism. I have tabulated information therefore regarding the modes of primitive production and distribution in this Table III. In regard, first, to the production of such food as game, cattle and flocks, common effort seems the exception rather than the rule. Where it does exist, however, it seems to go hand in hand with common distribution according to customary rules. Common production of vegetable foods, e.g. gathering of roots and berries, or cultivation of grain, is exceedingly rare. At all culture stages emphasis appears to be placed more upon individual or family production of the food supply, with a correlative family or private distribution thereof. This table, however, should be read in conjunction with information tabulated in the *Simpler Peoples,* since tables in the latter indicate that distribution of game and grain by customary rules, no matter by what manner its production, is widespread among certain peoples of the Hunting and Agricultural stages. From Table III it is evident that it is among the Australians, the Eskimo, the pastoral Yakuts, several Melanesian and several African agriculturals, that a certain approach is made to a restricted communism in the production and the distribution, or in both of these phases together, but not in the consumption, of food.

[1] Cf. Rivers: *History of Melanesian Society,* ii, 396, 452–453, and his *Instinct and the Unconscious,* Appendix viii, 268–269; Malinowski: *Argonauts,* 116–120; *Mailu,* 619; *Crime and Custom,* 20–21.

TABLE IV.—This table indicates the modes of disposal at death of various types of property objects and thus directly shows the degree to which exclusive control is exerted by the individual over such property. The salient feature of this table I take to be the fact that though full control may be enjoyed during life, nevertheless the group culture patterns rarely allow full and unrestricted right of bequest or alienation at death. Property is usually disposed of at death according to customary tribal rules. This emphasis on customary regulation extends to all types of property. Occasionally we find the right of bequest is exercised, but still qualified by necessity of clan assent before the settlement is allowed. In some cases there is material destruction of property, e.g. house, implements, personal ornaments, cattle or horses. What is not destroyed is disposed of according to custom. Tahiti appears as a notable exception to such rules, for here, according to Ellis, there appears to have been absolute right of bequest exercised over all property by means of a primitive form of a testament or will.[1] Among another Polynesian people, the Maoris, bequest applied only to personal property, otherwise customary distribution of the estate took place. With most savages there is no analogy to the will; bequest usually operates through death-bed word-of-mouth instructions. And thus it is not unnatural for clan representatives to step in and subject such absolute control to their approval. Among Hunters and Gatherers alienation or bequest could not embrace clan lands. Owned by the clan, such lands remained the permanent possession of the clan. Only among the Veddas do we find a qualified right of bequest operative over individually owned hunting lands.

Again, it is exceedingly rare to find tribes where women inherit on equal terms with the men of the group. Mostly the women are regarded as property and inherited along

[1] Cf. Ellis: *Polynesian Researches*, iii, 115–116.

with the rest according to the rules prevalent in a particular group. Finally, where, as among the West African monarchies, all property, we are told, is, in theory, the absolute property of the king, there could exist no right of bequest. At death, property reverted to the king, who had the right of appointing heirs to administer the estate as life tenants. In practice, heirs usually inherited according to customary rules; yet their control over the property was to a degree temporary. It depended upon the absolute discretion of the king to appoint whom he willed.[1]

With knowledge derived from a consideration of these four tables as a background, I wish now to discuss the social patterning of property values among one or two groups of primitive peoples at different economic and cultural levels of development. With the peoples I have selected I wish to show, first, the complex fashion in which the web of common ownership is interwoven with the woof of private, individual ownership to form the fabric of social life, clothing and moulding sentiment and impulse in conformity with the group pattern. And second, I wish briefly to indicate the attitude of primitive groups to the acquisition of wealth and the rôle which such wealth plays in the economic organization of a people. It will be well here to bear in mind the implicit contrast of the primitive attitude to wealth with that prevalent to-day in the Great Society. Finally, to evaluate the economic organization of savage society in terms of Communism or Individualism, I recall to mind the definition I have above of Communism. It is that organization of society where there is common ownership of the means of production and common participation in the means of distribution and consumption.

[1] General discussions on the primitive attitude to inheritance may be found among the following: Westermarck: *op. cit.*, ii, 44–49, 52–57; Rivers: *Social Organization*, 116; Sumner and Keller: *op. cit.*, iv, 56; Lowie: *Primitive Society*, 232–235; Art. "Inheritance," in *Hastings' Dictionary*.

Let me consider first the economic patterns of a culturally low hunting people like the Andaman Islanders. Here the group unit is constituted by ten families together with a few unmarried males and females. A. R. Brown suggests that the life of such a local group approaches to a sort of communism based on the notion of private property. Strange communism this! What, in effect, are the facts of the case? It seems that the hunting land of the group is the only property that is owned in common. Over the hunting grounds all members of the local unit have equal right to hunt game; intruders from other local groups are rigidly excluded from hunting or fishing the lands or waters without having first been granted express permission. Along with this common ownership there goes private ownership of fruit trees and of trees used in canoe-making and of the resulting canoes.

As regards the production of food, game and fish and honeycomb belong to him who obtains them; to the woman belong the roots, seeds, fish, prawns and molluscs which she herself gathers. The man owns his own weapons, the woman her own domestic implements. Personal property of man or wife may not be disposed of without permission. There is thus private production of food. Along with this, however, the culture patterns inculcate a ready generosity in the distribution of food. Everyone is expected to give to those who have not. An older married man reserves for himself sufficient for his family and gives the rest to his friends. A younger man is expected to give the best of what he gets to his elders. "The result of this custom is that practically all the food obtained is evenly distributed through the whole camp, the only inequality being that the younger men do not fare so well as the elders."[1]

Individualism is prominent, on the other hand, in the consumption of property and wealth. As I have said, each owns his own weapons or domestic implements. The canoe

[1] I am summarizing A. R. Brown: *op. cit.*, 29, 36, 41, 43, 50, 413.

is private property. Adultery is looked upon as a form of theft. Each family erects and repairs its own hut. Even the communal hut is not, in fact, common to the whole group, since each family is looked upon as owning a certain portion of the finished hut (though all co-operate in its construction), and it is the family that keeps this part of the hut in repair. Again, while all members of a family take their meals together, a married man is only permitted to eat with other married men and bachelors, but never with any women save those of his own household, unless, indeed, he be well advanced in years. Bachelors and spinsters are required to take their meals apart with those of their respective sexes.[1]

Characteristic, however, of the Andaman Islanders, as of several Melanesian peoples, is the custom of constant interchange of presents between members of the same group and between local groups. This custom is often interpreted as giving rise to an effective communism. Yet the fact that no gift is given without the expectation of a gift of equivalent value in return seems to negate this interpretation. Thus it is considered a breach of good manners ever to refuse the request of another. If a man be asked by another to give him anything he possesses, he will immediately do so. If the two men are equals a return of about the same value will have to be made; if they are unequal, the younger man will not always expect the return gift. Canoes, however, are rarely thus given away. They are usually lent by the owner to his friends. It is interesting to note, too, that Man regards this gift system as a species of barter. No transaction is carried out without equivalence of giving and receiving.[2]

[1] Cf. E. H. Man: "Aborigines of the Andaman Islands," *Journal Anthropological Institute*, xii, 344.

[2] Brown, *op. cit.*, 42–43; Man: *op. cit.*, 340. The idea that the giving of presents is a type of exchange-trade seems prevalent among another people of about the same cultural level as the Andamans. Thus of the Nootka Indians, Bancroft writes: "Even their system of presents is a species of trade, the full value of each gift being confidently expected in a return present on the next festive occasion." *Native Races of the Pacific States*, i, 192.

One may sum up, then, the relevant culture patterns of such a hunting people as the Andamans by suggesting that there is common ownership of land; private production of wealth; distribution of food according to customary rules; private consumption thereof; a gift system which is based on mutuality of response, but individual ownership of the gifts rendered or received. The result is that the rights of private property are so far recognized that no one would, without permission, appropriate or remove to a distance anything belonging to a friend or neighbour. These culture patterns do not suggest any complete approach to group communism.

Shifting now the focus of our enquiries from the Indian Ocean to the Pacific States of North America, we find an attitude to wealth among the West Coast Indians of British Columbia that may well have originated in the custom of gift exchange. I refer to that attitude which looks upon wealth in blankets, guns, pots and pans, knives, beads and other trinkets as no more than an expression of social status and not, as among ourselves, as an expression of social power or a tool for the fulfilment of personal desire. This attitude to wealth finds fullest expression in the institution of the potlach. This institution has been well summed up in these words of Niblack: "To procure a wife; to enter the ranks or obtain the influence of medicine-men; to become a great chief; to give social standing to one's children; to take on oneself the name of a paternal ancestor; to become a respected member of the community; to atone for a wrong done; to resent an insult—property in some form or other must be sacrificed either by destroying it to show one's rage, grief, or disregard of wealth, or by giving it away to obtain the good will of others."[1] In a word, through the operation of this institution, property is not valuable as riches are, to procure comfort, luxury or the services of other men.

[1] A. P. Niblack: *Report of the U.S. National Museum* (1888), 365–366; cf. also 308.

Its value lies in the social prestige that goes with its distribution.

For the potlach itself is really a feast given by one individual to another or to the clan, at which the guests are presented with articles of native wealth, or witness the destruction of much property. The more sumptuous the presents, the more lavish the destruction of wealth, the greater is the feast, and the higher the esteem accorded to the feast-giver. The value of property, in fact, is estimated in terms of the social prestige which comes to the owner when he gives away or destroys his property. A good example of this attitude is found in this description of a potlach among the Thlingets Indians: "For vainglory they often destroy their own property. We have seen fine canoes demolished with an axe in a few moments of time; dishes, stoves and other household goods smashed by their proud owner, just that he might be considered a greater man than some other. In the days of slavery, owners of slaves vied with one another in the sacrifice of slaves. Slaves were property and the owner who destroyed the most was considered the greatest man. Potlachs were given more for vainglory than for anything else. Public praise and honour are the objects in view."[1] It is evident, therefore, that the accumulation of property beyond the necessities of life, among these West Coast Indians, is only considered desirable for the purpose of distributing it or destroying it on the occasion of great feasts and thereby establishing social status, satisfying vanity, triumphing over a rival unable to make a similar brave show, and acquiring a reputation for generous liberality.[2]

[1] L. F. Jones: *Thlingets of Alaska* (New York, 1914), 93; cf. 95–96.

[2] For further information on potlach ceremonies reference may be made to the following: Goldenweiser: *Early Civilization*, 59–61; Kane: *Wanderings of an Artist in N. America* (1859), 221; Bancroft: *op. cit.*, i, 134; Swanton: *The Haida*, 155–181; Wissler: *The American Indian*, 185. Sapir: *op. cit.*; Landtman: *idem.*, 79, 87–88.

The concepts of wealth amongst ourselves and the West Coast Indians, if not possessing utterly distinct connotations, are at least measurably distinct. The point I stress is that the nature of this difference is to be sought not in differences of psychophysical make-up between civilized and savage, but in that total patterning of life in the two communities from which this particular pattern of wealth and its acquirement has been extracted. That this is so is indicated even more strongly by the fact that in startling juxtaposition to the customs of the West Coast Indians we have the example of a Central North American tribe like the Sioux, where a chief obtained his influence not through wealth but by his wisdom, courage and eloquence. Of the Sioux chief Neill remarks that "the individual who desires to improve his condition is not only laughed at but maltreated. Moreover, if he acquires any property (beyond a common level) there is no law which secures it to him and it is liable to be taken away at any time by any ill-disposed person."[1] A survey of the degree to which savage peoples accord power and influence to those possessing wealth without other socially successful qualities, e.g. courage, wisdom, the expert's skill, shows that to a large extent it is only among the highest cultural grades that wealth spells influence in tribal affairs. Prowess in war, hunting, magic, personal factors or hereditary claims are not infrequently the causes of influence and authority being afforded to the chiefs of the tribe or group.[2]

For comparative purposes it is of interest to include in our survey of the patterning of economic behaviour brief

[1] Neill: *History of Minnesota* (1873), 86.

[2] Specific reference to the relative factors upon which primitive authority and influence rest may be found in the following typical studies: Hobhouse Wheeler and Ginsberg: *The Simpler Peoples*, 50 (tables and quantitative data). For the Australians: Roth: *Ethnological Studies*, 141; Thomas: *Native Tribes* (1906), 143; Nieboer: *Slavery as an Industrial System* (1910), 235. For Polynesians: Firth: *op. cit.*, 284–285. For Melanesians: Seligmann: *The Melanesians*, ch. xxxvi. Landtman: *Kiwai Papuans*, 166–169. For Borneans: Hose and McDougall, *op. cit.*, i, 66.

reference to the life of a nomadic pastoral people like the Yakuts of Siberia. Before contact with Russian civilization the basis of Yakut existence was the breeding of horses, a nomadic life which imposed its structure upon Yakut arts and crafts, songs and legends, and the system of their group life. In these earlier days, the Yakuts had scarcely any permanent dwellings. Nomads, they carried with them all of the house save its framework, which later comers, in their turn, might use. The land was not even common property. It was free as the air, belonging to nobody. The herds were the common property of each nomadic group, though their nominal owner was the head of each group.[1]

The diffusion into Siberia of Western civilization has meant a certain change of life. Family groups have settled on plots of land and there has developed a conflict between roving pastoralists and settled tillers of the soil. Thus, with regard to both meadow lands and pastures and woods, a type of co-operative society has developed, in antithesis to an earlier communism. There are frequent re-allotments of land between various clan and family groups for purposes of equalization, but a certain portion of meadow land, apportioned to each homestead, is regarded as the inalienable property of each householder. Other strips of meadow, lying farther off, are subject to periodic division. Pasture and woods, on the other hand, remain almost everywhere for the undivided use of all members of the local group. In general, however, civilization has brought about the formation of new culture patterns. Whereas in earlier days there was common participation in production; to-day, the clan-group has reconciled itself to the individual disposal of land won by clearing woods or meadow, by draining swamps or ponds, when this right has been established by prescription. Apart from the homestead plot, individually appropriated

[1] In this account of Yakut organization I am again following Sumner's translation of Sieroshevski. Sumner: *op. cit.*, vol. xxxi.

land is inherited with the qualification that the land may not be too large an area, and must all be utilized by its owner.

In former times, however, as I have suggested, the social organization of the group approached very near to a complete communism. In regard to the distribution of food, for example (and of other wealth besides, since this consisted mostly of things subjected to immediate consumption), everything was shared among members of the group. Slaughtered beasts, meat, viscera, fat, entrails, and again, sugar, vodka, tobacco, flour, milk, and cream—all these were divided into portions of equal or unequal size and distributed among the neighbours. (Even the poorest to-day, we are told, are ashamed to take money for lodgings or food.) Travellers in winter took hay from stacks in the meadows to feed their animals. For themselves or beast they feared no hunger since it was their right to be supported by others in time of need. So again, in regard to common habitation. The family group lived together in a sort of communal dwelling. Anyone who entered at any hour of night or day might stay as long as he desired to drink tea, eat food or pass the night. Sumner states that these notions were so insistent that the nominal master or head of the house did not dare to drive from his dwelling, without overwhelmingly adequate reasons, even one who was thoroughly offensive to him.[1]

To a large degree, then, among the ancient Yakuts we find a prevailing community of ownership. As among all nomads, there was land in abundance, no pressure of population, and so no rights to the ownership of land, either in common or in private, were recognized.[2] There was,

[1] Sumner: *op. cit.*, 70.

[2] Further consideration of the pastoralist attitude to land may be found among the following: Sumner and Keller: *op. cit.*, i, 288–291; iv, 98–102; Lewinski: *Origin of Property*, 6–7; Descamps: *op. cit.*; Renard: *Le Travail dans la Préhistoire*, 258–259. Where, as among the Todas, land must be closely settled, there is more than common use of the land; there is common clan ownership. Cf. Rivers: *The Todas*, 541, 557–558.

however, common participation in production; custom enforced in large measure the distribution of wealth by the 'haves' among the 'have-nots.' And among the enlarged family group, extending even to all who wished to participate, there was a definite community of consumption. Wealth was not of particular value to its owner. He who grew rich in seasons of abundance shared his wealth with the starving in seasons of scarcity. If any were to starve, Yakut philosophy indicated that all should starve together. Of course, as I have suggested in a footnote above, this insistence upon common participation was in no way the outcome of a conscious attempt to set to right the ills of an acquisitive society. It was due, I suppose, to that economic determinism which brings about the prevalence of certain culture patterns among hunting peoples and pastoralists.[1] There are no known means of preserving food or wealth for future consumption. Therefore the fundamental grouping of the local unit consists of groups constituted upon the basis of a convenient, common participation in the distribution and consumption of a product of a proportionate number of animals. Customs of the Yakuts merely serve to emphasize that at certain economic levels of development, where there is a population substantially equal, a large measure of communism is not incompatible with the maintenance of a definite standard of group life. The individualism of human nature does not rebel against this communism. It is itself definitely moulded by the prevalent culture patterns into a characteristic group-complex necessary for the survival of the local unit in a particular type of environment.

[1] This note of M. Sieroshevski may be added to that of Sumner (cf. *supra*, note 1, p. 209). Of the Yakuts the former writes: "Les groupes qui se développaient le mieux étaient ceux qui pouvaient manger à la fois toute une bête tuée. Leur facilité de mouvement était plus grande, car ils n'avaient pas besoin de traîner avec eux leur fardeaux et la nourriture n'était pas exposée à se gâter." See Sumner: *Journal Anthropological Institute*, *op. cit.*, 108, note 1.

So far we have been considering the economic patterns of primitive groups at a relatively low stage of cultural development. It may be as well, therefore, before concluding this chapter to shift our attention to yet another part of the world, and to a group of peoples who gain subsistence mainly by agriculture. I refer to the Melanesians. It is all the more important also to pass in review the life of those groups in the Pacific because not a few investigators, at one time or another, without first defining their terms, have suggested that many Melanesian units are communist in social organization. Turner was an early sinner in this respect, in regard to a people closely akin to the Melanesians, but generally classified as Polynesian, e.g. the Samoans.[1] And Rivers' ascription of a wholesale communism to the natives of Banks Island and neighbouring islands is another case in point. It does not seem an unnecessary task, therefore, for us to examine in the light of our criteria of communism the culture patterns of one or two typical Pacific Island groups and to determine, as far as possible, the exact nature of these patterns.

First, then, let us consider the ownership of land in Melanesia. Among some peoples, e.g. the Koita, Southern Massim, D'Entrecasteaux and natives of Mailu Mainland, it is fairly clear that ownership of garden lands and the bush is vested in the clan. The individual usually cultivates his garden plot himself; it descends directly to his heirs. But if he has no descendants his land reverts to the ownership of the clan. Over the non-cultivated tracts of bush land all members of the village clan may range in search of fish, game or fruit. Each hamlet, however, resents any individual

[1] Reference may be made here to Firth's careful analysis of the economic organization of the New Zealand Maori. After examining various authorities who are at one in ascribing 'communism' to the Maori, Firth concludes: "Here we are confronted with a 'communistic' society with private property in land and also . . . monogamous marriage with exclusive sexual appropriation—surely a somewhat inconsistent state of affairs." The reader may well agree with Firth's conclusion. Firth: *op. cit.*, 356.

of another section hunting on its land and usually reserves to itself the exclusive right to some produce of the soil, such as, for instance, water, clay or minerals. Along with the enjoyment of the usufruct of plots of clan garden land, the individual will own his own house, the corresponding village site and coconut and betel-nut plantations.[1] Opposed to this preponderating type of clan ownership we have, on the other hand, systems such as those prevailing on Mailu Island, on Murray Island, and on those of the Trobriand group, where it appears that, in general terms, the land is entirely subdivided amongst individuals, each owning his own tract, where he and his wife make their garden. There may be a general overright on all the garden land, vested in chief, sub-chief, or garden magician, and carrying with it the exercise of certain ceremonial rights. But, taken by and large, the owner cultivates his own plot, apportions it to his children for separate cultivation, or leases it to someone else under a complicated system of payment. Firewood is collected by each woman on her husband's ground; clay and waterholes are still used by the whole community jointly.[2] Finally, among the natives of Banks Islands we have a system which combines the previous two. As regards garden land and village sites, this is never the absolute property of the individual, cannot be alienated, and is looked upon as vested in the clan, the member of which enjoys the usufruct of such land during his lifetime. At death such land descends to the sister's children or maternal kinspeople, all of whom have a collective interest in it. The case is different, however, with bush land cleared and cultivated by the individual. This is owned absolutely by

[1] For the Koita and S. Massim, cf. Seligmann: *Melanesians*, 87–88, 467–468; cf. also Malinowski: *The Mailu*, 592–595, 598, 635; Jenness and Ballantyne: *op. cit.*, 72.

[2] Malinowski: *Mailu*, 595; *Ibid.*, "Primitive Economics," *Economic Journal* (1921), 4; Haddon: *Torres Strait Expedition Reports*, v, 284–287, 289–290; vi, 163–164, 165–168.

such an individual and passes at death, not to his sister's children, but to his own sons. The latter will divide this land into separate lots, cultivate it separately and refuse to recognize any right of the kin group over it. Similarly trees planted on clan garden lands will go at death to his sons—the eldest will take the oldest plantation, the youngest the latest—though the land itself is the collective property of his nephews.[1]

From this brief survey of land ownership it will be at once evident how difficult it is to generalize regarding communal ownership. The facts are too complex to fit neatly into one classification. The difficulty is not decreased when we recall that along with the widespread use of taboos and personal marks to protect property in fruit trees and coconut plantations,[2] there is evident everywhere strong condemnation of theft and fairly extensive rights to personal private

[1] Codrington: *The Melanesians*, 62–66; Rivers: *History of Melanesian Society*, i, 209; ii, 96–99. Rivers talks later (*op. cit.*, ii, 147, *Psychology and Ethnology* (1926), pt. iii (b), ch. v) of land on Eddystone Island as being communally owned, because it is "free for the use of any of the groups of persons who call one another *taviti*, . . . any of whom have the right to use it as a garden without asking for permission of the rest." Yet Rivers tells us such land "is not common to a social group which can be regarded as a clan, but belongs to a group of persons brought into relationship with one another by kinship . . . other kinds of property in this island are largely owned by individuals." This type of communal ownership as developed on Eddystone has little to do with 'communism,' as Rivers would believe. It is rather the common ownership of garden land by members of a family or extended family group. As such, it is misleading to class this type of ownership with communal ownership by the group or tribe. Similarly Rivers finds evidence on Pentecost Island, New Hebrides, for believing that all property in land once belonged to the *verana*, a family subdivision of the moiety, of which social grouping, however, Rivers confesses he "was able to discover very little" (*Melanesian Society*, i, 209; ii, 146). Presuming one had adequate knowledge of the *verana*, the critic may reply, this would only be evidence for the common ownership of land by a family group, and not evidence for the existence in Melanesia of a communistic social grouping as a whole.

[2] Cf. Seligmann: *op. cit.*, chs. xi, xliv; Malinowski: *Argonauts*, 425–426; *Crime and Custom*, 117–118; *The Mailu*, 586–587; Jenness and Ballantyne: *idem.*, 41, 74–75; Codrington: "On Social Regulations in Melanesia," *Journal Anthropological Institute*, vol. xviii, 312.

possessions in pigs, dogs, ornaments, weapons, implements, trade goods, canoes, drums and fishing nets.[1] It may be remarked in passing that on Murray Island Haddon discovered this sentiment of ownership to extend even to personal or family ownership of certain stars and of local legends![2] Apart, therefore, from one or two isolated examples of the customary distribution of game or fish,[3] I think it is fair to say that the term 'communism' has been misapplied in Melanesia (sometimes under the stress of theoretic exigencies, sometimes through failure clearly to understand the connotation of the term) to various examples either of common family participation in distribution of goods, as in the D'Entrecasteaux, or of common participation of certain closely related kin members in the consumption of certain articles of wealth, as among the Koita or on Banks Island.

Let me elaborate the argument of this last sentence. Common family participation (if we assume that the *taviti* of Eddystone and the *verana* of Pentecost were probably some such family groups) in the ownership of land is to be found on these two islands in the Pacific. But in itself it is not communism. Likewise it is not possible to interpret an example that Jenness and Ballantyne give of the family distribution of the 'trade' of a returned work-boy as communism.[4] It is no more than the workings of that culture

[1] For typical examples of Melanesian attitude to theft among Koita and S. Massim, cf. Seligmann: *op. cit.*, 133, 572–573, 698; among D'Entrecasteaux, Jenness and Ballantyne: *op. cit.*, 76–78. Inventories of private property are given by Seligmann also, 88–90, 160–163, 513–524; Malinowski: *Sexual Life of Savages*, 20–23.

[2] Haddon: *op. cit.*, vi, 167, note 1.

[3] Cf. Haddon on Western Islands of Torres Strait, *op. cit.*, v, 289–290, vi, 168. One should recall also the elaborate ceremonial connected with *sagali* food distributions as described by Malinowski for the Trobriands; and the fact that on Waga Waga (S. Massim people) there is an elaborate system of food distribution which ensures that a goodly portion of the spoils of fishing or hunting expeditions falls to the share of the *pouluma* or club-house of the village elders. Seligmann: *op. cit.*, 454–455, 460.

[4] Jenness and Ballantyne write of the work-boys' 'trade': "It belongs to all the family in common, and as many as can will gather round to see it

pattern which ensures that the wealth of the individual in these social groups where there is a strong sense of family responsibility shall strengthen and augment the wealth of the kin group. Following up this idea of kin participation in distribution, we find that other examples of communism, often given by Rivers, for instance, seem to involve no more than the fact that closely related kinsmen, i.e. nephew and maternal uncle or paternal aunt, participate to a certain degree in a common ownership, sometimes common use only, of certain articles of one's kinsman's wealth. Thus on Mota Island any of an uncle's property may be freely used by his sister's son. "It was said that even the most valuable possessions, such as pigs or canoes, might be taken in this way, but there is little doubt that this is a prescriptive right which is not put into practice."[1] There is also a certain community of goods between a man and his father's sister.

This condition of affairs may be paralleled by those obtaining among the Koita of New Guinea, where kinsmen who are reciprocally *raimu* (*raimu* = maternal uncle), *siba* (brother- and sister-in-law) or *waru* (father-, daughter-, mother-, son-in-law) freely take food from each other's gardens and borrow each other's canoes and nets. "As a rule," says Seligmann, "such borrowed property is returned in as good a condition as when borrowed; thus a man who lends his brother a net would expect the latter to return it in good condition, and if it be torn, not to return it until he has mended it; but this rule does not apply to relations-

opened." It consists of loin-cloth, belt and knife, mirror, pair of scissors, red-shell ear pendants and tobacco sticks. "His elder brother presides at the distribution of all this wealth and the rest of the kinsfolk aid him with copious suggestions; as for the boy, he must content himself with looking on and taking, with proper gratitude, the tiny fraction of all his gains that may be allotted to him." *Northern D'Entrecasteaux*, 95–96.

[1] Rivers: *Melanesian Society*, i, 37. The fact that this 'prescriptive right' is rarely put into practice shows that in the Banks Islands, at any rate, this community of wealth existed more in theory than in customary practice. Cf. also i, 39, 225, 291.

in-law, and a relation-in-law might, if he wished, return a torn net with the scantiest apology, without exceeding his rights."[1] It will be seen that this community of property exists only between members of close kin groups and more particularly between those members whom the classificatory system of relationships recognizes as standing in the closest family relationships, i.e. son and mother's brother. As such, one is justified in speaking of a common participation in the consumption of native wealth among a limited kin group. But this, according to our definition, may not, strictly speaking, be termed 'communism.' It implies that within this kin group individualism is modified by culture patterns which serve to stress the fact that participation in common property strengthens the unity, coherence and mutuality of the primitive family grouping.[2]

I shall return to the Melanesian attitude to wealth in a moment or two. To complete this discussion of communism, however, among Pacific peoples of common cultural development, I may add a brief word about the Polynesians of Samoa. Writing in the early 'eighties of last century, Turner tells us at some considerable length that the member of a

[1] Seligmann: *op. cit.*, 68. Seligmann reports similar customs among the S. Massim, on Waga Waga, and in the Louisades. Cf. this of the Waga Waga: On the occasion of marriage during the *muri* or exchange of presents between the parents of the bride and bridegroom, "a man's wife's sister, whether she be older or younger than his wife, can take anything she likes belonging to her brother-in-law, and however unreasonable she is in this matter, or however severely she damages an article which she has only borrowed, he may make no objection and is supposed not even to grumble; this rule applies strictly to such articles as canoes, fishing nets, house furniture and personal jewellery, but does not apply to garden produce until it has been gathered." Seligmann, 505.

[2] It may perhaps be remarked upon in parenthesis that a certain community of property appears to be correlated with the collective responsibility of the family group among many African tribes at the same or slightly higher culture level as the Melanesians, e.g. among the Bechuana (J. T. Brown: *Among the Bantu Nomads* (1926), 48–49, 53, 60–61), where there is common property between son and maternal uncle (*maloma*); and again among the Ewe (Ellis: *Ewe Speaking Peoples* (1890), 208, ch. xiii, sect. 2, *passim*) and the Yoruba (Ellis: *Yoruba Speaking Peoples* (1894), 177).

tribe or clan had a "latent interest" in all the property of the tribe. "The system of a common interest in each other's property," he writes, "is still clung to by the Samoans with great tenacity. . . . They consider themselves at liberty to take up their abode anywhere among their friends and remain there without charge as long as they please. And the same custom entitles them to beg and borrow from each other to any extent. . . . This communistic system," adds the Victorian moralist, "is a sad hindrance to the industrious and eats like a canker-worm at the roots of individual or national progress. No matter how hard a young man may be disposed to work he cannot keep his earnings; all soon passes out of his hands into the common circulating currency of the clan to which all have a latent right."[1]

Reading this section of Turner's work, one would gain the impression that there existed in Samoa a fairly complete system of communism. Yet elsewhere we are told that there exist numerous classes of taboos, oaths, imprecations and conditional curses which are used to preserve private property.[2] We learn, too, that should divorce occur in the family all the family property is fairly divided between the man and woman; and finally, we are told that, as far back as Turner could remember, the Samoans had well understood laws for the prevention of theft, adultery, assault and murder, together with laws for such minor offences as pulling down a fence or maliciously cutting a fruit tree.[3] These three classes of fact alone would seem to indicate that a complete communism is far from representing a correct account of the culture patterns relative to property.

That this is so becomes at once evident when we compare Turner's work with that of a contemporary investigator like Miss Mead. From the latter's work it appears that each

[1] G. Turner: *Samoa* (1884), 160–161.

[2] Turner: *op. cit.*, 184–187, 276; cf. also J. G. Frazer: *Psyche's Task* (1913), 24–26, ch. iii, *passim*.

[3] Turner: *op. cit.*, 97, 178–179.

village consists of thirty or forty households, each presided over by a headman or *matai*. The composition of these households varies from the biological family group to households of fifteen or twenty people, all related to the *matai* or his wife by blood, marriage or adoption. It is the household, or family group, which is the economic unit of production, distribution and consumption, since in regard to the cultivation of gardens and the catching of fish all members of the group work on the plantations under the supervision of the *matai*, who, in turn, parcels out to them food and other necessities. All the family food for two or three days is cooked together in a circular pot of stones and all partake of the common meal.[1] Further, since such households may not be close residential units, but various members may be scattered over a village, it sometimes happens that family members, children mostly, often change their residence from one household or 'consanguineous refuge' to another.[2] This is perhaps what Turner meant when he stated that Samoans were at liberty to take up their abode anywhere among their friends without payment. They could: but only among closely related household groups.

This degree of community of property within the household group is limited by two other sets of facts. First by the Samoan system of classifying relatives in terms of sex groups. Relatives of opposite sex have a rigid code of etiquette prescribed for all their contacts with each other. Thus strict avoidance of each other applied to all individuals of the opposite sex within five years above or below one's own age with whom one was reared, or to whom one acknowledged blood or marriage relationship. Siblings might not touch each other, walk together, nor on any account use each other's possessions or property. This property was effectually tabooed as their own.[3] Again, within the family group in

[1] Margaret Mead: *Coming of Age in Samoa* (1929), 39, 40, 49–50, 269.
[2] *Ibid.*, 43; cf. ch. iv, *passim*.
[3] *Ibid.*, 44.

general there was no free and easy taking up of another's goods without asking permission. When property was given in response to another's request "careful account of the value of the property given and of the service rendered (was) kept and a return gift demanded at the earliest opportunity. Nevertheless, in native theory, the two acts are separate, each one in turn becoming a 'beggar,' a pensioner upon another's bounty."[1]

The reality of Samoan communism, then, would seem to be this: the loose household group, constituted by the three principles of blood, marriage and adoption, is bound together by common ties of everyday living. This common life involves a certain participation in the production, distribution and consumption of native wealth. Yet this participation is not completely communal since customs relative to taboos, disapproval of theft, and membership of sex groups, indicate the existence of a not inconsiderable amount of private property. And again, within the mutual give and take of the family group—the detailed obligations and duties traditionally required of one member by another—it was always understood that property was more private than common. Property was not borrowed or taken as a matter of course.[2] It was solicited as a favour. Refusal to oblige was not a violation of rights. It merely branded one as lacking in human kindness. Generosity was the virtue most esteemed among the Samoans as among other savage peoples.

Before concluding this chapter I wish to make brief reference

[1] Mead: *op. cit.*, 46.

[2] In olden times the beggar sometimes wore a special girdle which delicately hinted at the cause of his visit." *Ibid.*, 46. For Malinowski's analysis of the mutual obligations involved in Trobriand Society, cf. *Argonauts*, 174–175, and *Crime and Custom, passim*. I have followed Malinowski in supposing that the giving and taking of gifts and services does not obliterate, but on the contrary, enhances, the distinction between 'mine' and 'thine.'

to the prevalent attitude of the Melanesian towards the acquisition of wealth. To a certain degree, of course, this acquisition was put out of court by the fact that there was little individual hoarding of food. Common participation in the consumption of such wealth was the rule rather than the exception. Where, as among the Trobriands, the chiefs store up wealth in yams and other garden produce, this is not so much for the power that wealth gives, but because it is a means of providing abundant hospitality and paying for communal services. There was, second, little individual hoarding of personal ornament. Articles of value like arm-shells or necklaces were usually passed from relative to relative, either in payment of services or because of the customs of the *Kula* exchange. And finally, among some Melanesian peoples, e.g. the Koita, most of each man's possessions were destroyed on his grave at death—and thus each generation started the race of life with a minimum of possessions received from past runners. Family heirlooms, e.g. drums or precious ornaments, could not be used to augment the wealth of any one member of the group. They were usually inalienable and considered, potentially, the common property of the group as a whole.

In spite, however, of these considerations, we find among a Melanesian people like the Banks Islanders, the existence of institutions organized for the acquisition of native wealth. Two such institutions are particularly mentioned by investigators in Melanesia. These are the *sukwe* and the *tamate* societies found on the Banks and New Hebrides groups of islands. The *tamate* society is a club grouping which has two opposed influences upon the acquisition of property. On the one hand, members of the society are allowed to use croton leaf badges to protect their property from other than the members of the society, of which a particular arrangement of leaves is the distinctive sign. Thus a man belonging to a large society would find his badge of little use; but by belonging to many societies, and by combining their badges, a man may be able to protect his property against the rest of the population. One who takes property protected by the badge of a society to which he does not belong is forced to give a pig to the members of the *tamate* he has disregarded. On the other hand, however, there are occasions when *tamate* members arouse themselves to activity and go about the country injuring or destroying property, carrying off to their club-room all they want, robbing gardens, stripping fruit trees and cutting down coconut, breadfruit, or banana palms. Anyone who at any time has spoken or acted without due respect to the society will suffer in this way. *Tamate* members profess to pity such disposed owners, but the latter never complain and act as if they regarded the whole business as a joke.[1]

In both the *sukwe* and the *tamate* societies it is only the rich or those with rich friends who can advance far in the organizations. Thus, from one point of view, both types of grouping are means to the perpetuation and even the accentuation of differences of social rank in so far as this rank is dependent upon the possession of wealth. It is clear, however, that there are other deep-seated co-existing culture patterns active in the organization of society as a whole which prevent wealth from becoming the chief means of social differentiation and which, again, prevent wealth from assuming undue importance in the lives of the people. The manner in which *tamate* clubs periodically destroy village property is a useful check on the laying up of riches

[1] Cf. Codrington: *Melanesians*, 75 *et seq.*, 82–83. Rivers: *Melanesian Society*, i, 92–93, 122–125, 135, 142, etc. Rivers goes on to draw a suggestive analogy between occasions in savage society when at certain festivals there is a general relaxation of the most fundamental laws regulating the sexes—the laws being not only broken, but an excessive degree of relaxation allowed or enjoined—and the occasions when the *tamate* destroy property in a wholesale way; when there is, in fact, a general relaxation of the laws regulating the protection of property in which the *tamate* societies normally take so prominent a part. Rivers: *op. cit.*, i, 142.

and shows that the mere acquisition of wealth among the Melanesians, as among the Pacific Coast Indians, is probably wholly foreign to the patterns of a primitive people. In the *sukwe* clubs, for example, advancement from lower to higher grade can only come about by the payment of money to those who have attained the higher grade and by the giving of a feast more or less costly according to the rank to be attained. Wealth derived from a high position in the *sukwe* is regarded merely as a means to still further advance through the giving of popular *kolekole* feasts. The chief features of this feast are dancing, singing, the killing of pigs and payment to those who participate: "everyone will try to excel his neighbour in the splendour of the dance, the number of the slaughtered pigs and the liberality of payment."[1] A man, however high in the *sukwe*, would suffer social depreciation if he did not undertake social expense. He would be considered unworthy of respect and honour if he hoarded his gains. "To retain his influence and glory he must distribute his money by paying people to work for him in his gardens and by giving splendid *kolekole* performances."[2]

We may say, then, that in Melanesia, as among most other native peoples, the culture patterns of the group override any tendency to abnormal acquisitiveness or the hoarding of wealth. They seem admirably to serve the task of preventing the accumulation of wealth from being changed from means into ends of human activity. Culture patterns lay it down that to possess is to be great, and that, to a limited degree, wealth is the accompaniment and cause of social rank, an attribute of personal virtue. But the important point is that to possess is not to hoard, but to give. The native not unreasonably expects a man who possesses a thing to share it with other members of the group, to be its trustee and not its absolute owner. The higher the rank, the greater

[1] Rivers: *op. cit.*, i, 132; cf. also Codrington: *op. cit.*, 103–107, 110–112.
[2] Rivers: *op. cit.*, i, 141.

this obligation. The chief is expected to give food to any stranger, visitor or even loiterer from another end of the village. The more distinguished members of the *sukwe* club are expected to share their amassed wealth by giving popular dances and feasts to all members of the local unit. The culture patterns emphasize more the conception of wealth for use than that of wealth for power. Though, in Melanesia, a symptom of power is wealth, nevertheless the main symptom of power is generosity. "Meanness indeed is the most despised vice and the only thing about which the natives have strong moral views, while generosity is the essence of goodness."[1]

A backward glance over the contents of this chapter would seem to suggest, therefore, that although it is difficult to find among primitive peoples complete approach to a communistic grouping of society, yet it is equally evident that various factors converge to bring about a fairly equable distribution of wealth within the enlarged family group, the clan, or the tribe. Even in the higher grade agricultural societies, where we first find the phenomena accompanying the differentiation of classes, the rise of nobles and chiefs, we find evidence for the existence of group patterns which stress the social approval of generosity, of giving rather than keeping, and which thus promote equality of wealth. Culture patterns may stress the virtue of liberality; or the glory accruing to the group through temporary possession of *Kula* objects of incalculable value. And human nature does not rebel. It moulds its individualism into conformity with social ways of acting, its sentiments of ownership to group patterns of behaviour. The result is society without abnormal acquisitiveness, without clear-cut communism but co-operative, combining, through its customs, individual initiative with a not unequal distribution of wealth.

[1] Malinowski: *Argonauts*, 97.

TABLE I

TABOOS AND THEFT

	Taboos.		Theft reported and/or punished when committed.		
			A. Within Group.		B. Without Group.
	1. Personal Marks.	2. Magico-Animistic Signs, Curses.	1. Garden Produce, Food, etc.	2. Personal Property.	
Andamans	+		+	+	
Central Australians		+	+	+	—
Eskimo	+		+	+	—
Thlinkeet	No information		+	+	—
Haida	No information		+	+	+
Perak Sakai ..	+	+	+	+	
Keddah Semang ..	+	+	+	+	
Veddah	+			+	
Br. Guiana	+		+	+	+
Toda..	No information		+	+	+

Yakuts	+		+	+	—
Melanesians:					
Banks Is. ..	+	+	+	+	
Mailu	+	+	+	+	
Koita	+	+	+	+	
S. Massim ..	+	+	+	+	
Trobriand ..	+	+	+	+	
D'Entrecasteaux	+	+	+	+	
Kiwais		+	+	+	
Tahiti	+	+	+	+	—
Samoa	+	+	+	+	
Maoris	+	+	+	+	+
Sandwich			+	+	—
Bangala		+	+	+	—
Baganda		+	+	+	—
Kayan, Kenyah ..		+	+	+	+

TABLE II

HOUSES AND CANOES

	A. Houses.			B. Canoes	
	1. Common.	2. Family Houseroom.	3. Family and Individual.	1. Common.	2. Family and Individual.
Andamans	+	+	+		+
Central Australians	Natives purely nomadic		Each family occupies own shelter in temporary camps		
Eskimo	+	+	+ Summer tents		+
Thlinkeet	+	+			+
Haida, Ahts ..	+	+			+
Perak Sakai ..	+	+			
Keddah Semang ..	+	+			
Veddah	+ (caves)	+	+		
Br. Guiana			+		+
Toda..			+		
Yakuts	+	+			
Bageshu			+		

Melanesians:					
Banks Is.			+		+
Pentecost. . ..				+	
Koita			+		+
Mailu Is.				+	+
S. Massim ..			+		
Trobriand ..			+		+
D'Entrecasteaux			+		+
Kiwais			+		+
Tahiti	+ (Meeting-houses)		+	+	+
[8] Samoa	+ (Meeting-houses)		+	+	+
Maoris	+ (Meeting-houses)		+ (Dwelling-houses)	+ (War canoes)	+
Kayan, Kenyah ..	+	+		+ (War canoes)	+
Banyankole. . ..			+		
Bangala			+		
Ewe			+		
Yoruba			+		
Torres Strait, Mabuig			+		+

TABLE III

FOOD

	Production.				Distribution.			
	A. Game, Fish, Cattle.		B. Vegetable.		A. Game.		B. Vegetable.	
	Common.	Family and Individual.	Common.	Family and Individual.	Customary Rules.	Family and Individual.	Customary Rules.	Family and Individual.
Andamans.. ..		+		+		+		+
Central Australians	+	+		+	+		+	
Eskimo	+	+			+	+		
Thlinkeet		+				+		
Haida, Ahts ..		+			+			
Perak Sakai ..		+		+		+		+
Keddah Semang ..		+		+		+		+
Veddah		+		+		+		+
Br. Guiana ..		+		+		+		+
Toda		+ Cattle herds				+ Milk Butter		
Yakuts	+ Herds of Horses	+			+		+	
Bageshu	+			+	+			+

Melanesians:								
Florida Is. ..				+				
Banks Is. ..				+				
Koita				+				+
S. Massim ..	+			+	+			+
Trobriand ..				+				+
D'Entrecasteaux		+		+				+
Kiwais	+	+		+	+			
Tahiti				+				+
Samoa				+				+
Maoris		+		+		+		+
Banyankole ..				+				+
Bangala	+	(Fish) +		+	+	+		+
Baganda	+			+	+			+
Ewe				+				+
Yoruba				+				+
Kayan, Kenyah ..		+		+		+		+
Mailu Mainland ..			+					
Mailu Is.				+				+
Torres Strait ..	+			+	+			

TABLE IV

DISPOSAL OF PROPERTY AT DEATH

Inheritance, Destruction, etc.

People.	Land Held by—		Houses—	
	(1) Family Group.	(2) Individually Owned.	(1) House.	(2) House Site.
Andamans	—	—	Communal houses with family houseroom	—
Central Australians ..	Local tribal group	—	Native purely nomadic	—
Eskimo	,,	—	Communal houses with family houseroom	—
Thlinkeet	,,	—	,,	—
Haida, Ahts ..	,,	—	,,	—
Perak Sakai	—	—	Communal shelters	—
Keddah Semang ..	Family group	—	Private houseroom	—
Veddah	—	B and GC	Communal caves	
British Guiana ..	—	—	Family houses, individual houseroom	—
Toda	Clan lands	—	CR	—
Yakuts	Common access of group to grazing land	CR	CR	—
Bageshu	CR	B	CR	—
Melanesians:—				
Banks Islands ..	CR	CR	CR	CR
Florida	CR	CR	CR	CR
Koita	CR	CR	DM	CR

CR = Customary regulation of inheritance.
B = Right of bequest, of gifts, through death-bed wish.

TABLE IV—*continued*

DISPOSAL OF PROPERTY AT DEATH

Inheritance, Destruction, etc.

Stock, Cattle, etc.	Productive Trees, Palms, etc.	Canoes.	Rights in Fishing, Game Reserves.	Personal Property in— (1) Weapons, Implements, Ornaments.	(2) Dances, Songs, Privileges.	Heirlooms (Family).
Property disposed of by nearest relative. Generally divided among male relatives.						
—	—	—	CR	DM	CR	DM
—	—	CR	—	CR	—	CR
—	—	—	Held by group	—	Right vested in clan group	—
—	—	—	,,	—	—	—
—	B	—	—	CR	—	CR
—	B	—	—	CR	—	CR
—	—	—	B and CG	CR	—	CR
No information						
CR	—	—	—	CR	—	—
B	—	—	—	B	—	B
CR	—	—	—	CR	CR	CR
—	CR	CR + B	—	CR + B	CR	CR
—	CR + B	CR + B	—	CR + B	—	CR + B
—	CR	CR	—	DM	CR	CR

GC = Group consent required to attest legality of such right of bequest.
DM = Material destruction of property at death; usually burnt or broken.

TABLE IV—*continued*

DISPOSAL OF PROPERTY AT DEATH

Inheritance, Destruction, etc.

People.	Land Held by— (1) Family Group.	Land Held by— (2) Individually Owned.	Houses— (1) House.	Houses— (2) House Site.
Southern Massim:—				
Waga Waga ..	CR	CR	DM	CR
Tubetube	CR	CR	—	—
Bartle Bay ..	CR	CR	DM	CR
Louisades	CR	CR	DM	CR
Kiwais	CR	CR	—	—
Trobriand ..	CR	CR	CR	—
D'Entrecasteaux ..	CR	CR	DM	—
Tahiti	B (absolute)		B	B
Samoa	B. By Chief only subject to GC		Family houses CR	— CR
Maori..	CR	CR	CR	—
Banyankole	CR	CR	—	—
Baganda	CR	Right of occupation only from King	—	—
Ewe	CR	All land owned by King	—	—
Yoruba	CR	CR	CR	CR
Kayan, Kenyah, Klemantin	CR	CR	Communal houses. Family house-room. CR (room)	—

CR = Customary regulation of inheritance.
B = Right of bequest, of gifts, through death-bed wish.

TABLE IV—*continued*

DISPOSAL OF PROPERTY AT DEATH

INHERITANCE, DESTRUCTION, ETC.

Stock, Cattle, etc.	Productive Trees, Palms, etc.	Canoes.	Rights in Fishing, Game Reserves.	Personal Property in—		
				(1) Weapons, Implements, Ornaments.	(2) Dances, Songs, Privileges.	Heirlooms (Family).
—	CR	CR	—	CR + B	CR + B	CR
—	—	CR	—	CR	CR	CR
—	CR + B	CR	—	B	CR	CR
—	CR	CR	—	CR + B	CR + B	CR + B
—	—	CR	CR	Part DM, remainder CR	—	CR CR
—	CR	CR	CR	CR	CR	CR
—	DM + B	CR	B	Part DM, remainder B	—	CR
—	B	—	B	B	B	B
—	—	—	—	—	—	—
—	CR	CR + B	CR + B	CR + B	CR + B	CR + B
King nominally owns all herds	—	—	—	Pastorals CR	B + GC CR (Agriculturals)	— CR
CR	—	—	—	CR + B only with clan assent		
CR	—	—	—	CR. All property in theory owned by King		
CR	—	—	—	,,	,,	,,
—	—	CR	CR	CR	CR	CR
		Right of bequest indicated but not specified				

GC = Group consent required to attest legality of such right of bequest.
DM = Material destruction of property at death; usually burnt or broken.

PART III

The child is older than the adult in the sense that its traits existed earlier in the world than those that characterize the mature man or woman. The qualities of the latter were acquired and superposed later and are by long ages younger and more recent. . . . If it be true, as I hold, that the most complete knowledge of anything whatever, and especially of all that is vital, is an exhaustive description of its developmental stages from its origin up to the present, we are still very far from having a science of the soul of man. To this science child study has contributed a new method and new results. At every stage its conclusions must be correlated with those derived from the study of the mind of animals and of primitive people. To develop these three lines of investigation, using the results of each to shed light upon those of the other, is a far harder and more complex process than the mere classification or analysis of the adult consciousness, which is but one cross-section of the mind at only one of its many stages of unfoldment. The latter studies are valuable just as is the anatomy of the adult body, but genetic studies, like these, are the embryology of the soul. They reveal the secrets and processes of its making, show its faculties in perspective and thus bring the manifold elements into proper relations.

G. Stanley Hall

INTRODUCTION

In the previous two parts of this monograph I have discussed in some detail the biological and anthropological approach to our subject. I have been concerned with the nature of property interests in the animal world and have found that most animals tended to defend tenaciously their interests in food, nest or burrow, territory, in their mate and in their young. From the biological point of view I suggested that these objects might be regarded as primitive property values. They were of supreme importance to the animal concerned, not because of the drive of some acquisitive impulse, but because these objects served to satisfy the urge of fundamental needs. In this sense, each instinct is 'acquisitive' to a greater or less degree. 'Hoarding' behaviour in its distinctive sense, where it occurs at all, is found only among one or two orders of the animal world as a specialized development of an impulse to satisfy the need for food.

When I came to consider property values of the Simpler Peoples, I sought principally to show the formation of sentiments of possession about these original, naïve property objects, and the assimilation of secondary values to those of primary interest. It seemed of importance, further, to stress the fact that the organization of property in any social group might best be looked upon as the outcome of the interaction of two forces: one, the psychological make-up of man; the other, the complex culture patterns of that group, themselves the resultant of the complex interweaving of individual invention, historical causation and economic determinism. From this viewpoint it seemed that the drive of public opinion behind established culture patterns was of sufficient strength to mould the plastic stuff of human nature into conformity with group ways of acting, thinking and feeling. This viewpoint also seemed the most fruitful from which to discuss the nature of communism. I endeavoured to show the degree and nature of common ownership among primitive peoples, and the interaction of individualism and communism among peoples at different levels of culture organization.

In this third part of the book, I propose to shift the focus of my enquiry and study, in as brief a compass as possible, the development of property interests in the light of individual psychology. This study would seem to involve a consideration of four interrelated problems. There is to be considered, first, the actual course of the development of property rights as shown by the social behaviour of children in different age groups. In other words, I wish to study the process in child life, just as previously we studied it in the life of savage society, whereby original human nature is patterned by the *mores* of the family or wider social group to form socially acceptable behaviour. Second, and arising out of this first problem, it is of considerable importance for our subject to study the part that the acquisition of property plays in the development of personality. To-day, the statement that property is 'essential to the full development of personality' is, of course, a common phrase. It is a not unnecessary task, therefore, for us to discover what light the study of individual psychology throws upon such a conception as this.

The third problem involves a consideration of that behaviour, common both to children and adults, which is often taken to imply the existence of an instinct of acquisition and which generally finds expression in such collecting activities as, for instance, the collecting of stamps, post-cards, birds' eggs, or first editions. Here I will have an opportunity briefly to note psychoanalytic explanations of such behaviour and of the property interest in general. Finally, it will be relevant to our subject to discuss that apparent disregard for property rights shown in such anti-social practices as kleptomania and pathological stealing, and that heightened interest in property which is characteristic of the avaricious person and of the miser in particular. Here I shall attempt to argue that the explanation of kleptomania in terms of an acquisitive instinct will not accord with the facts of psychology, and that a correct understanding of such pathology is to be found along quite other lines.

It is hardly necessary to discuss in detail the advantages to be derived through a study of property interests from the viewpoint of the psychology of the individual. Child psychology enables us to study behaviour of a relative simplicity, behaviour which is characterized more by impulsiveness than reflection. It thus yields valuable insight into the complexities of general adult behaviour. Secondly, a survey of the relevant aspects of individual psychology will possibly enable us to correct sources of error arising from difficulties of interpretation that tend to weaken arguments drawn from comparative psychology. By bringing together evidence drawn from a study of the child, the adult, and the abnormal individual, one may best hope adequately to support those conclusions regarding the psychology of property to which we have come in previous chapters.

CHAPTER VIII

PROPERTY AND INDIVIDUAL PSYCHOLOGY

I CAN very usefully open my survey of property interests in the light of individual psychology by giving some consideration to the third and fourth problems which I have distinguished in the introduction to this section of my argument. It will be recalled that throughout the preceding chapters I have had occasion to discuss the evidence for the existence of an instinct of acquisition as the basis of property interests. It will be recalled also that my tentative conclusion has been, pending an examination of collecting activities in Man, that the evidence was not such as would justify the postulation of any such instinct as an adequate explanation for such behaviour. The opportunity, therefore, may now be taken to verify tentative conclusions by examining the nature of acquisitiveness and hoarding, both normal and abnormal, in children and adults, and to show how it is possible adequately to explain the facts already known in terms of psychological elements other than those involving appeal to the somewhat nebulous and over-simplified concepts of an acquisitive instinct. I will therefore begin this chapter by a brief survey of the all too few statistical investigations into the nature of collecting activities among children.

Though various references may be found in biographical literature to the fact that the subject of the study was possessed by an innate passion for collecting,[1] nevertheless

[1] Darwin writes of himself at the age of eight, for example: "My taste for natural history and more especially for collecting was well developed. I tried to make out the names of plants and collected all sorts of things, shells, seals, franks, coins and minerals. The passion for collecting which leads a man to be a systematic naturalist, a virtuoso or a miser, was very strong in me, and was clearly innate as none of my sisters or brother ever had this taste." *Life and Letters: Autobiography*, i, 28.

we owe it to Stanley Hall and his school that early surveys were made by quantitative methods of children's collections. In the first volume of the *Pedagogical Seminary* (1891) there is a brief report of data collected from 227 Boston schoolboys of 15 and 16 years. Of these boys, 19, or 8 per cent., never made collections of any sort; 144, or 63 per cent., collected at least two kinds of objects; 95, or 41 per cent., collected three kinds, and 28, or 12 per cent., collected four kinds, of objects. The most common objects of interest to these boys were marbles, stamps and coins.[1]

Up till very recently, however, the classic paper on the subject was based on an investigation by Mrs. C. F. Burk into the collecting habits of 1,214 Californian school-children.[2] Hall's well-known questionnaire method was used in obtaining the facts, and the results may be summarized somewhat as follows. Only 10 per cent. of the boys and 9 per cent. of the girls were not actively engaged in making collections at the time of investigation, while but 3 per cent. of boys and 1 per cent. of girls said they had never made collections of any sort. The children on the average were each making 3–4 collections. Many made more: 12, 13, 14, 15 collections per child were not uncommon. One boy was actively making 55 different collections. Mrs. Burk believed that there were discoverable well-defined age distributions, such that collecting manifested itself at 3 years, developed rapidly from age of 6 onwards, reached its greatest intensity between

[1] Wiltse and Hall: "Children's Collections," *Pedagogical Seminary* (1891), vol. i, 234–235. From these data Hall drew this conclusion: "It seems plain, however, that this instinct (of collecting) is a strong and almost universal force in human nature which the school should study and use more than it does. It is one of the chief juvenile expressions of the instinct on which the induction and specialization of natural sciences rests. Museums of all sorts and sizes, literary collections, and even the gathering of the above data about this instinct, rest on it"—a conclusion which is almost as startling as it is unscientific!

[2] Caroline F. Burk: "The Collecting Instinct," *Ped. Sem.*, vol. vii, 1900. Reprinted in Hall's *Aspects of Child Life and Education* (references to the reprint).

8 and 11 years, with 10 as the optimum age, manifesting an average of 4·4 collections for both boys and girls. From the age of 14 onwards, there is evidence of declining interest in collecting behaviour. Burk gives a list of over three hundred varieties of objects collected. Among the boys, cigar tags, stamps, birds' eggs, marbles and shells were most popular. Among the girls, picture-cards, buttons, cloth, dolls, books, rocks and leaves ranked the highest in interest.[1] Though she devoted attention to the part played by such factors as imitation and fashion, environmental opportunity and rivalry as stimuli to collecting, Burk had no hesitation in postulating an 'instinct of collecting' as the basis on which to explain the facts she brought together.[2]

In the absence of further statistical studies, it has been the practice of most writers on educational psychology to ground their remarks regarding the acquisitive instinct upon this investigation of Mrs. Burk.[3] In 1927, however, another quantitative study of the same subject was made by two American psychologists with five thousand South Kansas children, and the results seem to indicate both that Burk's data are the reverse of conclusive and that her conclusions need largely to be modified in many respects before they can be taken as representing an approximately correct account of the interest children take in making collections.[4] Lehman and Witty observe certain clear evidence of less marked interest in collecting activities among present-day children than was reported by Burk thirty years ago. Their method

[1] Burk: *op. cit.*, 207–216, 222–224. [2] *Ibid.*, 237–238.

[3] Typical accounts are to be found, for example, in Norsworthy and Whitley: *The Psychology of Childhood* (1920), or Kirkpatrick: *Fundamentals of Child Study* (1903), both standard textbooks on educational psychology. A more modern example utilizing much the same material is that of R. M. Ogden: *Psychology and Education* (1927), 59–61; cf. also Thorndike: *Educational Psychology* (1913–1914), i, 53–54, 267–268; and Thorndike: *Notes on Child Study* (1903), 43, 69–72.

[4] Lehman, H. C., and Witty, P. A.: "The Present Status of the Tendency to Hoard," *Psychological Review*, vol. xxxiv, 1927.

enabled the Kansas children, whose ages ranged from 8 to 22 years, to check over a list of play activities which they had voluntarily engaged in during the preceding week. One item in the list referred to collecting behaviour. By allowing for seasonal differences and by contrasting city and country children, these later investigators were able to gather together a large amount of relevant data.

Taking the average result of six investigations, Lehman and Witty find that the percentage of boys who indicated that they had engaged in making collections varied between 10·35 per cent. for 8½-year-olds, 10·69 per cent. for 12½-year-olds, 9·16 per cent. for 13½-year-olds, 2 per cent. for 19½-year-olds, and 0·5 per cent. for youths of 20½ years. With girls the figures were lower still: 4·4 for girls of 8½ years, 5·06 per cent. for those of 12½ years, 3·26 per cent. for 13½-year-olds, 2 per cent. for girls of 19½, and 0·0 per cent. for girls up to 22 years.[1] Further points are of importance. For example, Lehman and Witty could discover no marked interest in stamp collecting; they note that the transition from age group to age group is very gradual, so that they can detect "no age levels at which the interest in collecting and hoarding suddenly increases or decreases by spurts"; and finally, they note that marked seasonal differences are not revealed by the data in regard to the number of persons engaged in these collecting activities.

If now we compare the results of this later investigation with the earlier one of Burk, we discover that whereas Mrs. Burk found at least 90 per cent. of her children actively making collections, Lehman and Witty find that hardly more than 10 per cent. of children are so engaged. Of Burk's boys aged 7–14, more than 40 per cent. collected stamps; of those aged 9–11, more than 60 per cent. collected stamps; of those aged 8–16, more than 15 per cent. collected birds' eggs, while of those aged 12–14, over 30 per cent. did

[1] Lehman and Witty: *op. cit.*, 52.

likewise. Compared with these results, Lehman and Witty's evidence shows that at no age level were as many as 15 per cent. of the boys making collections of any sort whatever.[1] Agreement, however, with Burk is manifested on one point. Mrs. Burk found, it will be recalled, that collecting reaches its maximum intensity among ten-year-old boys. Lehman and Witty find that there is a slightly larger percentage of boys of this age level engaged in making collections; but in so far as they believe that the transition from age to age is very gradual, they emphasize the fact that a difference of one or two per cent. is not enough to justify the common assumption among educationalists and others that age ten is an age of individualism and that ages nine and eleven are to be characterized differently.

The conclusions one may draw from this comparison of earlier and later investigations separated in time by several decades are of quite supreme interest to our thesis. While one regrets the fact that there is not more statistical data to work upon, it is difficult not to conclude that if an instinct of acquisition were part of the innate make-up of the child as the earlier investigators so confidently asserted, working as a permanent factor in the play life of children, then one should expect to find a close correspondence between the incidence of collecting at one decade as compared with another. The comparison of results shows no such correspondence; results are even antagonistic when compared in detail. What, then, becomes of the instinct of acquisition if an instinct is *qua* definition a permanent element in the psychological make-up of similar age levels?

[1] In another paper on "The Play Behaviour of 50 Gifted Children," *Journal of Educational Psychology*, vol. xviii (1927), 259–265, Lehman and Witty emphasize the fact that among these children (I.Q. 140 or above, Stanford Revision Binet Simon Test Rating) there was manifest no noticeable interest in collecting or hoarding. The activities which appealed most to this gifted group were reading, watching sports or going to entertainments. And this result again should be compared with Burk's finding that 90 per cent. of her children actively collected and hoarded.

If we assume for the moment what I shall seek to establish later, the fact, namely, that collecting and hoarding behaviour is best explained as being due to the social patterning of a primitive tendency to obtain possession of those objects which serve to satisfy, directly or indirectly, the fundamental needs of the self, then it is not hard to explain why collecting activities should be prominent at one decade and not so prominent at another. The explanation is not to be found along the lines of far-fetched discussion of the waning and waxing of instinct. It is surely something of this nature: in earlier decades, there were few opportunities to use leisure along lines other than those of a conventionalized collecting, and so sentiments of ownership were formulated about the collecting of objects, standardized in each group, the possession of which brought power and a certain extension of personality. Present-day conditions, however, it may be suggested, present opportunities to use leisure which are more attractive to young people than are collecting and hoarding. Among certain sections of the social group, old-fashioned collecting activities will persist for a variety of reasons, and will be enforced by local practices and procedures. But where attendance at the cinema or the theatre is in vogue, or where dancing or listening to the wireless attracts modern youth, quite a different set of activities and interests are formed. Social patterning of youthful activities goes on from decade to decade. Owing to historical causation or scientific accident various diversions hold the field at any particular decade. Youthful activity finds an outlet in those amusements which appeal to its "time spirit."

The point I would try to emphasize is this: that deductions based upon studies of children's interests and inferences drawn therefrom as to the nature of the inherited equipment of man need to be made, if at all, with considerable caution just because such interests are often merely temporary ones. Both children and adults, for example, displayed much interest in cross-word puzzles during the winter of 1923–1924. Yet it would hardly be scientific to base on this datum inferences as to a possible specific instinctive foundation for such an interest. Conclusions would be applicable only to the time at which the study was made; and this would rule out of court appeal to specific innate postulated psychological elements in any attempt to explain such interests. The parallel with respect to collecting and hoarding activities is obvious. It is time definite use were made of Occam's Razor.

Before we proceed to consider in more detail other explanations of collecting behaviour, it is perhaps not inopportune here to make reference to a type of behaviour which is often taken to imply the abnormal or pathological manifestation of an instinct of acquisition, e.g. kleptomania, or pathological stealing and miserliness. A good example of the way some writers on the subject refer kleptomania to an acquisitive instinct is furnished by a leading American medical authority on nervous diseases. Quackenbos, discussing "Kleptomania, Causes and Treatment," urges us in all seriousness to seek its causation "in atavism, or reversion to ancestral chaos—the transmission of a predatory instinct from remote forebears through many intervening generations, to be revived from past centuries in an inexplicable manner as an earmark of plundering proclivities that were once normally human."[1] The same writer was able in 1918 to diagnose the Kaiser as suffering from an "inbred tendency to larceny, motivated by an inexpugnable passion for conquest."[2] Even such a cautious scientist as Rivers is not entirely free from suspicion in this respect. Thus he writes that "the most striking evidence in favour of the instinct of acquisition as part of Man's mental endowment is derived from patho-

[1] J. D. Quackenbos: "Kleptomania, Causes and Treatment," *Alienist and Neurologist* (1918), vol. xxxix, 230.

[2] *Ibid.*, 231.

logy. A leading feature of many psychoses is an impulse to collect, apparently with little, if any, regard for the nature or value of the objects collected. . . . Another pathological state which points in the same direction is the impulse to acquire which is known as kleptomania. This term probably denotes several different states or processes, but there seems to be little doubt that prominent among these is one in which a person has an uncontrollable impulse to acquire anything of value which comes within the purview of his senses. The various social factors through which such impulses are normally controlled are wholly insufficient to prevent these impulses from going on to action."[1] Finally, it may be remarked that even Burt's treatment of the problem in his volume on *The Young Delinquent* is sometimes not as clear as is to be expected from such an acknowledged authority on the subject.[2]

In opposition to the line of thought followed out by the above writers, we would suggest that almost the whole of the modern study of child and adult delinquency seems to point to the conclusion that the motivations of stealing and kleptomania are infinitely complex, and that it is a false

[1] W. H. R. Rivers: *Instinct and the Unconscious*, 266–267.

[2] Cf. Burt: *The Young Delinquent*, 450, where we are first told that an instinct of acquisition activates the commonest of human crime, e.g. stealing; and next that this is to over-simplify the case, since Burt finds that only 1·6 per cent. of his cases of stealing are due to "sheer inborn acquisitiveness"—whatever this is. Further down the same page Burt appears to recognize that his instinct is no more than a "mere automatic movement," yet in the next sentence he speaks of having one instinct working in the service of another, such that the child steals to satisfy an instinctive hunger, an instinctive resentment, an instinctive vanity. Burt finally aligns himself with Healy in recognizing that stealing is "a substitute reaction for some other impulse barred, baulked or suddenly frustrated," not an instinct itself, but an outlet for the banked-up energy of a baulked disposition (Burt: *op. cit.*, 450–451, 589–594, etc.). Burt apparently holds that the specific emotion correlated in the McDougall sense with his acquisitive instinct is an "avaricious thrill" (*Ibid.* 449). It is a pity that such an acute writer as Burt should become so confused through his uncritical acceptance of the McDougall instinct scheme.

simplicity which would reduce this complex motivation to the activity of one specific impulse. In point of fact, stealing seems to be the 'substitute' solution for mental conflict and its causes are to be found among the manifold elements that enter into such conflicts. It is the vice of the ownerless only because a lack of property means a starved and frustrated personality. When the personality is suffering from emotional conflict, stealing may very well become the besetting vice of the Man of Property as well.

We may follow up this point of view a little further by considering, first, some of the mental conflicts that give rise to stealing among children. A very interesting case of stealing due to scholastic inferiority leading to envy and jealousy of schoolmates is given by Burt. Martin G., a boy of 15½ years, in less than six months stole fifty-six pairs of spectacles. On analysis it transpired that the boy was jealous of his friends. He began to hide the spectacles of the studious myopes in his class, and finally stole money in order to buy spectacles for himself, as if the wearing of "the externals of those superior to him in work would somehow confer their ability."[1] Again, stealing may be due to unconscious motives arising from a general thwarting of personality. This is liable to occur not infrequently with children living in institutions or in orphanages and more particularly with the oncoming of adolescence.[2] But, indeed, stealing and delinquency is likely to characterize most children who receive no emotional or imaginative satisfaction, children of homes where parents are concerned not so much with living as with making a living, and where the children, in conse-

[1] Burt: *op. cit.*, 183–185. Another boy's obsession with spectacles was due to a different conflict. In this latter case the boy laboured under the impression that the fact that he practised masturbation was clearly visible in his face to those who looked closely. Hence the deprivation of his neighbours of their spectacles. Gordon: *Autolycus: or the Future of Miscreant Youth*, 18.

[2] Burt: *op. cit.*, 561; cf. also Tracy: *The Psychology of Adolescence* (1920), 167–168, 173–175.

quence, lack any sort of colourful experience and are prematurely encased in brick and stone. Routine is both dull and monotonous, need for adventure is not met. Or again, these children receive no attention, approval, affection, or the chance to win social esteem—all of them sources of the growth of personality. Such children, 'angering' for life, sublimate their energies in anti-social conduct.[1] Gordon gives an illustrative case. A girl, daughter of a gay, pleasure-loving woman, was brought up by an austere aunt, who never allowed her personal adornment of any sort, kept her as plainly dressed as possible and rarely lavished any affection upon the child. The girl went to a boarding school, where she was discovered stealing small sums of money, which were spent on ribbons and cheap jewellery to deck herself with in secret.[2]

Further fruitful sources of conflict giving rise to stealing are to be found in homes where there are veiled, but none the less real, struggles and antagonisms between the two parents, between the interests of the child and the adult, between parents and adolescent boys and girls.[3] The one motivation, however, which psychology has brought to light and which seems of overwhelming importance in giving rise to stealing, other delinquency, and kleptomania, is conflict due to obtaining forbidden knowledge on sex subjects. Healy gives numerous case studies which indicate fairly conclusively that stealing is very often due to that mental conflict which arises when newly gained sex knowledge clashes with conventional standards. There is a resulting depression because energy is locked up in the conflict. The individual obtains relief and at the same time excitement

[1] Van Waters, *Youth in Conflict* (1926), discusses this problem in some detail, 41–42, 51 ff. Cf. also Stanley Hall: *Educational Problems*, i, 255–257; Drummond: *Child Psychology* (1923), 137, and in general, appendix B, *Criminality in Children*, 383–387, of Havelock Ellis' study of *The Criminal*, 3rd ed., London (1901).

[2] Gordon: *op. cit.*, 16.

[3] Van Waters: *op. cit.*, 55 ff.

and interest by entering upon misdeeds which seem altogether less unworthy and reprehensible than gaining experience in the manner inwardly brooded over. "The child," writes Burt, "half automatically, half from a conscious horror, seems to be shunning what he considers the greater sin and indulging—by way of a distraction or a relief—in some lesser criminality, in some venial but forcible counterblast which opens up a channel of discharge. . . . Generally, through a connection unknown to the delinquent, through some blind filament within the brain, the substituted act is remotely linked to the original temptation."[1]

The type of stealing where the delinquent is more or less aware of the nature of his act and values the objects he steals is closely related from this point of view with sexual fetichism, on the one hand, and sexually motivated kleptomania, on the other hand. In obsessive cases of sexual fetichism the patient is impelled to the possession and repeated contemplation of some fetich object, or object charged with abnormal emotional excitement. Thus we find in the literature on the subject a workman who steals shoes, the cobbler who steals nightcaps, garters and underclothes, and a labourer who steals women's handkerchiefs.[2] Kleptomania, or pathological stealing, as Healy prefers to call it, is indulged in for its own sake and not because the objects stolen are needed or intrinsically desired. Where such pathological stealing is not the outcome of a genuine manic state it is almost invariably the expression of repressed wishes, or a substitute relief for inner conflict over sex matters. The objects thus

[1] Burt: *op. cit.*, 559. For a full discussion, reference should be made to Healy's work on this subject, e.g. Healy: *The Young Delinquent* (1925), ch. x, *passim*; *Mental Conflict and Misconduct* (1919), chs. x and xi; *Honesty*, etc. (1915), ch. ix, 120–159.

[2] Healy: *The Young Delinquent*, 405; Stekel: "Sexual Root of Kleptomania," in *Journal American Institute of Criminal Law* (1911), vol. ii, 241–242; Kiernan: "Kleptomania and Pyromania," *Alien and Neurologist* (1912), vol. xxxiii, 379 ff; Abraham: *Selected Papers*, ch. v, 125–136; McDougall, *Abnormal Psychology*, 321–322.

blindly stolen may either possess important associative value for the stealer, or stand as symbolic representations of what the patient desires rather than being actually the thing coveted, or else the objects have no symbolic value nor any important associative value, but are merely the first objects haphazardly stolen when excited sexual energy is diverted into channels of activity which end in stealing.[1]

I think this brief consideration of the light modern psychology throws upon the nature of stealing is sufficient for the purpose I have in mind. It is no more, of course, than an inadequate summary of a fascinating aspect of anti-social behaviour. But it clearly reveals my main point. At the risk of repetition I would once again stress this by suggesting that abnormal psychology, the psychology of neurosis and of pathological stealing, of conflict and its solution, can tell us nothing of the abnormal manifestations of an acquisitive instinct. Behaviour which on the surface seems due to an acquisitive impulse proves on closer analysis to

[1] The references to the subject of kleptomania are fairly scattered. See, however, Healy, the papers of Stekel, Kiernan, Quackenbos already referred to; also White: *Mechanisms of Character Formation* (1916), 198; Kempf: *Psychopathology* (1921), 641, 730–731; Abraham: *op. cit.*, 484–485; and a paper by Chadwick: "A Case of Kleptomania in a Girl of Ten Years," *Int. Journ. of Psychoanalysis* (1925), vol. vi, 300–312; Chadwick: *Difficulties in Child Development* (1928), 43, 366. Freudian literature abounds in references to collecting manias where the objects collected are sexual symbols according to Freudian interpretation. See Brill: *Psychoanalysis*, 3rd ed. (1922), 68–73; Pfister: *Psychoanalytic Method* (1927), 76–77. The psychology of stealing from departmental stores and bargain stores at sale time or at ordinary times deserves special study in any consideration of stealing. Bargain-store temptations seem to make special appeal to pregnant, climacteric or menstruating women. There is always the temptation of sudden impulse even to otherwise normal women. And the various factors discussed in the text must be taken into account before we have a complete understanding of this anti-social behaviour. Cf. Kiernan: *op. cit.*, 148 ff.; Stekel: *op. cit.*, 239–246; Ellis: *op. cit.*, 19–20, and an early reference in Griesinger to kleptomania: *Mental Pathology and Therapeutics* (1867), 293–294. The erotic element in stealing, the voluptuous titillation that fright and worry over detection give to women who plan more systematic thefts, Kiernan terms *Kleptolagnia*. Kiernan: *Alien and Neurologist* (1916), vol. xxxvii, 252.

have its roots far down in disorders of personality. Kleptomania, in fact, in the majority of cases, is an attempt to find relief from an intolerable mental conflict. It is unfortunate for the patient that this behaviour should be frowned upon socially. But psychologically, the relief mechanism serves the same purpose for the time being as the numerous other methods, some social, others anti-social, by which neurotics seek a substitute gratification for the burden of the conflict which is being fought out on subconscious battlefields.

We have so far in this chapter been content to set forth the facts about collecting as brought to light by a consideration of statistical enquiries and, second, by a discussion of stealing and kleptomania. The position we have now reached is that, while neither of these two lines of investigation supports the postulation of an instinct of acquisition (and thus they bear out tentative views formulated after our study of comparative psychology), nevertheless quantitative methods merely supplement everyday observation by bringing to our notice the fact that collecting behaviour is very common among the ordinary activities of child and adult. If we reject an explanation of these activities in terms of an acquisitive impulse, it seems that there is an onus on us to advance an explanation which shall build on known elements of human nature a psychological structure which is both more logical and more pragmatically satisfying than the theory we dismiss. In the remainder of this chapter, then, we shall consider two theories that may be advanced to explain man's interest in possession and in collecting.

In the interests of clarity it is of importance to consider, first, the Freudian explanation of collecting behaviour. In this, as in other fields of individual and social activity, Freudian theory has been extremely fertile when applied to the realms of social dynamics; and if an ultimate verdict is

Not Proven, at least one pays tribute to the ingeniousness with which the theory is worked out, the comprehensiveness of its scope and the pertinacity of its application. One may sometimes regret the absence of a sense of proportion in its exponents; but at least one will be sufficiently interested in its conclusions to keep watch for facts that may at some later date finally prove or disprove the theory.

In its essentials the Freudian theory would suggest that all interest in money, or in property of any sort, and all interest in collecting activities is to be derived from the elemental interest of the child in the products of its own body. Through the dual process of organic and social repression, this primitive interest of the child in bodily functions, their organs and products, is changed in the course of growth, and by the development of the libido, into the mature interests of the adult in money and other symbols of power. The evidence for this theory Freudians draw not only from analysis of children and adults, both normal and abnormal, but also from folk-lore; so that Freud can write: "In reality, wherever archaic modes of thought predominate, or have persisted—in ancient civilizations, in myth, fairy-tale and superstition, in unconscious thoughts and dreams, and in the neurosis—money comes into the closest relation with excrement."[1]

With this bald summary before us let us now consider the theory in a little more detail. Freud and his disciples regard the fact as well established that although the normal adult regards excrement as unpleasant to sense perception, and invests it with a negative feeling-attitude of disgust as for something unclean, nevertheless in the nursery this attitude is entirely reversed. Excreta arouse no aversion in the child; they seem precious to him as being part of his own body,

[1] Freud: *Collected Works*, ii, 49; cf. also his *Introductory Lectures on Psycho-analysis* (1922), 265–266.

though detached from him, yet all the time invested by that feeling of possessive animism with a strong sense of value and of interest, hardly less intense for a time than interest in eating and drinking. The child, that is, delights to contemplate his excrement, to take an affectionate interest in playing with it, and occasionally to regard bodily products as a love-offering, something given up to please the loved person.[1] In Freudian terminology, at the earlier and later anal sadistic stages of the development of the libido, there is a turning of the energy of psycho-sexual organization upon the excreta and a consequent narcissistic estimation of its value. It is urged further in support of this view that in various types of mental illness, and notably with hebephrenic dissociated personalities, where there is a process of repression, the individual shows a marked interest in faeces, even a desire to return to that later oral stage of libido development which is characterized by the aim of faeces-eating.[2]

The child is interested in the bodily product. He is also interested in the bodily functions themselves, because from them, as from his mouth, he obtains primitive pleasures and his first sense of power. Yet before long a social pressure is brought to bear on him which seeks to set up standards of cleanliness and so, by a process of education, to reverse the

[1] Klein: "Development of a Child," *International Journal of Psycho-analysis* (1923), vol. iv, 428–431; cf. also Chadwick: *Difficulties*, 185; Menzies: *Auto-Erotic Phenomena* (1921), 19–20, 27–30; Thom: *Everyday Problems of the Everyday Child* (1927), 102; Ellis: *Psychology of Sex*, v, 53–54; Hall: "Early Sense of the Self," *Amer. J. of Psychology* (1898), vol. ix, *passim*, also Hall: *Adolescence*, i, 116.

[2] Abraham: *Selected Papers*, 491–492, 495–497; Kempf: *Psychopathology*, 641 f., 662 ff; White: *Mechanisms*, 104. It is of interest to recall that Koehler observed among his apes an ambivalent attitude towards excrement. The apes were disgusted if by chance they came into accidental contact with faeces; filth on the surface of their body seemed to them a source of acute discomfort and was carefully removed with rag, straw, twigs, but never with the hand. Yet these same animals were all addicted to coprophagy and persisted in this habit in spite of punishment. Koehler: *op. cit.*, 6, 80–81, 96, 298.

primitive attitude of delight into one of disgust.[1] In adapting himself to the demands of education, the child for a space may resent efforts that are made to rob him of the massive pleasure of bowel movement. He may set up his own will in opposition to parents and educators and endeavour to retain individual control of his excreta as long as possible. It is from this desire of the child to control his own excretions that the Freudians would derive the various anal character traits, such as miserliness, economy, procrastination, obstinacy, and fear of losing possessions.

From this brief exposition it will be seen that Freud would consider it established that interest in money and other property, and interest in collecting, have a dual basis in the child's interest in the act of defaecation and in his further interest in the product of this act. In the course of growth, these two primary interests are so acted upon by factors of repression that the anal character traits are developed and alongside them adult interest in money. Fundamentally, however, the psychoanalysts suggest that the prototype of the tendency of the collector to gloat over his stamps, over his mental creations, his letters, his manuscripts, over his money and other wealth, is to be found in the tendency to contemplate excreta, "an ever new source of pleasure to many people and in some neurotics a form of psychical compulsion." This fact of libidinal over-emphasis upon the possession of faeces explains the difficulty, thinks Abraham, that certain people have in separating themselves from objects when these have no practical use nor monetary value. Such people collect all sorts of broken rubbish in

[1] In his latest book, *Civilization and its Discontents*, Freud emphasises the importance of what he terms organic repression in facilitating this education. When man became erect there was a twofold organic repression, one of olfactory stimuli in favour of visual as a means of producing sexual excitement and the other reversed a presumed primitive interest in strong excremental odours, p. 66 note 1. In its present form, however, the doctrine appears somewhat obscure.

attics, bits of paper, worn-out nibs, and other objects of no intrinsic value and seem incapable of getting rid of them. Then, on some particular occasion, they will get rid of the whole collection at once. "Their pleasure in having a mass of material stored up entirely corresponds to pleasure in the retention of faeces. We find in this case that the removal (evacuation) of the material is delayed as long as possible."[1]

As in all other character formations, Freudians trace ambivalent attitudes to anal erotism. Parsimony may exist alongside extravagance, procrastination along with extreme irritability and rashness of decision. Yet in sum, "all collectors," says Jones, "are anal erotics and the objects collected are nearly always typical copro-symbols: thus money, coins (apart from current ones), stamps, eggs, butterflies—these two being associated with the idea of babies—books, and even worthless things like pins, old newspapers, etc. In the same connection may be mentioned the joy in finding or picking up objects of the same sort, pins, coins, etc., and the interest in the discovery of treasure-trove."[2]

[1] Abraham: *op. cit.*, 385. On an earlier page Abraham gives a case in which "the connection between intentional retention of faeces and systematic parsimony is perfectly clear." It is that of a rich banker who "impressed on his children that they should retain the contents of the bowels as long as possible in order to get the benefit of every bit of expensive food they ate." Other examples of anal erotic parsimony are spending money on piano scores but not on concerts; neglecting to do up buttons in order not to wear out button-holes, *op. cit.*, 383–384, 387–388.

[2] Ernest Jones: *Papers on Psychoanalysis*, 3rd ed. (1923), 697. White has this very clear summary of the Freudian position: "One of the ways of securing and embracing the pleasure associated with the movement of the bowels is by retaining the faeces and so increasing the massiveness of the pleasurable results. The anal erotic is therefore characteristically constipated. This tendency to retain and accumulate is extended, and if well sublimated shows itself in economy, tendencies to collect, for example, to make art collections, collection of books, and in many other more or less useful ways. When not so well sublimated the tendency is towards penuriousness, avariciousness, miserliness and the collection of useless things." *Mechanisms of Character Formation*, 201–202. Cf. also Brill: *op. cit.*, 392–395; Coriat: "Note on the Anal Character Traits of the Capitalistic Instinct," *Psychoanalytic Review* (1924), 435–437.

So much for the anal erotism of collectors. It is of interest now to trace the stages involved in the Freudian formulation of the ontogenesis of interest in money. The first two stages are those we have already considered, i.e. childish interest in holding back excrement, and displacement of libido from organs on to the material which causes pleasure with consequent valuing of the excrement itself. Stage three involves the weaning away of childish interest in the name of cleanliness. The smell of excrement becomes disagreeable and disgusting (Freud's 'organic repression'), but since other attributes do not offend, the child plays with street mud, which is, in fact, deodorized dejecta. As the child's sense of cleanliness increases, even street mud becomes objectionable, so that the symbol of filth undergoes dehydration and the child plays happily with clean, dry sand. There is a regression to earlier stages, however, when the child mixes water with sand, or shows a liking for sticky materials with a characteristic odour, i.e. nail dirt or ear-wax. At this stage also, there is delight in moulding putty and bitumen, delight in the smell of gas and turpentine. Stages five and six complete this increasing detachment from playing with earthy things. Sand is unacceptable, so that the age of collecting pebbles, marbles, buttons, fruit pips, arrives. Soon, however, even stones begin to wound the child's feeling of cleanliness—he longs for something purer—and this is offered to him in the shining pieces of money, the high appreciation of which is naturally also in part due to the respect in which they are held by adults as well as to the seductive possibilities of obtaining through them everything that the child's heart can desire. Originally, however, it is not the purely practical considerations that are operative, enjoyment in the playful collecting, heaping up and gazing at the shining metal pieces being the chief thing, so that these are treasured even less for their economic value than for their value as pleasure-giving objects. The eye takes pleasure at the sight of the lustre and colour of coins, the ear at their metallic clink, the sense of touch at play with the smooth round discs. This is the main outline of the development of the money symbol. Pleasure in the contents of the intestines has become pleasure in what is nothing more than odourless, dehydrated filth that has been made shiny, portable, and economically valuable. At a further stage of development, corresponding with the growth of adult rationality, symbolic interest may be transferred to things in any way signifying value or possession—paper money or share certificates, for instance. But whatever form may be assumed by money, the enjoyment at possessing it has its deepest and amplest source in coprophilia. "The ontogenetic development of interest in money . . . while showing individual differences dependent upon the conditions of life, is nevertheless on the whole among civilized peoples to be regarded as a psychical process which seeks realization under the most diverse circumstances in one way or another."[1]

It is not possible adequately to criticize such a theory as we have just outlined within the limits of this chapter. It has such close connections with the general body of Freudian theory that any searching criticism would find it necessary to come to terms first with psychoanalytic doctrine as a whole before it could proceed to treat in detail the theory of anal-

[1] Ferenczi: *Contributions to Psychoanalysis* (Eng. trans., 1916), 279. I have summarized in this paragraph Ferenczi's interesting paper on "The Ontogenesis of Interest in Money." Cf. also Eder: "Psychoanalysis in Politics," in *Social Aspects of Psychoanalysis* (1924), 161–165; Jones: *op. cit.*, 638–639, 691–694. Jones even goes so far as to suggest that besides this interest in money, pleasure at manipulation of clay or plasticene, the setting up of printers' type, the development of photographic plates and cooking, "are all equivalent in the unconscious and are derivations of precisely the same primitive interest (in coprophilia)," *op. cit.*, 639. One searches Jones' pages in vain, however, for evidence to support such sweeping assertions. Other analysts hold that the relation of money to anal erotism is determined more particularly "by the association of the least valuable with the most valuable"—White: *op. cit.*, 201–202, 203 ff.—though why there should be formed this association we are not told.

erotic character traits and the theory of copro-symbolism. It would be necessary to raise, that is, the whole question of the value to be attached to evidence drawn from the psychoanalysis of very young children; and this problem, again, is related to problems of memory, of suggestion and personal influence, of infantile sexuality, primary sensory experience, of infantile curiosity, of interpretation of infantile phantasy, and of the nature of the wider theory of symbolism —and to raise such contentious questions as these is to involve one in almost endless dispute.

It may be suggested, however, that criticism like that of McDougall, when he speaks of the annexation of the acquisitive impulse to the sex instincts as involving "a remarkable display of perverted ingenuity" or of the Freudian 'assumption' that the child likes to play with his excreta as "strange and insubstantial," is quite out of court.[1] The time is long past when one could treat of analytic doctrine in terms of pure facetiousness or of unmitigated contempt, according to temperament or training. It must be recognized to-day, I think, that Freudian theory deserves to be treated as a serious contribution to the solution of some of the major problems of general psychology.

From this point of view, three aspects of the analytic theory of property demand consideration. These are, first, the degree to which children are interested in excrement; second, the derivation of various character traits from childish desire to control the evacuation of such excrement; and third, the nature of the scientific method displayed by psychoanalysts in drawing inferences from alleged facts.[2]

[1] McDougall: *Abnormal Psychology*, 163, note 2.

[2] For a consideration of wider aspects of criticism of Freudian theory, especially as applied to children, see Stern: *Psychology of Early Childhood* (Eng. trans., 1924), 281–282, 468–470, 511, etc. Mrs. Isaacs, however, writing on "The Function of the School for the Young Child," *Forum of Education* (vol. v, 1927), urges the fact that Stern's observations "are without value as negative evidence on any question of the native interests and innate trends of the child," 117. Reference should also be made to

It does not as yet seem absolutely established that children are interested in excrement. What is lacking here is a general body of observations upon the free-play activities of very young children and a close study of their interests and plays in an attempt to test Freudian theory. In the absence of such observation it may be apposite to recall here the fact that James was able to list among his instincts an instinct of cleanliness, marked by repugnance at "excrementitious and putrid things, blood, pus, entrails and diseased tissue."[1] Thorndike also speaks of 'original annoyers' or instinctive aversions, and among these he classes excrement.[2] Finally it may be remembered that Koehler's apes displayed an ambivalent attitude towards filth; and it is at least arguable that with these animals aversion to filth on the body is just as primitive and original a part of their nature as coprophagy—arguable, I mean, until further evidence is produced to show that one or other of these attitudes is not innate.[3] With young infants, again, it seems to be the rule that contact of excrement on the skin, when the child is wrapped in diapers, is a cause of considerable unpleasantness to the child. Even if, therefore, the infant is at first neutral in regard to excrement, it is not unlikely that it would rapidly become negatively conditioned to such an object after the repetition of unpleasant experiences. Further, the education of the young child in habits of cleanliness proceeds so rapidly after the first stirrings of self-consciousness that it is difficult to imagine the normal child being interested to any vital degree in his own faeces. These objections, however, would not stand if the analysts

Gordon: *The Neurotic Personality* (1927), 52–58, 62–64, for further criticism of Freud. MacCurdy's *Principles of Dynamic Psychology* is an interesting attempt to reformulate many of Freud's theories in the light of biology and psychiatry; while Wohlgemuth's *Critical Examination of Psycho-Analysis* represents the reaction of the more extreme experimental critic.

[1] James: *Principles*, ii, 434.

[2] Thorndike: *Educational Psychology*, i, 123.

[3] Abraham: *Selected Papers*, 491–492, 495–497, and Koehler: *op. cit.*, 80–81.

could produce irrefutable evidence of childish interest in, and valuing of, excreta. One must wait for this evidence before making a decision either way.

In regard to the derivation of character traits from anal erotism, one may perhaps understand how an emotional habit symbolizing interest in anal erotism may be present in later life as an overt expression of what is still active in the unconscious. Thus a child might develop habits of hoarding from struggle with his nurse to retain his faeces longer than she wishes. And when thrift becomes miserliness, it is not improbable that anal symbolism is invading consciousness. If the child, further, had no conflicts or contests with the adults who try to rear him other than those arising from his habits of defaecation, one could also understand stubbornness arising in the same manner as thrift. "But," remarks MacCurdy, "it would be a rare nursery that staged conflicts over just this one difference. The child is wilful and wants his way over many things, and consequently there is little *a priori* ground for expecting a rigid correlation between anal erotism and stubbornness; and so it is with the other characters which make up the general picture of egotism."[1]

Again, it may be argued that a coincidence of unconscious ideas does not necessarily imply immediate causal relationships between them. And so, although people with strong auto-erotic survival tendencies may show considerable evidence of unconscious anal erotism, nevertheless, until one can prove by observation of the child or by a clear case history the causal correlation of general anti-social characteristics with isolated anal erotism, it is just as logical to assign the genesis of these characters to auto-erotism in general or to a regression of the emotional attitude of the infant at the auto-erotic stage. MacCurdy urges that actual

[1] MacCurdy: *Principles of Dynamic Psychology,* 183. I have followed MacCurdy's argument in the next two paragraphs also.

observation of children shows that they may have no real irregularity and no greater interest in bowel function than in any other function or region of the body and yet show the general characteristics of the spoilt child. Such children, however, may not be free from other auto-erotic tendencies.[1]

In an attempt to criticize the Freudian assumption that gold is a faecal symbol, MacCurdy examined the nature of the property ideas of patients suffering from involution melancholia. He was able to show that out of the 67 cases he examined, delusions of poverty were coincident with anal erotism 11 times, with other auto-erotism 3 times, with no auto-erotism at all 14 times. This would certainly indicate that other types of unconscious interest may determine interest in property. "In two cases these delusions existed with an isolated anal erotism, and in one of them the evidence was strong for a causal relationship between them. Complaints of poverty disappeared as soon as the anal erotism appeared."[2] If, then, one is prepared to argue along these lines, it seems that anti-social behaviour should be derived not so much from anal erotism, but from looser associations with auto-erotism in general. Here again, however, evidence is not conclusive either way and judgment remains very much a matter of opinion.

Finally, it seems a not unreasonable criticism to suggest that Freudian argument would carry more conviction if Freudians themselves would use a more rigid scientific method than they at present display when it comes to the point of drawing inferences from the facts they bring to light. When, for instance, Abraham discusses the nature of infantile sexuality and its concomitant anal erotism, one obtains regrettably little information about the 'child' to whom his statements refer. Thus we are told that his excretions are, to the child, a "sign of enormous power"; or that

[1] MacCurdy: *op. cit.*, 184.

[2] Cf. MacCurdy, 185–186.

the child's pride in evacuation gives "a primitive feeling of power."[1] Yet the age of the 'child' whom Abraham is discussing is never explicitly stated; and we are left in the dark as to whether or no his statements are meant to have reference to a 'child' mentioned in previous pages[2]—obviously an infant excreting into diapers with hardly as yet the germs of self-consciousness—or to some other 'child' of more mature psychological development. Again, one is told that the 'child' places a supreme value upon the excreted products of his own body. Abraham supports this contention by the instance of an infant handed round the family circle and electing to wet a particular person with its urine. "This act," says Abraham, "is one of the most primitive marks of love and is far more primary than kissing or embracing, which the child learns only through imitation."[3] Maybe it is. But before one could be certain of this interpretation of the act as the giving of a supreme gift, it is surely of obvious importance to rule out other interpretations of such behaviour, e.g. that the micturition is due to unusual excitement, or the fear of unknown people, or to the automatic and uncontrolled opening of the sphincters in the course of physiological rhythm, since the infant is so young that it is not yet able voluntarily to control its excretions. One looks in vain for this elimination, by process or reasoning, of rival explanations of the child's behaviour. One is conscious throughout all one's reading of Freudian literature that a more vigorous use of a scientific method should at least have made a Freudian think a second time before he elaborated some far-fetched hypothesis. Surely, from this point of view, the Freudian has only himself to blame if his arguments meet with scepticism when he demands conviction, and reserved judgment when he is anxious to persuade. His treatment of some of the problems of child psychology is no exception to this rule. To be swept away by the

[1] Abraham: *op. cit.*, 374. [2] *Ibid.*, 372. [3] *Ibid.*, 291–292.

intoxication of a theory may be human, but unfortunately, it is not science.

We have been considering so far the Freudian explanation of collecting behaviour, and we have put it aside as definitely not yet proven. We may conclude this chapter therefore by bringing forward an explanation which builds upon a psychological foundation and which seems adequately to account for acquisitive activities. In terms of this theory, acquisitiveness is a habit complex resulting from an impulse to grasp those objects of interest to us in our environment which satisfy fundamental needs, the objects we collect being determined by our dominant root-interests as moulded by the prevailing culture patterns of our social group.

We may elaborate this theory more fully by considering first the nature of the grasping impulse. The study of the psychology of the immature infant renders it abundantly clear, I think, that one of the most important innate impulses of the child is the desire to grasp and to touch any large object which attracts attention and interest through the operation of fundamental needs, but which at the same time does not possess frightening, repelling, or disgusting features. Just as the jackdaw of an earlier page is attracted by bright peckable objects of its environment and endeavours to obtain them with its beak, so does the young child desire to grasp objects which arouse its native curiosity. When an object is grasped there is a further response to put it in the mouth, and, in general, to manipulate it and explore its surfaces. The sight of another human being reaching for the object or busied with it strengthens the tendencies towards possession. This process is the same throughout the whole animal kingdom, and the examples given on earlier pages will at once be recalled to mind. With the infant, again, whenever possession is resisted, the response is pulling and twisting the object, at the same time pushing away whoever or whatever is in touch with it. "Failure to get nearer, when one has moved towards such an object of attention, and failure to grasp it when one reaches for it, provoke annoyance, more vigorous responses of the same sort as before, and the neural action which produces an emotion which is the primitive form of desire."[1]

Although at first the child carries the objects it grasps to its mouth because the mouth is most frequently used in making adjustments in regard to such a primitive property object as food, nevertheless as development proceeds apace curiosity is satisfied first by handling merely, and later by the correlation of touch sensations with those derived from sight and hearing. In sum, however, the primitive impulse is to satisfy curiosity and attention by grasping and handling. As long as the grasped object continues at once to excite and satisfy interest, it is vigorously defended against any attempt to remove it from the child's reach. It is just because the child likes to handle things, once, twice, many times, for as long as they excite interest, that he stores them up and hoards them for future reference.[2]

This, then, is the germ of acquisitive behaviour: the innate impulse to grasp and to handle all those objects which in some manner or other serve to satisfy the fundamental needs of the organism. With the very young child these objects will necessarily be few, since the child is at first

[1] Thorndike: *Educational Psychology*, i, 51. Cf. also Drummond: *Dawn of Mind*, 32–33; Moore: *Mental Development of a Child*, pt. i, *passim*; Darwin: "Biographical Sketch of an Infant," *Mind* (1877), vol. ii, 287; Myers: "Reaching, Grasping and Handling," *Amer. J. Psych.* (1915), vol. xxvi, 525–539; Preyer: *Mind of the Child*, i, 241 ff.; Compayré: *Development of the Child*, 17–28. Reference should also be made to Pavlov's exposition of the conditioned "reflex of collecting." Pavlov: *Lectures on Conditioned Reflexes* (Eng. trans., 1929), ch. xxvii, 277–279.

[2] The point to be made clear is that the impulse to grasp subserves the more fundamental needs. It is the endeavour to satisfy those needs which is the basis of acquisitive activity, e.g. the obtaining of food to satisfy hunger. Grasping is not an impulse which stands on its own account. It is always active in the service of such needs as nutrition, the need of others, in sex and maternal behaviour, the needs of the mind and so forth. See ch. i, 5 *et seq.*

interested only in simple property objects, the feeding-bottle, for instance, the mother's breast, bright hanging objects, coloured balls, the rattle, toys, anything that the parents or nurse leave lying about. But with maturation and development of intelligence there will result a growing integration of values; growing curiosity and interest lead the child to pay attention to almost anything in its environment which has no repulsive features. Soon, however, there is a gradual specialization in the nature of the objects collected. This comes about through, and is influenced largely by, the fact that the child is drawn into a social group where fashions abound and where psychological factors like imitation and suggestion begin to mould into the pattern of the group the previous indiscriminate grasping and handling reactions. Along with this imitation of approved patterns, interest in the habit complex of collecting is stimulated by rivalry, by the desire for that admiration and approval which are lavished upon the child with better and more complete collections than his fellows; and again, by that desire to achieve, to exploit, to gain superiority and power, which is only the reverse side to the award of social approval.

At a later stage again, with the increasing organization and integration of mental processes, with the development of aesthetic discrimination, taste, and intellectual power, with the increasing importance of sex differences, with the specialization of environment, there results a further assimilation and integration of values, an integration, however, which still largely conforms to the patterning of the social group. Interest in accumulation for the purposes of comparison, enumeration, systematization may lead on to adult interest in scientific pursuits. In any case, the average individual will be led on by the fixing of his interests to pay attention to one or other property object, be it postage-stamps, family histories, old coins or books. This fixing of interest in external objects means an extension of personality, and to the degree in which our collection is superior to another's, it means that we taste the joys of superiority, power, and heightened self-esteem.[1]

The point, however, which I am seeking to stress is this: that the roots of acquisitive behaviour are to be found in the primitive impulse to grasp and to handle in the interests of the fundamental needs; that collecting behaviour is a habit complex whereby, on the one hand, the undisciplined and non-regimented character of the child's impulses is organized into a compact body of interests through play activities and participation in a social group; and on the other hand, a process whereby values are integrated, one with another, in conformity with group values, with developing intellectual interests, and, maybe, through the operation of some such ontogenetic developmental scheme as the Freudians put forward. Finally, I would emphasize the fact that whereas the child seeks all experiences because he has not yet had all experience, nor learnt to integrate his needs—and thus collects in an indiscriminate and unlimited fashion—the adult throws aside the once so valuable collections of childhood because the standards of value under which they were made are finally subsumed by a sterner and more insistent set of environmental needs and social patterns. Thus one does not need to call in the aid of an instinct of acquisition to explain human collecting activities. Starting with the native interests of the child and his innate impulse to grasp in their service, there results a progressive integration of random impulse and a similar integration of values. The agencies which favour this integration are

[1] Cf. Stanley Hall: *Aspects of Child Life and Education*, 7; Compayré: *op. cit.*, 22–23; Groos: *Play of Man*, 101; James: *Principles*, ii, 423; Gruenberg: *Outlines of Child Study*, 88–89. Groos is inclined to link up collecting activities with an innate impulse to construct. Thus he writes: "The disposition to appropriate and to cling to whatever attracts the attention . . . is a feature of constructive activity," *op. cit.*, 100. When applied to the collecting activities of some of the rodents, there seems a certain measure of truth in this statement. I have already considered it, however, in Part I of this monograph. The more correct view is, of course, that collecting activities are linked with all the fundamental needs, not simply with construction (the need for shelter).

factors of growth and development, and psychological factors like rivalry, emulation, desire for power, esteem. The final set of acquisitive activity results from the powerful pressure of the culture patterns of each wider social group.

It has been the aim of this chapter to consider the evidence bearing upon the existence of an instinct of acquisition in Man. I have surveyed the statistical examinations that have been made on various occasions; I have considered the nature of stealing, pathological stealing and kindred delinquencies. And I have concluded that no support may be obtained here for this alleged instinct. Yet since collecting behaviour undoubtedly occurs among human beings, I was led further to a consideration of an explanation of such activity which rejects the aid of an independent hoarding instinct. The Freudian hypothesis was briefly reviewed. Although it is both suggestive and ingenious, it is still far from presenting a satisfactory explanation of acquisitive behaviour. Finally, I suggested that this behaviour could be explained on the principle of the integration and assimilation of property values about the primitive impulse to grasp and handle objects of primitive interest; and that, in fact, collecting was a habit complex resulting from the interplay of impulse, culture pattern, and psychological mechanism. This scheme I outlined in general terms. Its elaboration is, I believe, a matter of everyday observation and so need not be considered in any detail at the present juncture. With this background of a general study of collecting activities, the way seems now clear for a consideration, on the one hand, of the development of property rights in the growing child, and on the other hand, for a further attempt to make clear the psychological reality behind the statement that property is necessary for the development of personality. I will consider this twofold problem in the next two chapters.

CHAPTER IX

THE GENETIC DEVELOPMENT OF RIGHTS IN PROPERTY

LEAVING aside for the next chapter a consideration of the part that ownership of property objects plays in the development of self-consciousness and the integration of sentiments about the self, I may proceed at once to a discussion of the second problem. This concerns the genetic development of property rights and the process whereby sentiments of ownership, built up about the enduring property values, are given full recognition in the life of others just as their recognition is demanded in one's own life. It is almost a platitude to say that this recognition of ownership in others is the outcome of a long educational process carried on by home, school, church and play-group. It is only through the forces of education, exerted by means of cultural institutions, that the conational make-up of the child is moulded and fitted so that it conforms to the prevailing culture patterns of that group in which the child has the fortune to find itself. The young child is a natural egoist, an extreme individualist driven by conational energy to satisfy its impulsive needs. It is only when the home and play-group step in, in the interests of social organization, that this individualism is modified, moulded, re-formed, re-patterned, and so adapts itself to prevailing folk-ways. The nature and principle behind this complex interaction is equally the same for all the major instincts. So sex impulses are organized into the prevailing erotic patterns of the group; so aggressive impulses are organized into the pattern of a head-hunting society, on the one hand, or into that of a Quaker group, on the other hand; and so likewise are organized into characteristic sentiments those impulses involved in the acquisition of primitive property values. We have studied this last process in regard to the social patterning of sentiments of ownership among the various grades of primitive peoples. We may now briefly consider the manner in which this patterning takes place in the life of a maturing child in a Western community.

For some time after birth the infant shows itself to be supremely indifferent to property distinctions. It is little more than the incarnation of appetite, knowing no restraint and yielding only to the undermining force of satiety. Thus it will seek to secure and enjoy for itself anything that attracts its attention and it will resent others participating in such enjoyment.[1] At first this interest will be purely a transitory phenomenon. It is only with the development of self-consciousness and with the maturation of memory processes that the child can in any way be said to lay the foundations of more permanent sentiments of possession. If the child names the animal in its picture-book or calls the doll 'my' doll, this can only happen because present sense stimulus calls to its aid the former occasions of a corresponding impression. Through memory, that is, the child develops its first sentiments of familiarity. Just as the mother's face becomes dear to the child, so in time, through a continued repetition of the complex perceptions of sight, hearing and touch, certain objects become dear and familiar. About the age of six months the child already has his own toys—a little ball, a rattle, a rag doll, rubber ring or feeding-bottle. Thus M(; 8) was given a go-cart and after he had ridden in it several times M(; 7) sat in it. M(; 8) cried, pulled his dress and hair until he got the cart back for his own use. This same situation appears in many records in regard to such objects as the child's rocking-

[1] Sully: *Studies of Childhood*, 231–232, 234.

horse, cradle or toy animals.[1] He may even know them so well that he resents a secret substitution of another plaything for any one of them.[2]

Yet in so far as memory processes are not well developed, and in so far as no clear and constant distinction is drawn between *meum* and *tuum*, in very young children up to the second or third year, the sentiment of possession will be largely the outcome of habit, intimacy and association, and so will not have any particular degree of continuity. The young child does not appear to feel keenly the absence of persons or things that have formed part of his ordinary environment. Out of sight is out of mind. Parents, nurse, favourite toys, or animals about whom the child may have shown jealousy the day before are forgotten the day after. It needs but little to revive his remembrance of them, but while so young, he never really misses them.[3]

From about the age of three years and onwards it is probably correct to suggest that the child begins to form more or less permanent sentiments of ownership focussed on his toys; and begins to fathom, in some dim, vague fashion, that other children have rights and interests in their own property. The two most important agencies which help to further this next step in the development of property rights, are the home and the play group. It is, of course, well understood that the age at which children develop this distinction between *mine* and *thine* can hardly be fixed save in terms of a range of years. The period in so many cases depends upon a variety of factors, upon innate mental abilities, upon opportunities for mixing in play groups,

[1] Cf. e.g. France and Kline, "Psychology of Ownership," *Pedagogical Seminary* (1898), vol. vi, 447, for cases of children whose ages varied between four and twenty-four months, showing rivalry over, and proprietary interest in, toys, clothes and food. Reference may be made also to Stern: *op. cit.*, 99, 385–386; White: *Mental Hygiene of Childhood*, 48; Gesell: "Jealousy," *American Journal of Psychology*, vol. xvii, 454–455, 475–477.

[2] Stern: *op. cit.*, 130–131, 213–218.

[3] *Ibid.*, 239, 508.

upon home discipline and control. Since, however, so much depends upon the last factor, it is to the particular household community that we turn first of all when we discuss the moulding of human nature to socially approved behaviour patterns.

Thus it is that much depends upon family life in this initiation of the child's conception of property rights. It is not simply a matter of poverty as compared with affluence in the home. Incidental factors may be of much greater importance. In this respect a child brought up in a family group where there is an unusual community of interests may find great difficulty in adapting itself to the rules of social intercourse and fail to perceive the stigma attaching to the appropriation of property outside the family circle. In point of fact, honesty and a consideration for the property rights of others is an acquired character trait only established by painful effort in the child's mind. In some of the examples I adduce below this is very evident. A child brought up without individual possessions, whether in a poor or a rich family, experiences both a material poverty and a psychological thwarting of its personality. On the other hand, a child whose ideas of life develop in connection with satisfactory, permanent, even though simple possessions has a very fair soil for the growth of the customary property rights of the group.[1]

Besides the home, however, the free-play activities of young children have an important rôle to play in developing a regard for social rights and duties. We are told that children coming to nursery schools, for instance, usually display one of two reactions towards the toys with which they play. Often they are entirely unused to sharing the toys. Their reaction is to grasp as many as possible and

[1] Cf. Healy: *Honesty*, etc. (1915), 15–18, 204; Thom: *op. cit.*, 232 ff.; Hall: *Adolescence*, i, 364; Gruenberg: *op. cit.*, 87–88; Russell: *On Education* (1926), 121–124.

hoard them. Sometimes this tendency is so strong that it definitely swamps a child's play interest; while at other times it involves him in disputes and quarrels with other children, since he feels it incumbent upon himself to question their right to the common toys. With other children, however, the reaction is one of avoidance, of reluctance to use the toys, and a tendency to give them up if another child approaches.[1] Since, however, the joint play of little children is largely a congeries of individual phantasies which sometimes fit more or less satisfactorily into each other and sometimes not, it usually happens that under the wise supervision of the teacher and the give-and-take of play life, haphazard play behaviour is a medium in which true social rights develop. The play group modifies, completes or reforms the influence of the home. As Mrs. Isaacs remarks on this point, social relations "grow through the actual experience not only of the fusion of interest by shared phantasy and common emotion, but, and perhaps more importantly, of the sharp clash of aims and discovered differences of desire leading the child to adapt to wills other than his own in order to attain his own satisfactions. Here, as elsewhere, negation, pain and lack of satisfaction are the potent factors in the development of the sense of objective reality. Such clashes of purpose are an effective stimulus to a movement away from ego-centrism and towards social adaptation." [2] In later childhood and adolescence the definition of rights in general, and of rights in property in particular, is finally stabilized by wider social contacts and the pressure of more powerful social institutions.

[1] Cf. H. M. Johnson: *Children in the Nursery Schools* (1929), 55.

[2] Mrs. S. S. Isaacs: "A Brief Contribution to the Social Psychology of Young Children." Unpublished MSS. I am greatly indebted to Mrs. Isaacs for her kindness in placing at my disposal relevant observations from those she accumulated during her work at the Malting House School, Cambridge. Those on a later page are part of her material shortly to be published in book form.

So far we have been reviewing this development of rights in property in general terms. It now seems desirable, therefore, to implement this survey by a brief consideration of typical situations in which, at various age grades, a growing consciousness of the existence of property rights becomes manifest in the mind of the growing child. With the young infant, as I have already suggested, extreme individualism is the common characteristic.[1] Those objects satisfying the senses are claimed on every occasion. Proprietary interest is shown in rivalry when another appears on the scene to claim the same object. Then there is aggressive behaviour displayed, and the attempt to reserve the valued object for exclusive use and control. The child up to three years, however, has no notion of an elementary right of another to property objects. Thus, as a typical example, we have Tiedemann's son, who, at two years, did not allow his sister to sit on his chair or to take any of his clothes. He called these "his affairs." But, on the other hand, he had no scruples at taking his sister's "affairs." An older writer, Legouve, summed up this age grade in the observation that "the child has not the instinct of theft, but he lacks all instinct of the property of others."[2]

It is just this "instinct of the property of others," this consideration for the interests and property of another as of equal importance and as deserving equal respect with one's own, that results from the give-and-take of home life and the social mixing of play life. The play activities of pre-school children, however, still display a large amount of individual aggressiveness where possession is concerned. The following examples, for instance, show both this individualism naked and unashamed and its later germs of

[1] James' words of the baby will be readily recalled: "His corporeal person and what ministers to its needs are the only self he can possibly be said to love. His so-called self-love is but a name for his insensibility to all but this one set of things." *Principles*, i, 321.

[2] Quoted Compayré: *op. cit.*, 201.

modification by some incipient understanding of the rights of others. Four examples from Mrs. Isaacs' MSS. are instructive:

"Miss B had given Dan (3;9) a pair of scissors, and when he had put them down and left them for a time she took them up to use them. He saw this and immediately screamed, 'Those are *my* scissors, I want them *now*,' and it took some time to quieten him and make him willing to let her use them."

A second example is this:

"While Dan (3;9) was occupied with something else, he saw Harold (5;2) take one of his engine books, which he had left on the shelf, to read. Harold put it down on the table and remarked that he was going to read it 'all the morning.' Dan immediately said: 'I want it,' and tried to take it from Harold, and screamed and cried. He took it away in the end."

A third example shows the same aggressive individualism at work:

"Theobald (4;11) had brought his scooter with him and all the children wished to take turns in using it. Frank (5;3) and Dan (3;9) squabbled about it, Dan being very insistent. Miss A suggested that Dan should get his own scooter and let all the boys take turns with it. He asked Miss B to get it out for him and to fix the wheel which he had taken off; but when he got it, he would not share it with any of the other boys."

A final example shows aggressiveness over non-material property values and is strongly reminiscent of similar behaviour among many primitive peoples:

"Harold (5;3) and Paul (4;0) often say to the other children: 'You are not to talk about Humpty-Dumpty,'—you are not to talk about so-and-so, referring to things they have in their books at home, or on the gramophone. They seem to look upon these as their own special possessions, like toys, and often forbid the other children to talk about them, or sing them. They say: 'It is in *my* book at home.' "

These examples show the egotism of pre-school children. A further quotation from another competent observer reveals the way in which children learn to show their feelings for, and understanding of, property rights through their use of play materials. (The ages of these pre-school children are unfortunately not noted.)

"Gertrude was playing with coloured wooden cubes. She was the only child to talk to the others and her words were entirely: 'No-No,' and 'You are bad' when any other child reached for her cubes. The children would not, even at the teacher's suggestion, use what cubes they wanted from a common pile, but rather each child took a handful which he defended as his and from which he drew to construct as he wished.

"Sylvia got the chalk and began to draw on the blackboard. Charles went up to her and began to write also. 'Don't, on my part,' Sylvia protested to him, and he moved further towards the other side of the board.

"The boys were building a house. They took all the unused blocks; then Peter took one aside to the girls' house. 'That's mine,' said Margaret, and Peter put it down. Albert took one from Gertrude's square, but after a moment's pause put it back, remarking: 'We can't take any more. The rest are hers.' "[1]

In the next age group we see this process of education in the nature of property rights proceeding apace. It is accelerated not only by the cumulative effect of the give-and-take of the play group, but also through the extension of family altruism beyond the bounds of the family circle, and through the fact that as the maturing child learns to generalize its own feelings and desires, the feelings of possession are objectified and projected outwards on to other people; the result is that respect for the property of others begins to have a rational basis and the general notion of proprietary right obtains. An example or two will show these factors at work. This, from Stern, illustrates the modification of extreme individualism by altruism extended beyond the family circle:

"Scupin's child Bubi (5;2½) often went with us to take cast-off clothes to a very poor family. Before his first visit he was asked to take some of his toys to the three children of the family. But he objected at first, saying they were his own toys and he needed them,

[1] E. T. Verry: *A Study of Mental and Social Attitudes in the Free Play of Pre-School Children*, Iowa (1924), 37–46. Quoted Hart: *Science of Social Relations*, New York (1927), 92–93.

only going at last so far as to look out some damaged or old toys, long since put on one side. But when he saw how they delighted the children he himself began to take pleasure in giving. The very next time he was much more generous, looked out toys of his own accord and jumped about gaily in anticipation of giving and seeing the poor children's joy. Yesterday he reminded us on his own initiative that it was time to take the poor children something again, and we even succeeded in persuading him to give them a toy from which at first he would not hear of parting."[1]

Further examples show the increasing respect for property rights that is shown by older children from about six years onwards when they reason from their own feelings to those of others. The little girl, for instance, who could view her book, returned to her soiled, dog-eared and torn, and then cry: "I felt as though a large part of myself had been injured," would hardly be likely to treat inconsiderately the property of other children. Or again, we have the case of M (6;0), always very careless about books:

"The books were furnished by the school and he had ruined two books since he began going to school. His teacher gave him a picture-book for being regular in his attendances and he was very much pleased with it. He would not allow the other boys to look at his book or touch it unless their hands were clean. Soon after he was given this book he began to erase the pencil marks from his school book and said: 'I don't suppose teacher wants her books all dirty any more than I do.' "

Another case is that of M (10;), who was

"always careless with tools. Left them out at night or lost them, etc. One Christmas he was given a set of tools and he became very careful of them. Through this he was led to be careful of the tools of others."[2]

One must allow, however, that the records show what a long and painful process it is before children can realize just what is involved in this respect for the rights of others. Even in a play group, for instance, where the rule is rigidly

[1] Stern: *op. cit.*, 529.
[2] Both cases are from answers to a questionnaire sent out by France and Kline: *op. cit.*, 460–461.

enforced that particular property objects shall be for the common use of all, the struggle for individual possession, blind and impulsive, will occasionally break out. Two interesting observations from Mrs. Isaacs' collection are apposite here:

"Frank (5;6) took one of the rugs which Duncan (6;11) had been using earlier in the morning, and Duncan tried to get it from Frank, saying: 'It is *my* rug.' There was a struggle. Miss A intervened, pointing out that the rugs were for 'all the boys' to use, and that if Frank was using it now, then Duncan could not do so, but would perhaps get another; after a time he accepted this, but then, seeing Dan (4;1), who had meanwhile taken the second rug, he tried to get that from Dan, and Miss A had to make the same sort of intervention."

Duncan then found a third rug and took it back to the swings, but by this time

"Dan and Frank were both on the two low swings, and Dan was on the one that Duncan particularly regarded as his own. He tried to pull Dan off and gave his hair a severe tugging. When Miss A intervened he protested violently: 'But it is *my* swing—he has got *my* swing.' She said, 'Well you have another,' pointing to the third one. He said, 'No, I don't want that, this is mine.' Miss A remarked, 'The swings are for all the boys to use.' He said, 'No, they are not. It's mine, the swing is mine.' She said, 'The swing is for all the boys to use. Sometimes you use it, sometimes Dan uses it, sometimes so-and-so uses it,' mentioning each of the boys in turn. He then replied, 'But it was *I* who thought of making the swings,' and repeated this several times, clearly feeling that that gave him the proprietary right to the swing when made.[1] Miss A replied, 'But you did not make it, you thought of it. Miss B made it, and it was made with the wire that is in the garden for all the boys to use. You use it now and another boy uses it another time.' He kept on making hostile remarks, very disturbed, and trying to push a chair over on to Miss A, saying, 'I'll tell my Aunt on you,' and 'I don't like you,' and so on, but gradually he calmed down and appeared to accept the facts fairly well and went away to do something else. Later he was entirely calm and friendly."

Apart from these occasional outbursts of aggressiveness

[1] Cf. Robert the gardener and his disquisition to Emile. Rousseau: *Emile* (Everyman Edition), 62–63.

over the question of control of property objects it would seem that with normal children, at any rate, the passage from ego-centrism to social adaptation is well accomplished by the time adolescence sets in. With both the child and the adolescent reversions to aggressive individualism and to anti-social conduct in regard to property are not infrequently due to emotional troubles, to lack of understanding and sympathy on the part of parents and teachers, to the failure adequately to sublimate or otherwise adapt to social demands the maturing sex impulses, and to resulting subconscious conflicts. Anti-social behaviour arising from these causes I have already discussed in the previous chapter. In so far, however, as the period of adolescence is one of socialization and enlargement of experience, the process of 'objective reference' upon which the whole recognition of social rights is based, continues apace to teach the lessons learnt in the home and the play group.[1] The youth learns to see himself in relation to the wider social group. He realizes that social life can only exist in so far as there is a recognition of the value of personality. This can only mean that the wishes, desires, hopes, the experience, striving, and aims of another should receive from those in authority a consideration equal to his own if social life and the associations subserving the common good are to give to all some measure of satisfaction and happiness. But this can come about, on the one hand, only if there is an intimate contact between the life of the individual and the corporate life and authority of these associations, including the state, which subserve community life; and on the other hand, it can come about only through the recognition that rights, as conditions of social welfare, must be respected, if this social welfare is to be attained. Thus through the progressive development of this twin process of generalization and

[1] Cf. France and Kline: *op. cit.*, 430–433; Tracy: *The Psychology of Adolescence* (1920), 66–67, 124–128.

objective reference the aggressive strivings of the individual to gain property objects are modified and canalized into the channels of rights and duties prevalent in the Great Society.

Looking back, however, over the outlines of this development of rights, and of property rights in particular, one cannot but be impressed with the part played by culture patterning. One has first the aggressiveness and egotism of the young child, wanting all things that attract his attention, blindly defending the property objects he regards as his own from another's aggression, but himself recognizing no right in others to property values. Then through the influence of social life in the family circle, through play activities at home and at school, through the moral teachings perhaps of a church as well, the primitive stuff of his human nature is cut to the patterns of the rights and duties of the wider social life. Painful though this patterning may be, embroidered now and then with conflicts, backslidings, anti-social struggles, nevertheless it is remorseless. The individual either adapts himself to the particular ordering of social relations in his group or becomes a misfit. Yet it says much for the plasticity of human nature that it is probably only an accident of birth which is the original mark of difference between a Vedda child in Ceylon, a Yakut child in Siberia, a Soviet child in Russia, a Puritan child in America. Their original human nature is, as far as we know, roughly the same. They have the same complement of instinctive needs, they obey the same laws of development. It is the moulding of human nature by the culture patterns of the different groups which adapts one child to a communist organization of society and another to a Western capitalist society. Thus the brief consideration we have given in this chapter to the development of property rights in the maturing child forms a valuable supplement in favour of the thesis I have maintained in the previous chapters.

CHAPTER X

PROPERTY AND PERSONALITY

THE second of the two problems which I distinguished at the conclusion of Chapter VIII concerns the part property objects play in the development of self-consciousness and the integration of the elements of personality into an ordered system. I now wish to discuss the implications of this thesis in greater detail.

Though I have, for the purposes of exposition, considered separately the development of property rights in the child, nevertheless it is obvious that in point of fact the objectification and projection of property interests and consequent consideration for the rights of others as embodied in the *mores* of the group can only develop *pari passu* with a corresponding enlargement, extension and integration of the idea of selfhood. In other words, our attribution of selfhood to others and our respect for it in them is an offshoot of the process whereby we gradually build up an idea of the unity of our own self. This further discussion, then, of aspects of the development of personality is in large measure complementary to what I have already said above regarding the formation and projection of property rights.

The theoretical position is, I think, quite clear. Though the child may be born either a little Liberal or a little Conservative (as Gilbert was at pains to assure us before the rise of Labour politics), nevertheless it is not born with a single unitary soul or ready-made self, nor has it instinctive or intuitive knowledge during early years of the idea of any such self as an original datum of consciousness. In spite of the teaching of theologians and moralists the study of psychology makes it abundantly clear that the idea of self is a human construction, an hypothesis, as it were (and, like all hypotheses, never complete but always open to change), whereby, through the selective handling of environmental situations, the implicit underlying conational unity of the self is rendered relatively clear and explicit. This process of development results from the integration of emotional dispositions into stable systems of sentiment grouped about significant focal objects and ideas. It is my aim briefly to describe this development of self-consciousness and this integration of personality, paying special attention to the part played in the stabilization by property values and objects.

In terms of theory some degree of self-consciousness arises through the child's first attempts at adaptation to the external forces of inanimate nature. That is to say, there must be some sense of self as soon as any living being, in order to satisfy an impulse arising from its own nature, is aware that it is necessary to effect an alteration in an object presented to it. The object will appear to the agent as presenting a persisting inertia which has to be altered by the only means within the agent's control, that is, through such bodily movements as grasping, stretching or handling. A good example is the child motivated by hunger impulses and striving for food. The self is qualified by the impulse and is contrasted with the food object which must be manipulated and altered if the impulse is to be satisfied. In this qualification of the self by impulse and in this striving process, the germs of self-consciousness arise. Further, in so far as the object desired is a primitive property object and liable also to attract the attention of others, fuller feelings of heightened self-consciousness will arise should the object be defended from the aggressive movements of an opponent. And even where curiosity and interests are held in check by conflicting impulse, by fear, disgust or repugnance, this conflict will in some measure give rise to self-feeling. Therefore self-feeling will arise in all those states of grasping and handling which we have distinguished above as incipient phases of the collecting sentiment; and will be strengthened and given continuity to the degree in which the agent is active in pursuit of primitive property objects.

But in its more complete form, self-consciousness appears to arise as the result of a twofold set of relations to other living beings. Focussed about property objects these are relations of co-operation and of aggressive opposition. Co-operation probably first arises among animals in the rearing of offspring or the building of burrow or nest and in the consequent defence of such objects against intruders. Many of the play activities of young children display a primitive co-operation also. Aggressive opposition arises from individual or co-operative defence or offence. Where the self is successfully affirmed against opposing force, the level of the conscious processes is thereby raised through an accession of power. Where the self is unsuccessfully affirmed it will nevertheless be brought into consciousness through its submission to the outside force. In either case, impulsive elements will be integrated into the rapidly developing sentiment of self.[1]

This development of self-feeling is, of course, a slow process. Before the self is unified, memory must elaborate and co-ordinate experience. The web of conation must be woven into the woof of remembrance. The agent must develop the experience of being a causative force. Experimentation must proceed apace. Language must so develop that the conceptual distinction of *I*, *self*, *mine*, may be made exact and crystallized into meaning.[2]

[1] Cf. Allen: *Pleasure and Instinct* (1930), 116–120, 141–142.

[2] For the part that these factors play in the development of self-consciousness in the child, see Stern: *op. cit.*, 130; Compayré: *op. cit.*, 269–275; Preyer: *Mind of the Child*, ch. xix; *Ibid.*, *Mental Development of the Child*, ch. ix; Stanley Hall: "The Early Sense of Self," *American Journal of Psychology* (1898), vol. ix, 353–361; White: *Mechanisms of Character Formation*, 181–182, 228–229, 239 ff.

Throughout this process, whether in initial striving, in later experimentation as a causative force, or in those further relations of co-operation or aggressive opposition, the self organizes itself about those objects which are of interest because they satisfy fundamental needs. The sentiments that come to be grouped under a master sentiment of self are organized about those existing interests and values which, in so far as they are exclusively used, enjoyed and controlled, exist for that self as property objects. Thus, with the qualification that the unity of the self is based fundamentally upon an implicit relation of conational continuity, we arrive at William James' position: the sum-total of the empirical self is the objects of its regard, and self-feeling is the feeling of familiarity we have for the objects we regard as our own. In James' words, "To have a self that I can care for, Nature must first present me with some object interesting enough to make me instinctively wish to appropriate it for its own sake. . . . My own body and what ministers to its needs are thus the primitive object, instinctively determined, of my egoistic interests. Other objects may become interesting derivatively, through association with any of these things, either as means or as habitual concomitants; and so, in a thousand ways, the primitive sphere of the egoistic emotions may enlarge and change its boundaries. This sort of interest is really the meaning of the word *mine*. Whatever has it, is, *eo ipso*, a part of me."[1] Elsewhere James writes: "It is clear that between what a man calls *me* and what he simply calls *mine*, the line is difficult to draw. We feel and act about certain things that are ours very much as we feel and act about ourselves. Our fame, our children, the work of our hands, may be as dear to us as our bodies are, and arouse the same feelings and the same acts of reprisal if attacked. . . . In its widest possible sense, however, a man's Self is

[1] James: *Principles*, i, 319, 324.

the sum-total of all that he can call his, not only his body, and his psychic powers, but his clothes and his house, his wife and children, his ancestors and friends, his reputation and works, his land and horses and yacht and bank account. All these things give him the same emotions. If they wax or prosper, he feels triumphant, if they dwindle and die away, he feels cast down—not necessarily in the same degree for each thing, but in much the same way for all."[1]

I have quoted James at length, as much for the felicitous phrasing in which he summarizes the problem as for the acuteness of his analysis. It is of interest now to consider more closely, first, the nature of the psychological bond that binds self to acquired property value; second, to stress the closeness and intimacy of this relation of self to object through a discussion of the changes of personality brought about by accession or loss of property objects; and third, the nature of the elements which go to form the acquisitive sentiment centred about money interests.

The nature of the bond binding self and property object is again well expressed by James when he remarks that "a great part of our feelings about what is ours is due to the fact that we live *closer* to our own things and so feel them more thoroughly and deeply."[2] This living closer to our own things, this intimate realization of, and deep feeling towards, our own property, this appreciation of 'the details and shadings' of our own, as compared with 'the coarse outlines and rude averages' of others' property, would appear to be an expression of man's tendency towards animism: that magical tendency he everywhere displays to equip the inanimate objects of his environment with the psychic qualities which he himself possesses as a living being. I have already discussed the nature of this magico-animistic tendency in our consideration of the part it plays in giving a fuller meaning to ownership among the Simpler

[1] *Ibid.*, i, 291–292.

[2] *Ibid.*, i, 327.

Peoples. Magic and Animism operate in the same fashion and to the same purpose in strengthening the bonds of ownership among children and adults of any civilized community. The sense of ownership, in fact, is a special form of positive magico-animistic feeling, the theoretical nature of which I need not consider in further detail here. I need only point out that Freudian psychology has made us familiar with this feeling and process under the name of 'ego identification': the soul of the object is an imaginary partial projection of the libido of the ego; and we value the object just because part of our ego is narcissistically incorporated within it.[1]

Examples of this possessive animistic aspect of the sense of ownership are to be found by any close observer of the manner in which children regard their property objects, their toys, school books, badges, possessions.[2] The same tendency is at work when the workers and machine tenders in the modern factory speak of the instrument of labour and the products thereof as their 'own.' In many cases the worker will rationalize in one way or another this identification of himself with the objects with which or upon which he works. But since he usually speaks of his 'love' for his machine or his tools, he shows that other than utilitarian considerations are influencing his relations with the machine he calls his own. Thus we have the case of the young girl whom an industrial investigator found sitting at a sewing-machine crying and sobbing violently. It turned out that the cause of her sorrows was that her 'own' machine had broken down and that she was required in the interval to

[1] Cf. what has been said above on the stages of libido development; or see Abraham: *Selected Papers, passim.*

[2] Cf. the little girl above who felt 'a part of herself had been injured' when she saw her borrowed book returned dog-eared and soiled. See also the examples collected by G. H. Ellis: "Fetichism in Children," *Ped. Seminary* (1902), vol. ix, 290–293; and G. M. Gould: "Child Fetiches," *Ped. Seminary* (1898), vol. v, *passim.*

use another machine in perfect repair and of identical make, capacity and efficiency.[1] Two cases from those collected by De Man are equally instructive. A machinist says: "I have always taken the utmost care of the machines at which I worked. They rewarded me for this by working well and accurately. When I had to change from one employment to another, or even when I had merely to change from one machine to another in the same works, I was always mournful from parting from my iron companion. I should never have believed that one could come to feel so humanly towards dead material." Another worker, a joiner, states: "As a rule, our employer supplies us with our tools. Nevertheless one usually acquires a sense of ownership. As long as a tool is fit for use, one is reluctant to let one's mate handle it, even on loan. In the case of the older and more highly skilled workmen, this feeling goes so far that they would rather throw up their job than accept transference from one bench to another. The machines are looked upon as assistants upon whose shoulders the heavy work is put."[2] Possessive animism in regard to the finished product of the machine occurs less often than in regard to the machine itself. Nevertheless, that the worker tends to regard the product of his activities as his own is disclosed by his pride when the products are satisfactory, and by his crestfallen attitude when they are not. They are so linked to his own feelings of self-respect and self-esteem that a negative judgment passed on the products is taken as a direct reflection upon the worker's personality.[3]

As in the sense of ownership, so in the sentiments centred about wealth accumulation do we find this animistic identification an important element. It is found, for instance, in the common identification of parent with child whereby

[1] Cf. *Industrial Psychology*, edited by C. S. Myers, 20–23.
[2] H. De Man: *Joy in Work* (Eng. trans.), 28, 31.
[3] *Ibid.*, 37–39.

the parent labours that the child may enjoy the result of the effort, amasses wealth that the child may have the power wealth confers. It would be interesting to learn what would be the effect upon this process of ego identification and the virtues fostered thereby—thoroughness, thrift, foresight, care and the rest—of measures designed to render illegal the transmission of property to heirs, or the increasing use of measures, such as heavier death duties, designed seriously to diminish the value of such property.[1]

In any case, however, as a matter of common observation, the process of possessive animism as I have described it on an earlier page, and the kindred process of ego identification, help to explain the relation of property object to the self, and the focussing of sentiment upon object of interest. Animistic feeling is the hidden thread, strong though invisible, which binds civilized as well as savage to the objects he regards as his own. It is the real core of ownership, the psychological basis of the philosopher's cry: "In making the object my own, I stamped it with the mark of my own person; whoever attacks it attacks me; the blow struck it, strikes me, for I am present in it. Property is but the periphery of my person extended to things."[2]

If one is correct in supposing that there is this close magico-animistic connection between self and property object, it is but natural to imagine that the accession or loss of property objects will have close corresponding effects upon the balance of elements which make up personality. It does not seem absolutely impossible to test the truth of

[1] Cf. Flugel: *Psychoanalysis of the Family*, 169–170. Van Waters gives several interesting cases of economic and mental conflict induced by parents so identified with their children that they considered they had vested property right in the latter and all they earned. The reverse process, that of children identified with parents, is, of course, not uncommon. Van Waters: *op. cit.*, 59–61.

[2] Jhering: *The Struggle for Law* (Amer. ed.), 55.

this inference. Take first the reaction upon the self of property in which the self is vitally identified. James has told us long ago that "there are few men who would not feel personally annihilated if a lifelong construction of their hands or brains—say an entomological collection or an extensive work in manuscript—were suddenly swept away. The miser feels similarly towards his gold, and although it is true that a part of our depression at the loss of possessions is due to our feeling that we must now go without certain goods that we expected the possessions to bring in their train, yet in every case there remains, over and above this, a sense of the shrinkage of our personality, a partial conversion of ourselves to nothingness, which is a psychological phenomenon by itself."[1] Good examples of this 'partial conversion of ourselves to nothing' are to be found among the records of art collectors forced to witness the break-up of their collection. Many commit suicide at the resulting depression; many refuse to attend their sales so as to avoid the agony of mind it would cause them. Some, we are told, unable to face depression at the last moment, have bought in all the lots by joining in the bidding themselves, afterwards relieving their financial distress by other means; and there has been at least one collector who allowed his collection to be dispersed and then laboriously brought it together again by buying it back from all the dealers and collectors into whose hands it had passed.[2]

[1] James: *op. cit.*, i, 293. Cf. also this quotation from Stout: "When we possess the means of commanding desirable or avoiding undesirable things, we can without let or hindrance imagine ourselves obtaining the one or escaping the other. The sense of impotence, on the other hand, is a check on the flow of ideas, restricting inward freedom, and so producing in many minds greater discomfort than the sacrifice of particular enjoyments which can only be gained by spending. To such persons, the loss of wealth is a curtailment of existence—a kind of mutilation of their conscious being." *Analytic Psychology*, vol. ii, 90–91.

[2] Cf. *Daily Express*, September 4, 1929; from an article on the break-up of the famous Simon art collection. Dr. Simon committed suicide rather than face the loss of his collection.

The same shrinkage of personality is to be observed among criminals and others confined in prison, where they must pass their days without the opportunity of asserting their personality through the medium of property objects. Through the continued inertia, monotony, and repression of personality, there seems to occur a state of emotional self-intoxication which results in violent and spontaneous outbursts of excited activity. Dostoieffsky, writing from personal experience of Siberian prison life, characterizes this activity as the "anguished, convulsive manifestation of personality, an instinctive melancholy, a desire to affirm the degraded ego, an emotion which obscures the judgment."[1] This same outburst of emotional excitement, resulting in destructiveness and incorrigibility, is often reported of charity or delinquent children unwisely and severely confined in homes, orphanages or institutes and, through mistaken motives of discipline, deprived of all personal property. When a little psychological insight is displayed and the worst of these children given property objects of their own to care for, such as books, toys, or animal pets, when, in fact, they are able to focus their energy upon primitive property values and so live freer and more independent lives, it is noteworthy that the anti-social child quickly adapts itself to social requirements.[2] Finally, it is not without psychological interest that monks, nuns and hermits, recognizing that the things owned by them are the material that makes up much of the personality, aim to subjugate this personality, to annihilate the self, by

[1] Dostoieffsky: *The House of the Dead*. Quoted Ellis: *The Criminal*, 172.

[2] Psychological literature on this point seems practically non-existent. I have been unable to obtain any complete records of the psychological observation of institutional children. Cf., however, the work of Healy and Burt, *passim*. Viteles, M. G.: "Children of a Jewish Orphanage," *Psych. Clinic* (1919), vol. xii, 248–254; Wyle, A.: "A-typical Children in Orphanages," *Journal of Delinquency* (1922), vol. vii, 169–191. I am indebted also to Professor H. J. Laski for one or two observations on this point.

making one of their triple vows, the vow of poverty.[1] In Soviet Russia also, among numbers of the Communist Party, where individuality is subordinated before the altar of the Great Collective, a large measure of poverty is enforced upon all who would serve the State.[2]

Just as we find a negation and shrinkage of personality through loss of property, so we may expect a corresponding enlargement and extension of the self through accession of wealth. This again is a matter of everyday observation. An accession of wealth may make a man irresponsible, extravagant, snobbish, generous, idle, dissipated; or it may bring increased self-confidence, enterprise, pride; or again, it may lead to avarice, miserliness, and kindred abnormalities. France and Kline, who investigated a limited number of cases by the questionnaire method, found that of sixty cases reported to them of men who had recently acquired sudden wealth, 10 per cent. continued in the even tenor of their way without noticeable change of personality, 8 per cent. turned spendthrifts and prodigals, pleasure intoxicated, so to speak, 20 per cent. became very generous and made a point of remembering old friends, while 38 per cent. are described as becoming suddenly haughty, proud, arrogant, forgetful, neglectful of friends, harsh, unsociable or cruel to servants. Two examples are typical: M (60) inherited a moderate fortune. "The first thing he did was to tell all his friends and invite them to supper. Before this he had been rather a quiet man, and not given to pushing himself into anything. Now, suddenly, he was heard from in most enterprises." On the other hand,

[1] Reference may be made to G. G. Coulton: *Five Centuries of Religion* (Cambridge, 1923–1927), vol. i, 214, for the rules of Benedict; vol. ii, 124–136, for the rules of St. Francis, on this subject. See also for general statements as to the nature of this vow of poverty, Coulton: *Life in the Middle Ages* (Cambridge, 1929–1930), vol. iv, "Monks, Friars and Nuns"; and Eileen Power: *Medieval English Nunneries* (Cambridge, 1922), 315–340.

[2] Cf. H. N. Brailsford: *How the Soviets Work* (New York, 1928), 122–123; and Dorothy Thompson: *The New Russia* (New York, 1928), 111 ff.

M (45) "came suddenly into possession of a great deal of money. He became very disagreeable socially and was considered mean in business; his family was about as bad off as before, for his new wealth made him stingy."[1]

These changes in personality are, after all, what we might expect. Where there is no morality of inwardness which may enable a man philosophically to accept the responsibilities which accession of wealth brings in its train and consciously to control the direction of his life in regard to newly gained wealth, it would seem inevitable with many that the power which wealth provides should be used in irresponsible and thoughtless fashion. Unprepared for sudden power, the personality becomes at first disorganized and unbalanced; in the flux of conflicting interests it is not unlikely that it should single out new interests about which it may stabilize itself; and when, at last, some measure of integration is attained among these conflicting sentiments and desires, the resulting personality pattern has been woven afresh. With the wise, the self will have enlarged itself through incorporation of wider experience, larger interests, extended powers; with those of lesser clay, the self may have altered in some less creditable fashion, through inability to preserve the old balance of elements and lack of skill in forming a new harmony.

On a more minor scale we have the effect of dress and ornament on the sense of self. With children, a change of dress often involves a change of disposition, sometimes almost of character itself. With the adult the same effect is noticeable though to a lesser degree. When we seek to be highly formal in our social relationships, we assume dress clothes. When we desire to impress with a sense of strength of character, we assume less formal, but quiet, well-cut, precisely tailored lounge suits; and when the time for holiday relaxation arrives we assume loose-fitting, prefer-

[1] France and Kline: *op. cit.*, 463.

ably old, sports clothes. New clothes of any type heighten self-feeling, seem to inspire increased self-confidence, and invoke a pleasant feeling tone.[1]

From what I have said on this subject I think it is fairly plain what sort of changes in self-consciousness we may expect from the acquisition or loss of wealth. The fact that such well-marked changes occur is proof of the manner in which we objectively identify our self with the objects that we regard as our own, and is some evidence of the closeness of the animistic bond between self and property object. We may now proceed to characterize some of the factors that reinforce this irrational ego identification in the various acquisitive activities of the Great Society.

The sentiment which fosters the accumulation of capital involves in its organization a number of more primary impulses and emotions. It includes, for instance, the need for the materials of subsistence and the desire for increased physical comfort and for a higher standard of living; it involves the activity of constructive impulses and includes also the sentiments centred about the desire for social esteem. The love of family, the identification of parent with child, the desire to hand on wealth to the next generation, interacts with a refined form of fear such as prudence to add stability and strength to the sentiment. Finally, another important motive is that aggressive desire for power and superiority which comes from rivalry and business competition. The desire for physical comforts and for subsistence is more urgent with those classes habitually employed at

[1] On the intimate connection between clothes and self-consciousness, and the effect of dress on personality, see Lotze: *Microcosmus* (Eng. trans.), i, 592, and, for a psychoanalytic treatment, Flugel: *The Psychology of Clothes* (1930). A related problem of some interest is the effect upon a married woman of losing her maiden name and assuming that of her husband. Until the self adapts itself to the change, there seems to be the peculiar feeling that the self has lost a part of itself, that the new name is somehow aliently imposed upon the old self, and that the new self is somehow not at home with the old. Presumably this feeling of newness, strangeness, loss, is fairly universal among women.

manual labour. With regard to those classes in the community chiefly concerned in the accumulation of wealth, it would seem that this incentive of physical comfort rarely plays any considerable part. The dominant motives to wealth accumulation would thus seem to be prudence, the love of family, the desire for social esteem and invidious distinctions founded on wealth, and lastly, desire for power, and the aggressive control of others. The desire for economic goods, therefore, the response to the bribe of wealth, is always complex.[1] It is a value supported by a strongly organized system of sentiments and interests, the joint product of the interaction of impulse and emotion with the economic culture patterns of the material and social environment. So important, however, is this group patterning that it is hardly unfair to say that man is acquisitive because his environment makes him so.

This is not the place to consider the historical and economic determination of the economic culture patterns of the Acquisitive Society. We may therefore leave this problem in the hands of students of economic history.[2] We may, however, consider a little further the psychological basis of this acquisitive habit complex. It would seem that the motive which dominates all others in these accumulative activities is the desire for power, the desire to attune a

[1] See Z. C. Dickinson: *Economic Motives*, 19, 123; Wright: "Evolution of Values from Instincts," *Philosophical Review* (1915), vol. xxiv, 173. One might note also that the accumulation of money may call into play complex and persistent mental activity, which of itself is sufficiently engrossing to constitute a motive which may demand some measure of gratification for its own sake. Cf. Stout: *op. cit.*, ii, 88, 91. Chess, for example, may exercise a similar fascination over its devotees.

[2] Reference may be made to Mr. Tawney's authoritative study: *Religion and the Rise of Capitalism* (London, 1926); to Weber's equally authoritative work: *The Protestant Ethic and the Spirit of Capitalism* (Eng. trans., London, 1930); and to various relevant essays in *Property: Its Duties and Rights*, edited by Bishop Gore (London, 1922). Veblen's volume on *The Theory of the Leisure Class*, together with Hobson's study of *Wealth and Life*, should also be consulted. An interesting summary is to be found in Müller-Lyer: *History of Social Development*, 292–296.

greater or less number of wills to one's own. Mr. Wells has given us a valuable analysis of the motives of the business man in his portrait of Lord Edensoke, one of the dominant characters in his novel *Meanwhile.* This business magnate had no religion, no patriotism, no passion for science or for beautiful things. His great satisfaction in life was winning a game. He was not avaricious simply, "but he liked to get, because that was besting the other fellow. His business was his great game. He liked to feel his aptitude, his wariness, to foresee, and realize, and let other people realize, the shrewd precision of his anticipations." "Besting people and feeling that the other fellow realizes or will presently find out that he has been bested was subtler and far more gratifying" to Edensoke than any other activity. The profits of his business were a secondary consideration, important only like scoring points in a game.

This is shrewd characterization and psychologically exceedingly acute. Veblen terms the same motive pecuniary emulation,[1] while Professor Laski writes: "Men may begin to acquire property to safeguard their lives from want, but they continue to acquire it because of the distinction that comes from its possession. It satisfies their vanity and their lust for power; it enables them to attune the will of society to their own."[2] Combined with other motives distinguished

[1] Veblen: *op. cit.*, ch. ii, *passim.*

[2] Laski: *Grammar of Politics*, 175. Money still has allurements even for professing young Russian Communists. One, outwardly a model Communist, was expelled from the Union of Communist Youth for writing a letter to his friend, part of which reads as follows: "I am tired of building up all the time without end. I want to live. And what is the obstacle that stands between me and real life? Money. For money I shall acquire glory, power, beautiful women, and happiness. For money I shall create for myself an earthly paradise, and the road of my life will be covered with flowers. Money—that is my ideal." Besides indicating the difficulty of Communists in warding off the gradual infiltration of apathy and scepticism into their own ranks, this letter shows a very vivid realization of motives leading to wealth accumulation, and illustrates the inertia and 'lag-over' of culture patterns characteristic of the earlier economic and social regime. For the letter, see the *Observer*, Moscow Correspondent's dispatch, July 21, 1929.

above, aided by a certain unscrupulousness, a complacent conscience and a little good fortune, the business man's desire for power over others will usually enable him to accumulate a large fortune and thereafter to bask in the sun of society's approval.[1] I do not suggest, of course, that the business man will display these motives in every social relationship. In relations other than those concerned with business, for instance in committee or charitable work and the like, the capitalist may draw on large reserves of public spirit and be actuated mainly by a desire to be of service to the community at large. Indeed, sufficient credit is not always given to him in this connection. But in the main, my point is that in the accumulation of wealth the desire for power is the mainspring of economic activity.

As in the accumulation of money, the same sentiments support the other non-pathological collecting activities of adults. But the possession of property will not reach a high degree unless the possessions themselves are such as to yield some feeling of value. The objects collected may be rare and difficult to get, symbolizing valuable qualities such as strength and skill displayed in obtaining them; or they may be valuable only because they are sought by other people as well, and their possession then registers the scoring of points in the game. Both factors operate in accumulating and hoarding behaviour to reinforce other motives and to pattern those primitive possessive tendencies I have already discussed. The articles collected have a certain initial rarity. Others compete in trying to get them. When a fashion has been started in collecting, either among

[1] Sombart, in his volume, *The Quintessence of Capitalism* (Eng. trans., 1915), ch. xii, describes the modern 'undertaker' in terms not dissimilar to mine. Sombart's excursion into psychology, however, particularly his analysis of business psychology in terms of such genetic 'ideals' (values) as physical bigness, quick movement and novelty (*ibid.*, p. 176), seems to me rather unhappy and quite the reverse of convincing.

adults or children, the intrinsic interest of the articles is of little importance. The main value of a collection consists in the fact that it symbolizes successful competition and the ability to exhibit before others that collection which signifies the fact of success, power, gratified ambition, and heightened self-esteem.[1]

Where hoarding activities become an end in themselves, and accumulation of wealth, for instance, is carried on without reference to social factors like competition or emulation, we have to recognize that wealth is desired by the miser simply as an end in itself and apart altogether from its value as a means to the purchase of economic goods or because possession brings social esteem. Collecting manias may be motivated entirely by those unconscious factors which the Freudians are concerned to stress; and miserliness over wealth may be merely the expression of an anal character trait.[2] This psychoanalytic evidence is suggestive, if not at the present moment entirely convincing. But in more general psychological terms it would appear fairly clear that extreme avariciousness is not unusually the outcome of delusions of poverty brought about by such factors as mental shock, loss of friends, or incipient manic-depressive states. Where an object of affection, solicitude or companionship is lost, and interests are turned away from personal relations, it is natural to imagine that habit may concentrate

[1] An extract from the *Literary Digest*, September 12, 1925, is apposite here. The writer tells how he remembered spending an afternoon with a great R.A. who was contemplating paying the sum of £400 for a piece of early Persian pottery, the value of which as a work of art was hardly more than sixpence. As the R.A. remarked: "It simply means that if I do pay £400 for the saucer I shall be envied its possession by about four men in Europe. And on the whole, I think it's worth while." He bought the saucer for his collection. Probably it has not been looked at more than once a year since. One sometimes wonders how much aggressive rivalry motivates those American millionaires who pay such enormous sums of money for rare books, old furniture, and *objets d'art*, which can hardly interest many of them beyond the fact that they have them and not their rivals.

[2] See *supra* and again Brill: *Psycho-Analysis* (1922), 73.

these interests upon money.[1] The permanent sense of power bound up with the possession of money is preferred to the fugitive enjoyment of it. Negatively there is a stronger aversion to the loss of this power than to the sacrifice of this or that particular gratification. Sentiments of possession supporting the identification of the ego with money are reinforced by poverty complexes. The want of money will then seem to the avaricious man to occasion a painful restriction of the personality, a negation of all his impulses. An accumulation of wealth comes to be regarded as a permanent reserve against this possible thwarting of the self, giving rise to feelings of security, strength and power. Thinking of the indefinite possibilities of his hoarded possessions the miser prefers what Stout terms 'free ideal activity' to all the possibilities and gratifications of actual use. So long as he hoards his wealth under his immediate care his personality suffers no subjective restrictions. He cares nought for present gratification so long as the personality-property relation continues fixed, stable and secure. The miser's interest in his wealth becomes a master sentiment which integrates impulse, emotion and desire into an ordered, but not therefore an admirable, character. He has found only one sheet-anchor for personality development because he has bartered the potential harmonious unity of the self for the unlovely malformation of a permanently twisted character.

[1] See Maudsley's *Pathology of Mind* (1895), 75, 331–333, and the same writer's *Physiology and Pathology* (1868), 235, for vivid though somewhat rhetorical characterization of the miser. France and Kline, *op. cit*, 467–470, speculate variously also as to the motives which make men misers.

CHAPTER XI

CONCLUSION

I HAVE attempted in the last chapter to present a psychological analysis of the intimate relation between property and personality. It is, of course, a familiar plea on behalf of private property that its possession is necessary for the full development of all the powers of the individual and that it is the most effective stimulus to the growth of character. I think we are now in a position to understand the psychological reality and basis of this appeal and in some measure at least to judge of its validity.

In this concluding chapter it is my aim to indicate the importance of my earlier analysis for the study of property in its wider philosophical context. Before I do this, however, it may be well briefly to state what I understand to be the general nature of the theory of social rights and duties. Property is usually spoken of in terms of a specific right. How, then, are rights to be conceived?

By rights I mean claims made by individuals upon the common good, claims to the conditions requisite for the fulfilment of personality in harmony with this common good. The individual, that is, has claims upon society for such conditions as are necessary for the realization of his functions: rights are thus claims to the satisfaction of functional needs. The rights of the individual are the duties of the community, and the rights of the community are those duties owed to it by the individual. Rights therefore are integral elements in social welfare and can be in no sense independent of a particular set of social relationships.

This is a somewhat dogmatic statement of a view as to the nature of rights which has been convincingly argued by

Hobhouse and others. Taking it as my theoretical standpoint, I wish to ask what is the functional need involved in the right of property. This question I can best answer in the light of a short summary of the conclusions of the preceding chapters.

First, I have suggested that to speak of an instinct of property or of an instinct of acquisition is to import a false simplicity into what is essentially a complex set of facts. Acquisition *per se* is not a fundamental need of the self. It is one aspect of each fundamental need. The lower animals acquire food and a mate; they defend nests, burrow, territory or offspring from the aggressive behaviour of other animals. When, through the drive of fundamental needs, these objects are used, controlled and defended against aggression, I have termed them primary property values. When interest is focussed by an act of attention (and further strengthened through an act of seizure) upon these property objects, trains of feeling or reactions attendant upon, or subsidiary to, fundamental needs are thereafter called forth in response to this object rather than to others. Among the lower animals attention will continue to be focussed so long as the object remains the end-object satisfying impulse. With human beings, this centering of interest is strengthened after acquisition by greater or less magico-animistic identification of the self with the object of regard.

With all animals, the dog with its bone, the bird with its nest, the jackdaw with its cache, the insect with its hive, the rodent with its burrow and storehouse, and with man himself, the appropriated object becomes a permanent basis of action, something that the individual can count upon and go back to at need. For man, in addition, his property becomes something that he can rely upon as a permanent home, permanent means of subsistence and enjoyment, permanent means for the exercise of power and the winning of social esteem, permanent elements in that integration of personality which alone can yield some measure of order and stability to life.

Thus the study of property interests in man emphasizes the fact that these are more than the resultant of a blind instinct to keep that which satisfies fundamental needs. With the operation of intelligence the various impulsive factors directed toward the acquisition of some property object are ordered, through permanent association, into a relatively stable sentiment. Sentiment is connected with sentiment just as one property value involves another. The development of self-consciousness is materially assisted by the integration of those sentiments about property values made permanent through their incorporation within the orbit of the self's activity. One may no longer conceive of property as we did among the lower animals simply in terms of the end-object satisfying basic need. The self has developed sentiments of possession and of ownership centred about primitive property values and the acquired values assimilated to these. Animistic identification of the self with this property strengthens to a further degree this personality-property sentiment relationship.

This study has led me also to stress the importance of what I have termed the culture patterning of property values. The organization of property values in a Yakut community of Siberia differs greatly from that prevalent in a modern Western European Community, or even from that of a comparatively highly cultured African agricultural community. Yet we may probably in all reason suppose that the inherited fundamental needs, somewhat similar in kind and degree, of Yakut, European and African adapt themselves with more or less equal ease to the patterns of their respective social organizations. The *mores* of these groups are the complex resultant of economic, historical, psychological and social forces. But each set of *mores* moulds the raw stuff of human nature into conformity with its own demands and practices. There is more than a little truth in the paradox that human nature is unchanging but always changeable.

The point that the study of this aspect of the problem has brought out is that although it is as true as ever to say that some measure of property is an integral element in both the free life and the ordered life of purposeful activity, nevertheless one may lay down no hard and fast rule as to the amount of property required to secure this order and this freedom. Psychologically speaking, the individual will suffer little real thwarting of his personality in so far as he has free access to, and permanent control of, those primitive property values necessary for the satisfaction of his fundamental needs. What he will demand beyond this minimum will depend upon the type of social grouping in which he finds himself and the amount of property which the patterns of this group allow him to secure through the status he occupies and the function he performs in its economic organization. Beyond this minimum, that is, the Trobriand Islander will find social esteem awarded him for his possession of large stores of food, or of valuable *Kula* exchange articles which he knows he must soon pass on to friends in another group. The Pacific Coast Indian, again, will find that the culture patterns of his group allow him to accumulate native wealth only on the implicit understanding that he distributes all of it to his friends on the occasion of the numerous potlach ceremonies. The Yakut of Siberia grows up in a milieu which does not permit the accumulation of wealth. It is a case of practical communism, and if there is scarcity of food, all must starve together. Finally, the Western European adapts himself to that Great Society where unlimited acquisition of wealth is permitted, encouraged and esteemed, where wealth is a measure of worth, and where it is a matter of each for himself and the devil take the hindmost in the race for the possession of riches.

This, then, I take to be the measure of psychological truth

embedded in the convention of property worked out for Western Europe by Roman and Byzantine jurists. The 'right' to property is indefeasible and unchanging just to the degree that if the individual does not enjoy permanent control of those end-objects satisfying certain of the fundamental needs he will live a thwarted life. But from the point of view of social theory, after allowance is made for this conception of the psychological minimum, one must argue that property is neither unchanging nor indefeasible. It is, in reality, an instrument, expedient or convention, adaptable and changing in accordance with varying needs (just as is any expedient), and must be so changed, if needs are to be satisfied, in conformity with the requirements of a dynamic society. The truth of this statement gains support from even the most cursory glance at the history of Western Europe. This history shows very clearly a gradual development in the culture patterning of property values. There is, for instance, a difference in the modern as compared with the Elizabethan attitude to property in slaves. There is, again, an increasing growth of testamentary freedom in England as compared with the reverse process in France. Or, finally, in contemporary Russia, among the agricultural communities, there is being waged a battle between old culture patterns, habits and traditions, highly individualistic in outlook, and the new culture patterns which have for their aim the communization of peasant life. From what I have suggested in previous chapters it will be evident that new culture patterns will only take the place of old if it is possible to overcome the inertia of old habits of thought and action, the pressure of an older social heritage, and the recalcitrant will of a coerced minority. That this is a difficult process the American experiment in liquor control bears eloquent witness. But for the social psychologist, in his capacity as psychologist and not moralist, both experiments are of extreme interest in the light they throw upon that moulding of impulse by culture pattern which has been the main thesis of an earlier chapter.

So far I have been attempting to indicate the nature of the functional need whose claim to satisfaction is implicit in the recognition of a right to property; and I have been concerned briefly to summarize the psychological nature of this need. Psychology, however, touches the field of social philosophy when one endeavours to link up the study of fact with the problem of social values. The question that then faces us is the nature of the principle which will give some measure of ethical justification for the distribution in the community of wealth and property above the psychological minimum. I have hardly space here to enter into debatable realms of social philosophy or to attempt philosophically to determine the ultimate principle by which the fruits of industry may be most justly distributed among those sharing in their production. Such questions as these may be best left for discussion elsewhere. All I would say now is that it would appear that a justification of private property must depend not upon *a priori* principle or appeal to indefeasible right or to the alleged virtues of full-blooded economic individualism, or, again, to some hypothetical psychology of human motives—not upon any of these but upon the fact that property in a society based upon ethical principles is to be judged by its social effects, by its contribution to that common good which is in essence the harmonious realization of human capacity.

I cannot give a detailed discussion of the ethical justification of this principle in the present context. It should be noted, however, that such a principle would follow inevitably from the conception of the nature of rights which I have already briefly sketched. The function of any right is its place as an element in social welfare. Such a right derives its moral authority precisely from the fact that it is, in general, necessary for the realization of the common good. The first and most general social function of property is to provide that undisturbed use of material things without which man can do nothing that is consecutive or purposeful. This control of property objects by an assigned agent is necessary further to prevent disputes and misuse. The reverse side of this assignment is that control carries with it a measure of liberty and a definite degree of responsibility. So long as the direction of one's life and the ability usefully to employ one's capacity depends upon the free use, enjoyment, and control of property objects, just so far does it depend upon one's undisturbed possession of such property. This is true of the individual as of the corporate association. Freedom of choice, freedom to direct one's own development freedom of enjoyment, will thus rank along with a sense of security and permanence as some of the more complex constituents of the sentiment of ownership. Though this freedom, however, does away with certain obvious responsibilities, it imposes on the owner of property the particular kind of responsibility involved in self-dependence. It thus brings with it the necessity for foresight, prudence, self-control. It teaches the individual the price he must pay to satisfy his fundamental needs. In a word, since property is the economic basis of freedom and personality development, the possession of individual property above what I have called the psychological minimum is a desirable thing; and not only for individuals, but for any corporate body that has to direct its own affairs.

What sort of property and under what conditions is another question. As Hobhouse has pointed out, property may be for use; but also it may be for power. What may confer freedom on one owner may at the same time give him so much of power that he destroys the freedom of another. In any community, therefore, which aspect—of freedom or of power—is more important depends on the nature of the property and its distribution. Communism would reserve to the State all control of property for the purposes of power; the individual would have property for use and for freedom. If one rejects this type of social organization, the problem of the community, relative to property, resolves itself into the best way of working towards general economic freedom and reconciling this freedom with power. One way is the method of individualist production—a method not without merits in certain social groups, but one which, it may be argued, has little to commend it under the present regime of large-scale production. The other way is the expression of liberty and of property in terms of social function, and in ultimate resort as dependent upon social control. Under this method, that is to say, while the individual may control property for the free ordering of his personal life just to the degree that he performs a useful social function, property as an instrument of economic power will be vested in the self-governing community.

There is no need to say more of the individual aspects of this wedding of power and liberty. Of the social aspect, however, it may be remarked that during the last few years a form of property control has been evolving, a form which at least points the way to the method in which this vesting of economic power in the community may proceed to its logical conclusion. The public utility company, for instance, is a form of 'will-organization,' developed in recent years, which harnesses the drive of self-interest to the wheels of public need. Profit and interest, say the school-men of economics, are oil and water and will not mix. The semi-autonomous public authorities which are already conducting successfully such diverse enterprises as the business of a great port, the distribution of electric current, the broadcasting of instruction, education and entertainment, and the management of hotels and inns, have already mixed them. One sees in this development of the public utility organization, along with the spread of co-operative enterprise, the commencement of a process which will ultimately reconcile economic liberty and power. To the degree to which the community accepts this process and this newly evolving will-organization, and by so doing, constructs a new pattern of thought and action in regard to social ownership, one may witness the gradual development of a new economic culture pattern. And, after all, the ultimate reason for the study of the psychological foundations of property is to be found in the faith that the great task of the social thinker of to-day is consciously to create, foster and develop culture patterns and social institutions more in harmony with present needs than those of the century that is past.

BIBLIOGRAPHICAL NOTE

For two reasons I have not thought it advisable to include here a complete bibliography of the Psychology of Property; principally, I think, because completeness is hardly to be attained in the literature of a study such as this which is the first of its kind, and which is, in fact, an excursus into the border-country lying between psychology and sociology; and secondly, because the footnotes are in themselves a sufficiently full guide to this literature. By consulting them, the reader will find for himself ample material with which to form his own opinion upon the points at issue.

Further references, however, to the psychology of the subject may be found in the volumes of the *Psychological Index* (Princeton, N.J.); and for the more specific anthropological aspects, to the bibliography contained in Hobhouse, Wheeler and Ginsberg: *The Material Culture and Social Institutions of the Simpler Peoples* (London, 1930).

For a general orientation to the problem the reader may consult, first, the treatment of property contained in classic philosophical works, and then, for more modern discussion, the following: Lafargue: *The Evolution of Property* (5th ed., 1908); Letourneau: *Property: Its Origin and Development* (1892); Lewinski: *The Origin of Property* (1913). Tawney's treatment of property in *The Acquisitive Society* (1921) is, of course, a masterly survey of the place of property in a Functional Society. Graham Wallas has a valuable discussion of property as a 'will-organization' in *The Great Society*. Finally, reference may be made to two essays: one by Bosanquet on "The Principle of Private Property" in *Certain Aspects of the Social Problem* (1895); the other by Graham Wallas on "Property Under Socialism" in *Fabian Essays* (1931—1st ed., 1889).

INDEX

GEORGE ALLEN & UNWIN LTD
London: 40 Museum Street, W.C.1
Cape Town: 73 St. George's Street
Sydney, N.S.W.: Wynyard Square
Auckland, N.Z.: 41 Albert Street
Toronto: 77 Wellington Street, West